Queer Timing

WOMEN AND FILM HISTORY INTERNATIONAL

Series Editors
Kay Armatage, Jane M. Gaines, and Christine Gledhill

A new generation of motion picture historians is rediscovering the vital and diverse contributions of women to world film history whether as producers, actors, or spectators. Taking advantage of new print material and moving picture archival discoveries as well as the benefits of digital access and storage, this series investigates the significance of gender in the cinema.

A list of books in the series appears at the end of this book.

Queer Timing

The Emergence of Lesbian Sexuality in Early Cinema

SUSAN POTTER

UNIVERSITY OF ILLINOIS PRESS
Urbana, Chicago, and Springfield

Publication of this book was supported in part by a grant from the Australian Academy of the Humanities.

1 2 3 4 5 C P 5 4 3 2 1
∞ This book is printed on acid-free paper.

Library of Congress Cataloging-in-Publication Data
Names: Potter, Susan (Film historian), author.
Title: Queer timing: the emergence of lesbian sexuality in early cinema / Susan Potter.
Description: Urbana: University of Illinois Press, 2019. | Series: Women and film history international | Includes bibliographical references and index.
Identifiers: LCCN 2018048169 | ISBN 9780252084249 (pbk.)
Subjects: LCSH: Lesbianism in motion pictures. | Lesbians in motion pictures. | Motion pictures—History—20th century.
Classification: LCC PN1995.9.L48 P68 2019 | DDC 791.43/6526643—dc23
LC record available at https://lccn.loc.gov/2018048169

Ebook ISBN 978-0-252-05130-2

Cover illustration: Loïe Fuller dancing photographed by Samuel Joshua Beckett (ca. 1900). Metropolitan Museum of Art Gilman Collection, Purchase, Mrs. Walter Annenberg and The Annenberg Foundation Gift, 2005.

Contents

Acknowledgments

THE PUBLICATION OF *Queer Timing* is generously supported by the award of a Publication Subsidy from the Australian Academy of the Humanities and a Research Support Scheme Grant from the School of Literature, Art and Media, the University of Sydney.

The book's trajectory of development is evidenced by the other financial and institutional support it has attracted over the years: a New Zealand Tertiary Education Commission Bright Future: Top Achiever Doctoral Scholarship; a University of Auckland Faculty of Arts Doctoral Research Fund grant for overseas archive and library research; the Dame Joan Metge Post-Doctoral Research Award, awarded by the Kate Edger Educational Charitable Trust; and several grants toward presenting at international conferences from the University of Auckland Department of Film, Television and Media Studies, and the University of New England (Australia).

Libraries and archives provided access to essential research services, materials, and image duplication services, including: the inter-library loan services at the University of Auckland, the University of New England, and the University of Sydney; the British Film Institute National Archive and National Library; George Eastman House; Institut Lumière; Library of Congress Moving Image Research Center; Margaret Herrick Library, and especially Kristine Kreuger of the National Film Service; Minneapolis College of Art and Design Collection; Museum of Modern Art Film Study Center and Libraries; New York Public Library of Performing Arts; UCLA Film & Television Archive; and the University of Tennessee Libraries Special Collection. I also thank Garry Malvern and Mike Haritos of moviemags.com for providing last-minute high-resolution images.

Thanks to my former colleagues in the School of Arts, University of New England, who showed an interest in the project and who supported it in large and small, and material and immaterial ways: Alan Davison, Jeremy Fisher, Yvonne Griggs, Elizabeth Hale, Jennifer McDonell, Jane O'Sullivan, and Dugald Williamson. I'd especially like to thank the Researchers Anonymous Group—you know who you are. Thanks to Louise Noble for supporting this project through the early career researchers writing workshop, and to Jo Chipperfield, Sarah Lawrence, and Kate Wright for reviewing draft chapters.

For counsel on writing and publishing, and scholarly companionship, thanks go to my colleagues in the Department of Art History at the University of Sydney, especially my Chairs, Mark Ledbury and Catriona Moore; my neighbor, both professionally and personally, Donna West Brett; my companion in AAH awards, Stephen Whiteman; Roger Benjamin for linguistic advice; my Film Studies colleagues, Bruce Isaacs and Richard Smith; and all-round departmental champion, Lucy Baird. I shared the corridors of summer revision with Chiara O'Reilly and Anna Lawrence. Thanks also to Lee Wallace for always-astute writing and career advice and for introducing me to my writing partner, Thushara Dibley. But more than these acts of mentorship, my intellectual debts to Lee go further back to "Sexual Narratives," a course that first introduced me to the brain-exploding concepts of queer theory and the history of sexuality, and without which I would never have gone down this track.

While I have had the opportunity to present work on this project at a number of conferences and departmental seminars, I need to thank in particular the participants and organizers of the Women and the Silent Screen conferences, the first of which I attended back in 2008. These conferences have introduced me to a brilliant and collegial network of feminist film historians. For various conversations over the years, however brief or long, about papers that I've presented or the field more generally, I thank in particular Mark Lynn Anderson, Victoria Duckett, Maggie Hennefeld, Minette Hillyer, Laura Horak, David Mayer, Drake Stutesman, and Yiman Wang. Thanks are due as well to Shelley Stamp who has kept the imminent publication of this book on her radar in the context of an astonishing command of the broader field of feminist media histories and its global scholarly networks.

This book sustains an argument concerning the cinematic representability of same-sex desire that I was not able to imagine when I first started this project. Its development owes much to early generative conversations with Annamarie Jagose, a patient and generous interlocutor who also modeled a commitment to intellectual projects that productively push us to the edge of our capabilities. Heather Love and Jackie Stacey read the manuscript in an earlier iteration and their generous and helpful comments have stayed with me as I have revised and clarified its arguments. I am also grateful to the two reviewers who not only took on the manuscript to read but who also understood—despite my sometimes cryptic sentences—the intellectual aims of this book.

I am honored to have *Queer Timing* published in the Women and Film History International series. It has been a pleasure to work with the University of Illinois Press, including Julie Laut, and acquisitions editor, Daniel M. Nasset, whose warm and encouraging emails have helped an author go that one step further in revising her manuscript. Parts of this book have been published in slightly different forms elsewhere. An earlier version of Chapter 4 was first published as an essay in *Screen* and it appears here in revised form courtesy of Oxford University Press. A version of Chapter 6 was published in *Framework: The Journal of Cinema and Media*, and it appears here in slightly extended form courtesy of Wayne State University Press.

Behind the scenes, I would like to thank some people who in one way or another supported this project in its development, even if they didn't quite realize it at the time: Cassandra Barnett, Pansy Duncan, Emma Kelly, Irene Lee, Jani T. Wilson; Shannon Brown and Susan Wilkinson; Marty Molloy; Alison and John Potter; Liz Nicholson. Never last nor least: Fiona Ward who has experienced secondhand, and for too many years now, what it takes to write a book.

Queer Timing

Introduction

We're never at one with our queerness;
neither its time nor its subject is ours.
—Lee Edelman, "Theorizing Queer Temporalities"

THIS BOOK IS A COUNTER-HISTORY of the emergence of lesbian sexuality in early cinema. It proposes that the representability of a minoritarian sexual identity has something to teach us about cinema's role in the history of sexuality as a modern normativizing phenomenon. While studies of lesbian representation in film might be understood generally as counter-histories, in that they seek to make visible a history of others occluded by dominant histories, this book is a counter-history in a more specific sense: it reorients conceptually the historicity of lesbian sexuality in early cinema as a site through which to also reconsider the historicity of all sexualities.[1] The appearance of figures cinematically intelligible as lesbian across the 1920s and 1930s, from briefly glimpsed extras to fully fledged psychological characters, registers sexuality's queer timing: such figures are only the most visible and belated signs of an array of strategies of sexuality. The retrospective identification of cinematic figures or on-screen relations as lesbian without any further elaboration of how they come to be sexually intelligible—or not—risks sustaining the regulatory and normative effects of sexuality in the present. As many historians of sexuality and queer theorists have taught us, such knowledge does not guarantee transparent historical insight since it is one of the means by which sexuality arises and is sustained, from the contradictory epistemologies of new disciplines such as sexology to its entanglement in everyday and seemingly benign forms of visual pleasure. This reoriented understanding of the historicity of sexuality requires a different methodological approach: put negatively, this study does not undertake a more thorough survey of lesbian representation as evidenced by early films and other materials preserved in the archives, nor does it aim to revise the chronology of the emergent legibility of a minority sexual identity. Rather, across a series of case studies, *Queer Timing* asks its readers to move beyond the identification of figures already intelligible as lesbian and to suspend their sexual knowledges and attendant pleasures, in order to trace the contradictory and unexpected sexuality effects of cinema in the first decades of its intermedial development and institutional consolidations.

The book's main title gestures toward its central argument, that the emergence of lesbian representation and spectatorship in early cinema is not a linear progression and consolidation but rather arises across multiple sites in dispersed forms that are modern and backward-looking, recursive and anachronistic. A heterogeneous early cinema sustains and reconfigures older same-sex erotic styles, relational idioms, and knowledges, and establishes nascent forms of modern lesbian intelligibility, both systematically and accidentally, in ways that are visible and invisible—or thinkable and unthinkable. In other words, early cinema's sexuality effects shape a discursive terrain that contributes to the emergent legibility of lesbian sexuality in often negative and paradoxical terms: as accidental or incidental attraction; as homoerotic spectacle premised on both sexual ignorance and knowledge; as opaque character motivation; as almost undetectable and momentary erotic orientation; as characterological sexual identity intelligible in terms of contradictory epistemologies of the present and the past. Early cinema's contribution to the intensification of modern sexuality has other consequences too that disturb and reorient sexuality's more repressive effects. It generates structures of representation and spectatorship—a disembodied and depersonalized moving image aesthetic; a dispersed and fragmented structure of identification, recognition, and shared feeling—able to sustain queer subjectivities that are not exactly lesbian but that are enabled by the disparate forms of its emergence.

Queer Timing contributes to one of the major projects of feminist film history: the investigation and recuperation of women's contradictory and ambivalent pleasures in the cinema. A consensus has developed that the institutionalization of cinema in the major film-producing territories of the early twentieth century generated diverse pleasures for an expanding female audience, even as those enjoyments were also disciplined through the development of gendered structures of spectatorship, film-specific modes of exhibition, conventions of narrative cinema, star systems, and practices of censorship.[2] This book proposes that tracing the different orders of legibility, articulation, and regulation of same-sex desire should be central to an understanding of cinema as an alternative, albeit compromised, public sphere for women. Early cinema's regulation of homoerotic visual pleasure may be just as salient a historical transformation as the privileging of the male gaze for emergent forms of female sexual intelligibility and modes of spectatorship. A counter-history of the emergence of lesbian representation and spectatorship is thus inevitably a partial history of a more privileged, yet historically less visible, sexual identity and discourse, a seemingly timeless heterosexuality.[3] Lesbianism in this respect is not opposed to or distinct from heterosexuality—however much their everyday instantiations make them seem so. Rather, they are closely related cultural formations whose historical cinematic intelligibilities are governed by different, and differently valued, temporal orders.

The case studies assembled in *Queer Timing* focus on both canonical and obscure films and figures from the late nineteenth century through to the late 1920s, during the transition to the sound era. This chronological span extends beyond the disciplinary periodization that typically designates "early cinema" as the moment of film's emergence and institutional consolidation, from the 1890s to the mid-1910s. As an ostensibly periodizing term, "early cinema" draws within its purview micro-periods in the history of silent cinema while adumbrating now well-accepted and conventional (in the disciplinary sense) temporal demarcations: the cinema of attractions (1895–1907), transitional cinema (1908–1915), late silent cinema (1916–1930), and early sound cinema (1927–1931).[4] These periods both reflect and sustain a dominant field orientation to significant transformations in the institutionalization of cinema as a distinctive medium and form of entertainment.[5] Their temporal boundaries, some of which are still subject to debate, are organized by a historical attention to material practices such as the advent of movie theaters, the rise of narrative feature filmmaking, industrial standardization, and changes in technology and exhibition. That individual case studies in this book are situated within or on the cusp of these fine-grained film historical periods is an indication that some of the sexuality effects that each tracks are synchronized to the aesthetic and industry transformations that those periodizations privilege. Nevertheless, other sexuality effects are calibrated to different timelines. In extending the term "early cinema" to the whole of the silent cinema period, *Queer Timing* follows the counter-periodization strategy of feminist film historians.[6] As Jennifer M. Bean writes, to employ the term "early cinema" across these micro-historical periods is to insist on the "longevity of heterogeneous, aleatory modes of [gendered and other forms of] address and reception across the whole of silent cinema's parts."[7] This enlarged timespan reflects not only *Queer Timing*'s genealogical approach but also a queer-feminist perspective that keeps to the foreground cinema's articulations of homoeroticism, same-sex desire, gender, and sexual identity.

After the History of Sexuality

To undertake a counter-history of the emergence of lesbian sexuality in early cinema is not a straightforward enterprise. The emergence of new kinds of sexual identity from the mid-nineteenth century as the means by which erotic behaviors and desires are disciplined and normalized is precisely what defines sexuality as modern.[8] If we follow Michel Foucault's *History of Sexuality: The Will to Knowledge, Volume 1*, the history of sexuality involves more than an attention to the advent of novel sexual categories and identities: it requires tracing a vast network or apparatus of power that constitutes and individualizes people as its sexual subjects.[9] This understanding of sexuality and its history as a complex assemblage of discourses and material practices is critically distinct from—though it also encompasses—its more everyday meanings as sexual identity, orientation, or sexual acts and practices. David Halperin summarizes most astutely the radical implications of Foucault's project:

> The history of sexuality . . . is not a history of the representations, categories, cultural articulations, or collective and individual expressions of some determinate entity called sexuality but an inquiry into the historical emergence of *sexuality itself*, an attempt to explain how it happened that in the eighteenth and nineteenth centuries sexuality gradually came into existence as *a conjunction of strategies* for ordering social relations, authorizing specialized knowledges, licensing expert interventions, intensifying bodily sensations, normalizing erotic behaviors, multiplying sexual perversions, policing personal expressions, crystallizing political resistances, motivating introspective utterances, and constructing human subjectivities.[10]

That first italicized phrase, "sexuality itself," is more than a little ironic. As an object of critical-historical inquiry, sexuality in this sense remains stubbornly opaque—and not only because of its diverse strategies, pervasive operations, and forceful reality effects.[11] Sexuality itself can be difficult to apprehend because it operates through forms that seem to promise something else—knowledge—or nothing more because it is an end in itself—pleasure. It may register in historical forms now unrecognizable to us, and so they might pass us by; or it may take hold in forms and cultural locations that seem to have nothing to do whatsoever with sexual identity or sexual discourse.[12] Though some of those claims rest on the subsequent insights of historians of sexuality and queer theorists, Halperin's retrospective and secondary account returns us post-Foucauldians to an important articulation of the history of sexuality as an intellectual project.

While Foucault's radical conception of the history of sexuality continues to be a touchstone for this book—we are not past or over Foucault just yet—*Queer Timing* moves beyond *The History of Sexuality* in several senses.[13] The book is most obviously concerned with the intensification of sexuality beyond the immediate domain of the medical and sexual sciences and governmental discourses and practices. By the late nineteenth century, sexuality had become an increasingly central problem of human life, and early cinema is not quarantined from these developments.[14] Mary Ann Doane puts it most aptly when she states: "The cinema's central role as entertainment does not preclude its intimate relation with new epistemologies, its inextricability from the reorganization of knowledge taking place in modernity."[15] Early cinema remediates sexual discourses already in circulation in culture and draws upon those same discourses as a ready-made epistemological framework through which to make sense of its subjects and themes, while also developing institutional and medium-specific modes of articulating sexual knowledges and pleasures. In the latter regard, *Queer Timing* contributes to a diverse set of studies that have drawn on and extended Foucault's inaugurating project to historicize early cinema's sexuality effects, such as the co-implication of sexuality and stardom as systems that sustain a will to know the truth of the body.[16] A focus on the body remains important for this book since sexuality exploits its self-evident nature as a sexual, desiring body in order to enable, as D. A. Miller has observed, pervasive sexual ideologies to seem "less arbitrarily imposed."[17] Yet, the sexualization of bodies in early cinema is not an evenly distributed or stable process, nor is it gender neutral.[18] It is the female body that bears the greatest pressure of these transformations. As Linda Williams argues in her still critically energizing essay, "Film Body: An Implantation of Perversions," the generation of new visual knowledges that constituted the gendered body in motion, through proto-cinematic technologies such as film motion studies and Muybridge's zoopraxiscope, was inextricably bound up in the simultaneous generation of new forms of visual pleasure that expanded and sustained the new regime of sexuality.[19] In its critical attention to the sexed and gendered body, *Queer Timing*, like other feminist projects, seeks to redress Foucault's notorious lack of attention to gender in his foundational work on the history of sexuality.

This study also aims to complicate the post-Foucauldian feminist project inaugurated by Williams and others in a slightly different way. While early films may take up and disperse the logics of new forms of body-centered scientific and medical knowledges, their sexuality effects remain contingent and unpredictable, particularly in terms of the articulations to one another of sexual difference, hetero and homo forms of eroticism, and emergent sexual subjectivities. One of this book's key arguments is that the proliferating forms of visual scrutiny of the female body bear a less acknowledged relation to the emergence of a same-sex oriented subjectivity that would, on its face, seem to be excluded by an erotics organized in terms of sexual difference. Such a claim depends in part on a pervasive but contradictory epistemological structure by which lesbian sexuality can be known. As several queer and lesbian studies scholars have persuasively demonstrated in relation to different historical periods, women's same-sex desires have been rendered knowable by being coded, paradoxically, as invisible, impossible, or secondary to other modes of erotic life.[20] The persistence of such cultural logics in the modern period functions, as Annamarie Jagose argues, to secure the fantasy of heterosexuality's primacy and authenticity and sustains a corresponding disavowal that the very same logics—of derivation, for example—underpin all sexualities.[21] These critical insights augment an aporia in Foucault's *History of Sexuality* by highlighting, as Judith Butler has pointed out, how the production of domains of sexual knowledge simultaneously generates domains of "unthinkability and unnameability."[22]

As a post-Foucauldian project, this book considers the inventive and resistant responses of queer people to the intensification of sexuality. While the diverse strategies of sexuality may seem oppressive, they are not automatically so. The regime of sexuality has, perhaps paradoxically, also generated varied and enriching forms of queer subjectivity and culture. Like the studies of lesbian cinematic representation that have inspired and informed this book, *Queer Timing* can be understood from this perspective as partly engaged in a recuperative project of queer cultural history.[23] This interest is aligned with and develops Foucault's articulation of the possibility of *reverse discourse*, a theoretical term whose evocation of a unilinear inversion of power's oppressive effects has been considerably complicated by histories of sexuality and queer theorizations of time, discussed later in this Introduction.

Finally, but also as a way to signal a different point from which to begin, *Queer Timing* joins other post-Foucauldian projects in revising and complicating the historical timelines of the emergence of sexuality, and the centrality of sexual identity as the means by which modern erotic life is ordered. While Foucault famously dates the "birth" of the modern homosexual to 1870—a date that in any event we ought to read polemically rather than historically—there is now, as Susan S. Lanser has noted, "copious evidence that erotic practices did come under intense scrutiny in the eighteenth century, implanting the notion of 'perverse' sexualities even earlier than Foucault believed."[24] This extension of the period boundary of modern sexuality a century earlier has been accompanied by a corresponding recognition that the centrality of sexual identity to modern sexuality may be more recent than previously imagined. This point is partly demonstrated by the history of "lesbian" as a word, since it is only in the 1920s that it is consolidated as the go-to sexual term that signifies erotic attraction between women rather than a geographical identity—an inhabitant of the isle of Lesbos—or a heterosexual dalliance.[25] Even then, as Laura Doan's study of sapphic public culture in early-twentieth-century England suggests, the "very concept of 'lesbian' as a specific category of identity or as a subcultural style had not . . . sufficiently cohered within the public consciousness."[26] Histories of the belated emergence of modern lesbian identity are further complicated by the persistence of nineteenth-century erotic categories and relational idioms by which women's same-sex desires could be organized—whether the gender-transgressing sapphist, romantic friendship, or other kinship models.[27] Each makes same-sex identity or desire legible according to incommensurable logics of difference (masculinity) and similitude (femininity), figuration (the sapphist), relationality and kinship (romantic friends, mother/daughter, and so forth). The tenacity of what seem like relics of earlier same-sex erotic practices, identities, and relational idioms has permitted the critical recognition that prelesbian models of erotic life continue to structure the incoherencies of the modern sex/gender system.[28]

These more elastic and nuanced historical timelines respond to a different understanding of Foucault's distinction between the regulation of sex in terms of acts and identity. Rather than being totally aligned with and characterizing two different historical periods, the premodern and modern, acts and identities name (in simplified terms) "two different discursive styles of sexual disqualification."[29] Though sexual identity remains an important if not defining feature of modern sexuality, intensified by the weird but potent effects of the homo/hetero sexual binary, historians following Foucault's line of thinking have pursued a more careful attention to the mutual co-articulations of acts and identity across different historical periods.[30] The critical consequences are demonstrated by Halperin in a brief comparative analysis of the "conceptual entities" assembled under the sign of homosexuality:

> (1) a psychiatric notion of a perverted or pathological *orientation* . . . an essentially psychological concept that applies to the inner life of the individual and does not necessarily entail same-sex sexual behavior or desire; (2) a psychoanalytic notion of same-sex *sexual object-choice* or desire . . . which is a category of erotic intentionality and does not necessarily imply a permanent psychosexual orientation, let alone a pathological or deviant one . . . ; and (3) a sociological notion of *sexually deviant behavior* . . . which

focuses on non-standard sexual practice and does not necessarily refer to erotic psychology or psychosexual orientation.[31]

This careful disaggregation draws attention to the incommensurable logics by which sexual acts and concepts of selfhood are related—or not—to each other across cognate sexual sciences. From this perspective alone, the definition of lesbianism, as a gendered version of the category of homosexuality, remains contradictory and incoherent. Historians working on social and cultural histories of sexuality in the late nineteenth and early twentieth centuries, the timespan within which *Queer Timing* is also situated, have responded in turn by approaching sexual identity as a non-unitary phenomenon in which gender, class, and race, among other factors, may be more important than sexual object choice and the hetero/homo binary.[32] *Queer Timing* does not claim to attend to those aspects evenly across its book-length project but considers each as they arise as salient elements in relation to the specific case studies that it pursues.

As these revised historical perspectives indicate, the term "lesbian" remains a capacious and incoherent critical category. Yet its powerful discursive and identitarian effects should not be discounted. As a contemporary category of identity, the term "lesbian" risks "[bringing] into 'the real' the very phenomenon that [it claims] to name only after the fact."[33] Why then continue to use a term that cannot help but accommodate the ahistorical and ideological tendencies of its worst disciplinary deployment? Despite such critical risks, this book retains the term lesbian for conceptual and pragmatic reasons. It indicates, if very coarsely, the sex/gender specificities of the book's concerns in relation to the intertwined histories of early cinema and sexuality. This same coarseness also allows the term lesbian to become a usefully flexible historiographical category. At one moment, it may reflect the retrospective application of a modern sexual category to an early film or figure in relation to which it has little conceptual purchase. At another point, its use might acknowledge the material force of an emergent sexual subjectivity. By retaining the term in the book's subtitle and across its chapters, I walk a kind of critical-revisionist tightrope: making lesbianism the book's primary focus even as I remain committed to historicizing and denaturalizing its effects. The term "lesbian" should be taken to mean less a definitive sexual category or identity than a provisional, even inadequate, term that names a sexual subjectivity in formation. As an always potentially anachronistic term, "lesbian" gestures to a central but paradoxical historiographic strategy pursued in this book: the suspension of contemporary sexual knowledges in order to make the historicity of sexuality critically perceptible. What does such a suspension involve, and what does it enable critically? Is it even possible?

Opacity as Method

Queer Timing endeavors to suspend present-day sexual knowledges in the encounter with early films and other extrafilmic archival materials. In other words, it presumes initially that the sexual legibility of any film or material artifact is opaque to us "sexual moderns." In some respects, this is to adapt one of the strategies of film historians in the celebrated encounter with early cinema at the 34th FIAF conference in Brighton in 1978: to endeavor to suspend (or at the very least recognize self-reflexively) contemporary enculturations in particular modes of viewing and in turn to reconsider early film not in terms of the present-future but in terms of its historically specific representational forms, modes of reception, and broader institutional and cultural contexts.[34] An initial presumption of sexual opacity aims to bring attention to our present-day sexual subjectivities and enculturations in the modern sex/gender system and naturalized modes of knowing that shape habits, practices, and methods of interpretation. To presume, at least before critical work commences, the sexual opacity of early cinema is to start from the position that the past is different from the present, particularly in terms of sexual subjectivity but not to accede to a homophobic denial of the historical existence of same-sex desire or queer ways of living and being. As a historiographical tactic, it draws inspiration from queer modes of speaking and writing that refuse the double binds of the closet and its lose-lose epistemologies.[35] It is akin to Eve Kosofsky Sedgwick's notion of reparative reading, as opposed to paranoid reading or a hermeneutic of suspicion.[36] The former approach has a temporal aspect: to inhabit a reparative rather than paranoid stance in one's engagement with the historical archive is to be attuned to the possibility of alternative patterns and experiences of time, to the ephemeral and contingent rather than the inevitable or teleological, without assuming in advance their ideological consequences.[37] The book draws on these queer modes of inquiry, interpretation and communication in order to sustain an openness to historical otherness, to being surprised, and to the uncertainty of not knowing.

Suspending our sexual knowledges as queer heuristic returns us to fundamental questions about not only what we know but the discursive and material conditions that shape what is able to be known in the first place. Initially this requires reviewing the conceptual terms that are pertinent to lesbian representation and spectatorship, not only the term "lesbian" as already considered, but other critical concepts such as identity, desire, and subjectivity. As Valerie Traub has argued, in an agenda-setting essay on lesbian historiography, it behooves scholars to be clear about what each critical category entails and its overlapping or intersecting conceptual, theoretical, and historical coordinates.[38] For example, a perspective attuned to the historical emergence of modern sexuality understands that homosexuality as novel sexual discourse, premised in part on logics of sexual similitude and mutuality, puts into crisis dominant social distinctions based on sexual difference and related cultural structures reliant on maintaining a difference between identity and desire. More than advocating a careful attention to the theoretical and historical implications of terms commonly deployed in studies of lesbian representation and spectatorship, Traub argues that lesbian historical projects need to historicize—by critically identifying and analyzing at a more granular level—the specific discursive forms by which women's bodies and erotic bonds are epistemologically organized. Drawing on an extensive cross-disciplinary literature of lesbian history, Traub sets out a list of "substantive themes"—which she readily acknowledges is unwieldy and far from comprehensive—through which a lesbian historiography might better understand the meta-logics that structure recurring but always different formations in the history of female-female desire. Even a select list indicates the varied focus and scope of these themes and their potential relevance to rethinking early cinema's instantiations of lesbian sexuality:

- the relationship between erotic acts and erotic identities;
- the quest for the etiology of erotic desire in the physical body . . . ;
- the relations of love, intimacy, and friendship to eroticism, including the defensive separation of sex from friendship;
- the fine line between virtue and transgression, orderly and disorderly homoeroticism;
- the relation of eroticism to gender deviance and conformity;
- the symbolic and social functions of gendered clothing;
- the relevance of age, class/status, and ethnic/racial hierarchies to erotic relations;
- the relationship of homoeroticism to homosociality;
- the dynamic of secrecy and disclosure, including covert signs, coding, and open secrets;
- the attractions of aesthetic conventions of erotic similitude versus erotic difference and/or hierarchy;
- the effects of narrative, poetic, and visual form on representations of homoeroticism;

- the gendering of propriety, emotion, and sensibility;
- the derivative, secondary order of lesbian visibility, which underpins conceptual misrecognitions such as lesbian "impossibility" and "imitation";
- the potential threat that female-female eroticism poses to patriarchal relations and male dominance.[39]

As Traub is at pains to note, "It is less that there exist transhistorical categories that comprise and subsume historical variation than that certain perennial logics and definitions have remained useful, across time, for conceptualizing the meaning of female bodies and bonds."[40] Some of those logics and definitions are more salient across the timespan considered in this book, and others arise that are not included in Traub's nearly exhaustive list, such as the possibility that a sexual identity might be organized across differences of sex and gender, perhaps because it is one of the givens of modern sexuality and operates, of course, to subsume precisely those more specific logics and definitions to which Traub's list draws attention. To the extent that *Queer Timing* endeavors to disarticulate and track the development of these specific discursive effects in early cinema, it can be understood to offer an alternative periodization of the emergence of lesbian sexuality as a fragile, incoherent sexual category. What appears from one critical perspective as a consolidation, such as the appearance in an early film of a lesbian-identified character, from another perspective registers more disparate, sometimes antagonistic transformations that cannot be neatly assembled into a legible totality.

One queer historiographical approach that elegiacally demonstrates the historical outcome of such a multivalent approach is Patricia White's carefully theorized essay that recuperates actress and director Alla Nazimova as lesbian auteur.[41] Focused on Nazimova's film *Salome* (dir. Charles Bryant, Nazimova Productions, United States, 1922), White demonstrates how the lesbianism of its director and her film only signifies at the intersection of certain historical discourses and critical perspectives. Cognizant of the productive effects of an anachronistic interpretation of the archive, White figures her project in terms of the veil, a critical trope that emphasizes the eroticized dynamics and affective investments in such revelations and concealments. Demonstrating the fragility of her historical reclamation while remaining alive to the desires and fantasies that animate a retrospective lesbian view, White's essay draws attention to the significance of not only identity but also identification for queer historiography.

In not requiring that we set aside our identities and identifications in order to read the past properly, and yet requiring the suspension of present-day sexual knowledges, the method advocated by *Queer Timing* is a deliberately queer and paradoxical formulation.[42] In endeavoring to sustain this methodological orientation, the book is aligned with Valerie Traub's "low-level" historiographical tactic of "maintaining a state of uncertainty regarding meaning and a state of contradiction regarding method," which as she writes promises to "paradoxically achieve more exactitude than privileging a single method or designating certain authors, texts, or analytics as queer."[43] Across the past two decades queer scholars have been reconsidering the historiographical value of asserting the difference between past and present and the value of critical procedures of anachronistic identification that depend in some form on a scholar's sexual identity.[44] From a queer perspective, history's disciplinary ban on anachronism ambivalently enforces an ideological binary: between a bad transhistoricist if not ahistorical identification, and a good historicist disidentification.[45] Identification as historical error or anachronism puts us out of sync with the disciplinary demands of present-day scholarship, an outcome shaped in part by the history of homosexuality itself. In an argument that draws attention to the lingering homophobic effects of a historical discourse of sexuality, Valerie Rohy suggests that the rhetoric against historical anachronism bears an uncanny resemblance to the sexological and psychoanalytic theories that constitute homosexuality as always out of time, unsynced from sexuality's most proper and normative sequencing.[46] Heterosexuality finds innumerable ways to straighten time in order to claim its epistemological and cultural privilege, but as Rohy indicates, "While straight culture at its own convenience finds homosexuality primitive or derivative, too early or too late, it is the old idea of queer retrogression that most clearly echoes in the complaint against scholarly anachronism."[47] Here "history" doubles around on itself: the history of homosexuality as sexological discourse belies the apparent ahistoricity of the prohibition on anachronism.

The disciplinary ban on anachronism occludes the critical efficacy of identification and the pertinence of queer experience and its unruly temporalities as a potential resource for developing new forms of historical knowledge.[48] In their effort to revise and reverse—or to queer—a suspect disciplinary prohibition on anachronism, Fradenburg and Freccero query whether identification across seemingly incommensurate time periods always determines a conservative historical and critical outcome: "What has to be asked is whether the observation of similarities or even continuities between past and present inevitably produces an ahistoricist or universalizing effect."[49] In other words, a psychic process implicated in sexual subjectivity can encompass an analytical and historiographical function. Anachronistic identifications, as several queer scholars have argued, can have cognitive value in the way that they permit the recognition of similitudes, resemblances, continuities, and echoes between past and present.[50] As Valerie Traub writes, what is promising about identification is "the possibility of dissociating the *apprehension* of similarities and continuities from their possible *effects*."[51] Identifications, when considered in terms of sexual subjectivity, will never be clear-cut. In psychoanalytic understandings, difference is a structurally necessary condition for identification to take place, one that in turn produces self-recognition and identity.[52] As David Halperin has pointed out: "if other people weren't *different* from us, what would be the point of *identifying* with them?"[53] In this regard, opacity as method pushes into territory in which identification signifies another kind of opacity, of the sexual subject to herself. Such identifications are already historical in the sense that they are shaped, if not wholly determined, by both personal and impersonal social histories. While the anachronistic temporalities of identification are not commensurate with the historical times of conventional historiography, the odd temporalities identified by psychoanalysis—such as the well-known *Nachträglichkeit* or *afterwardness*—can provide a conceptual vocabulary not only for describing subjective time but also possible connections between lived and historical forms of time. The queer lived and felt time of anachronism potentially disrupts and reorganizes historical time, that is, disciplinary discourses of temporality by which the past, present, and future are articulated to one another. The following section of the Introduction further pursues this claim and its implications for *Queer Timing*'s counter-historiographical methods.

Queering Historical Time

Queers already know that different historical times, as Peter Osborne notes toward the end of his book, *The Politics of Time: Modernity and the Avant-Garde*, "encode" some possibilities and experiences of history while foreclosing others.[54] The sense of a linear continuity between past and present has provided many lesbian historical projects the means of ensuring the future possibilities of lesbian identity and culture, even if we might argue that they are premised on a retrospective misrecognition of the historicity of sexual subjectivity. For such continuist histories, the archives offer, as Anjali Arondekar writes in a different context, "a temporally ordered seduction of access, which stretches from the evidentiary promise of the past into the narrative possibilities of the future."[55] Such histories are necessarily forward-looking utopian enterprises that have faith in a continuous, linear historical time. More radical queer perspectives, while not denying the urgency of such desires and the material conditions that subtend them, critique the political effects of such forms of historical time and instead propose alternative temporalities that draw from queer experiences of lived time and their cultural forms. Carolyn Dinshaw summarizes the temporal dimension of queerness as "forms of desirous, embodied being that are out of sync with the ordinarily linear measurements of everyday life, that engage heterogeneous temporalities or that precipitate out of time altogether."[56] The nonnormative modes of inhabiting time that characterize and structure queer life are understood to be opposed to, even if partly constituted by, the schedules of normative time: clock time, calendar time, rationalized linear quantifiable time. The lineaments of queer time include anachronism, feeling backward, a dilated present or "continuing moment," an asynchronous "temporally multiple world in the *now*," and moving sideways rather than forward into a normative reproductive future.[57] The latter "no future" queer time might be read in one way as a dilation of the queer temporalities that structure the present, while it points to a "refusal of futurism" shared across divergent queer projects engaged in thinking historical time otherwise.[58]

Queer thinking on time has been challenged recently in relation to several problems: the scholarly forgetting of alternative Western traditions of thinking time; the oversimplification of disciplinary conventions of historical time; and the slippage between or conflation of sexual subjectivity, temporal experience, and historical time.[59] As Dinshaw points out: "No historian believes that time moves punctually forward, for example, emptily, evenly, and always progressively toward a single goal."[60] In a thoughtful and generously argued critique of what she calls the new unhistoricism in queer studies, Valerie Traub points out that: "Neither straight identity nor heterosexual desire is the same as linear time. Not every diachronic or chronological treatment of temporality needs to be normativizing, nor is every linear arc sexually 'straight.'"[61] More than identifying these problematic conflations, Traub has diagnosed in some recent queer studies a tendency toward a "teleoskepticism" that tends to misconstrue the complexity and history of debate concerning teleology, chronology, and historical time.[62] Rohy has also contributed to this rethinking of queer temporality by demonstrating that the normative or nonnormative effects of different orders of time—the ephemeral, the dilated present, even clock time—are always "contextual and contingent."[63] Rather than choosing one time or another, or rather than one time or another being indelibly queer, Rohy exposes their co-implication and the impossibility of choosing between ordinary (chronological) and extraordinary (other) times.[64]

The co-implication of queer and normative temporalities is further complicated when we consider that experimental inhabitations and rethinkings of time across the twentieth century are mediated by, and respond to, new forms of time-consciousness specific to the social and material forms of modernity, including cinema.[65] For example, anachronistic viewing practices, perhaps even an empathy with "outmoded" styles of film production and reception, continue to be important for lesbian critical spectatorships. Theorizing her relation to a later film style and period, Hollywood classical cinema, Patricia White coins the neologism "retrospectatorship" to describe the distinct temporalities that shape her relation to the film archive as both lesbian spectator and film scholar.[66] Emphasizing the always already retrospective nature of our objects of study, retrospectatorship allows White

> to diagnose a nostalgic impulse in spectatorship theory; to name my own use of classical film history; and to describe the irreducible play of past and present, the joining of audiences and artefacts, in the subjective and (sub) cultural experience of viewing and writing about films.[67]

Though White's mode of lesbian critical spectatorship might not seem translatable to a project focused on early cinema, her final point usefully keeps in view film's complex temporal orders and the identifications across time that it sustains. The temporal folds of past-present that persist in the encounter with a historical film text are not problems to be overcome by particular methodologies, but are rather part of the enabling conditions of critical spectatorship—and especially queer critical spectatorship. Heather Love's observations about the historical and present significance of feeling backward, for example, are generated in part from a consideration of a documentary film on the history of gay and lesbian representation in cinema, *The Celluloid Closet*, one instance of the productive anachrony of film's remediations and spectatorships in the present.[68]

Seen in the wider context of the impacts of new imaging and storage technologies not only on film culture but also scholarship, such queer modes of historiography might also be understood as parallax historiography, a term developed by Catherine Russell to name a transformative turn in the field of feminist film history.[69] For Russell, parallax historiography is "a discursive formation premised on the archival function of new technologies that enable us to rewrite film history; and . . . this rewriting constitutes a valuable revision of the modernity of cinema as a site of shifting identities and viewing positions."[70] Despite its utopian dimensions, parallax historiography resonates with the alleged deficiencies of historical anachronism, that is, with reading present-day identities and politics back into the past. It is this sense of historical anachronism, manifest in the secondary meaning of *parallax*—"the fact of seeing wrongly or in a distorted way" according to the *Oxford English Dictionary*—that haunts Russell's perceptive analysis.[71] From a queer perspective, parallax historiography evokes a different scale of historical time to which anachronistic modes of queer viewing might be articulated: a structural and contingent sense of historical times, of the present and the past held in suspended, discontinuous, and dynamic relation to each other.

While *Queer Timing* remains particularly attuned to temporalities such as anachronism and the ephemeral in early cinema, it remains initially agnostic as to whether they evidence or structure specific sexuality effects. One of the fundamental strategies of sexuality itself, for example, has a temporal valence: it attempts to stabilize and fix ephemeral erotic experience. José Esteban Muñoz's theorization of ephemera as a queer kind of evidence—a slightly different historiographical articulation of time than I have just been discussing—is valuable in this context because of how he redefines ephemera as evidence, and articulates its particular relation to representations of queerness as nonnormative, minoritarian, sexual, and relational.[72] In his challenge to conventional historiography, Muñoz expands the term *ephemera*, emphasizing its immaterial qualities and its different relation to dominant domains and structures of knowledge: "Ephemera, as I am using it here, is . . . a kind of evidence of what has transpired but certainly not the thing itself. It does not rest on epistemological foundations but is instead interested in following traces, glimmers, residues, and specks of things."[73] Muñoz's last poetic line of thought, which gives Chapter 2 of this book its title, evokes the importance of the ephemeral in terms of queer historiographical modes of identification and selection, and the valuation of those materials, texts, and media that evidence a mode of being or erotic relationality that may no longer exist or be perceptible from a present-day perspective. Part of what *Queer Timing* tracks in early cinema are moments in which the fleeting durations of ephemeral time, ostensibly a quality of all erotic experience, are discursively retooled to regulate certain forms of homoeroticism and not others (see Chapter 2) or strategically enlisted to more queer-positive representational modes (see Chapter 4). In relation to what I am calling opacity as method, ephemera as evidence recognizes the difficulty of suspending current sexual knowledges while drawing attention to the close relation between the values attached to certain kinds of historical evidence and the historical narratives that they support, in particular to efforts to render certain forms of eroticism—most often heteroeroticism—as more solid and weighty, as mattering more than others.[74] But ephemera as Muñoz defines it also conveys a double meaning in its organization of historical time: it is evidence of something that is already past, and an always secondary mode of encounter in the present that seeks to avoid reproducing the sexual norms or disciplinary procedures that might otherwise contain or destroy it.[75] If *Queer Timing* seems at times hesitant, or unable to sustain a definitive historical interpretation, it is because it aims to inhabit this queer (and Muñozian) critical perspective.

Timelines

Queer Timing is organized thematically in three parts. The first, "Queer Historiography: Suspending Sexual Knowledges," comprises two chapters that together reconsider the historical narrative of the emergence and consolidation of lesbian representation. Each chapter resists deploying current sexual knowledges to make the past sexually intelligible, while critically redeploying the incoherent identifications that indicate our present-day enculturation in modern sexuality for their cognitive rather than epistemological value. The first chapter, "Troubling Sexual History: The Anachronistic Lesbian of *Pandora's Box*," considers the critical, historical, and cinematic temporalities that structure the sexual legibility of the lesbian character in *Die Büchse der Pandora* (dir. G. W. Pabst, Germany, 1929). The Countess Geschwitz has been apprehended as a particular kind of pathological, sexual, and erotic figure, even as the shifting discursive fields that render her intelligible have not been exactly commensurate or coherent across the decades of her dramatic creation and subsequent cinematic representation and reception. Paradoxically, any narrative of the emergence of lesbian cinematic representation is problematized by the very sexual identity that such a narrative claims to historicize. The Countess turns out to be both modern—lesbian, polymorphously perverse—and backward—sexual invert, romantic friend—her sexual legibility temporally desynchronized from any single or singular historical period. Not only registering a historically specific set of incoherent sexual discourses that continue in different ways to inflect lesbian identity, the temporally burdened figure of the Countess also indexes a critical disavowal of the historical accumulations that comprise all modern sexuality. The companion chapter, "Traces, Specks, and Glimmers: Regulating Same-sex Attractions," turns to reconsider a related historical narrative: the absence of any recognizable lesbian figures in the early cinema archive. Given the claim that the intelligibility of lesbian figures on screen is already a belated effect of a complex assemblage of prior strategies of sexuality, the chapter aims to trace some of those strategies particular to early films at the turn of the twentieth century in the context of a heterogeneous culture of spectacle and entertainment. Early cinema evidences a capacity for generating unruly and multivalent forms of erotic attraction and visual pleasure, even as it also registers transformations in sexual knowledge and experiences of embodied desire and erotic identity. "Traces, Specks, and Glimmers" argues that attempts in early films to eroticize sexual difference and establish a gendered scopic hierarchy also represent a discursive effort to transform—by visually de-privileging, suppressing, or eliding—the differently ordered homoerotic visual pleasures and practices of looking of the late nineteenth century. These often forgotten moments of disrupted same-sex intimacy or voyeurism demonstrate the expansion of discourses of sexuality, and nascent efforts to discipline the erotic, even as their effects remain fleeting and unpredictable.

Part II of the book, "Bodies: Form, Genre, and Sexuality Legibility," comprises a pair of chapters that together consider how film-specific modes of representation—that is, narrative form and genre—render the female body intelligible as a sexual body with particular kinds of desires. The sexuality effects of early cinema depend in part on the capacity of cinematic narrative to represent human figures as characters, that is, as embodied narrative agents whose actions are intelligible in terms of some kind of unseen, internal motivation. The first chapter in this part, "Queer Character: *A Florida Enchantment*'s Ambivalent Sexual Motivations," argues that the development of a specific narrative film style—recognized in retrospect as the Hollywood classical style—and the concomitant industry drive to ensure the legibility of longer-form stories for audiences marks a small but significant turn in the disciplinary effects and representational possibilities of early cinema and its spectatorship. Often recuperated as an example of the representation of sexual inversion and lesbian desire in early cinema, the sex-change comedy *A Florida Enchantment* (dir. Sydney Drew, Vitagraph, 1914) offers an ideal case study of early cinema's novel sexuality effects. The chapter argues that a female figure tangential to the main narrative, and whose erotic desires or orientations remain puzzlingly opaque, demonstrates how the reliance on even rudimentary forms of motivated character action to sustain narrative clarity is also productive of novel, albeit nascent, forms of sexual legibility. This effect cannot be considered in isolation from a second, in which the coding of heterosexual desire as transparently legible depends paradoxically on forms of both knowledge and ignorance pertaining to the sexual import of homoerotic forms of intimacy.

Turning to focus on the generic conventions and institutional structures of Hollywood classical cinema, "Mobilizing Genre: The Sexual Kinesthetics of *The Wild Party*" considers the sexuality effects of a film released on the cusp of the transition to sound, which redeploys the codes of a nearly exhausted genre, the flapper film. While several scholars have read *The Wild Party* (dir. Dorothy Arzner, Paramount Lasky, 1929) in terms of its lesbian subtext, a mode of interpretation shaped by a representational regime that postdates the film's release, this chapter traces how the visual erotics mobilized across the entire film render such scenes sexually legible. "Mobilizing Genre" argues that the site through which lesbian possibilities are paradoxically screened—that is, both projected and hidden from view—is the sexualized and kinetic body of the feminine flapper. In failing to anchor same-sex desire definitively to any one sexual category, *The Wild Party* demonstrates the centrality of same-sex desire to female spectatorships in Hollywood cinema and its intimate and productive relation to new erotic discourses of both homo- and heterosexuality.

The final two chapters turn away from the cinematic legibility of particular kinds of sexual figures, identities, and desires toward a wider range of same-sex erotic visual discourses, practices, spectatorial relations, and effects. Part III "Bonds: Spectatorship and Queer Subjectivities" comprises two chapters that consider the unanticipated effects of a regime of sexuality bent on disciplining and normalizing wayward forms of eroticism and sexual identity. Each addresses moments in early cinema in which sexuality's potentially repressive effects are short-circuited by processes of appropriation, reorientation, or refusal. The first chapter in this final part focuses on an archive that is emblematic of the intermediality of early cinema: the electric light dance performances of late-nineteenth-century celebrity, Loïe Fuller. Fuller's assemblage of various conventional forms of movement, dance, stagecraft, and costuming resulted in an innovative and spectacular stage show in which she "danced" encased in a voluminous, flowing, and sometimes translucent, robe onto which were projected colored electric lights, magic lantern slides, and photographs. While Fuller rarely performed in front of the camera, filmmakers were quick to exploit her popularity, producing a number of films of Fuller imitators performing, to varying degrees of success, her signature serpentine dance. The chapter argues that the Fuller performances and films represent a specific response to and transformation of conditions of vision, practices of looking, and voyeuristic modes of spectatorship for women. Fuller's visual archive—considered in an expanded sense as both her onstage performances and their cinematic copies—suggests how the developing sexual subjectivities of female spectators were already bound up in proto-cinematic forms of spectatorship that turned on the visual pleasures of the moving female body. Appropriating and reorienting the sexuality effects of late-nineteenth-century visual culture, they sustained a paradoxically disembodied and depersonalized homoerotic mode of spectatorship.

The final chapter of *Queer Timing* tracks sexuality's more dispersed impacts via the matinee idol Rudolph Valentino, a star figure whose appearance in a book dedicated to lesbian representability might seem unexpected or even antithetical to its stated ambitions. "Valentino's Lesbianism: Stardom, Spectatorship, and Queer Recognition" considers the terms by which Valentino's historical female spectatorship is shaped by both identifications with and desires for the feminized star. These entangled spectatorial relations are often associated with Valentino's negation of cross-sex desire, whether through his on-screen relationships with mannish or asexual female figures, or his off-screen relationships with well-known sapphic figures. The chapter argues that these and other elements of Valentino's contradictory image, though constitutive of his sexual ambiguity, comprise a more obscure fantasmatic supporting female same-sex desire and new forms of sexual identity shared by women and men. The spectatorial possibilities that accrue to Valentino are suggestive of the unpredictable but also generative possibilities of the Hollywood star system by which the seeming impossibility of desire between women might register in more diffuse terms as a kind of recognizable queer affect or structure of feeling.

Resisting the lure of writing a history that ends triumphantly in the representation of a coherent modern sexual identity, *Queer Timing* traces the disparate sexuality effects of what was once a novel material and social technology. Far from being a straightforward linear account of "emergence," in which some category or identity comes into view, the book delineates the process of the emergence of lesbian sexuality in early cinema as unevenly distributed and haphazard, and at other times increasingly systematized and continuous. In other words, the history of lesbian representation and spectatorship in early cinema is marked less by emergence and consolidation than by the aleatory timing of sexuality's disparate impacts. Via its historiographical reorientations, this book seeks to enable the articulation of a richer, queerer set of possibilities for thinking about the representation of desire between women, same-sex oriented erotic identities, and their diverse corporeal, aesthetic, and affective modes.

PART I

Queer Historiography

Suspending Sexual Knowledges

FIGURE 1.1. Alice Roberts as the Countess Geschwitz in *Pandora's Box* (1929).

1. Troubling Sexual History

The Anachronistic Lesbian of Pandora's Box

> The history of sexuality is, in some sense, always already anachronistic.
> —Peter Cryle and Christopher E. Forth, *Sexuality at the Fin de Siècle*

THE SEXUAL MODERNITY of the late silent film, *Pandora's Box* (dir. G. W. Pabst, Nero-Film, Germany, 1929), depends on the presence of one character: the Countess Augusta Geschwitz, played by Alice Roberts. Yet, critical commentary on the film tends to relegate the Countess to a marginal role in its history, or she is simply—or, in my case, perhaps symptomatically—forgotten. The first time I saw *Pandora's Box* at a film festival screening I barely registered her on-screen presence even though I have no doubt that it partially authorized my own erotic and identificatory investments in the central character of the film, Lulu—if not more especially the American actress who plays her, Louise Brooks.[1] More glamorous, seductive, and enigmatic than any of the film's other characters, the Lulu/Brooks cult star complex exerts a powerful centripetal force on both everyday and critical receptions of *Pandora's Box*.[2] It is possible that my initial forgetting of the character of the Countess was a defense against—or resistance to—the terms within which her character has most often been understood, a barely registered dis-identification with a figure whose diegetic relation to Lulu echoed my own cinema-induced fantasies. For even as the formal style and aesthetics of *Pandora's Box* establish Lulu as a figure who incites desire, the Countess is remembered less for being one of the many characters caught up in the erotic force field of Lulu's strangely vacuous screen persona than for what seems now a more prosaic, but for all that still more deadly, "fact": her status as the film's lesbian character.

The most influential scholarship on *Pandora's Box* tends to note the "fact" of the Countess's lesbianism in a way that sustains the character's marginality even as she remains a paradoxically necessary figure in the film's sexual schema.[3] Critical claims that the Lulu/Brooks figure instantiates an appealingly mobile and ambiguous screen eroticism inevitably rely on the celluloid presence of the Countess as a kind of sexual counterpoint, a figure whose sexual identity is apparently easily determined and fixed.[4] The identification of the Countess as the lesbian character of *Pandora's Box* exhumes her from the archive as a fully formed figure continuous with present-day sexualities while occluding the historicity of her sexual intelligibility. Turning away from the charismatic star configuration of Lulu/Brooks to attend to the forgotten figure of the Countess—a seemingly perverse endeavor that goes against the film's design and its predominant mode of reception—enables the historiography of cinematic representations of sexuality to be problematized.

The predominant signifier of Geschwitz's lesbianism is taken to be her "masculinization," a gendered state allegedly confirmed by what Mary Ann Doane describes as her consistent occupation of "the margins of a masculine scenario structured around Lulu."[5] Yet, aside from the too-easy conflation of a style of gendered embodiment with a sexual identity, the difficulty of relying solely on a gendered optic by which to read the discursive figuration of the Countess is foregrounded by Doane's other claim that "femininity constitutes a danger which must be systematically eradicated."[6] Her supporting examples comprise not only the early disappearance from the film's narrative of Schön's fiancée, and the death of Lulu in the eighth and final Act at the hands of Jack the Ripper, but also the demise of Geschwitz in the film's penultimate Act. Unable to discipline the figure of Geschwitz to one or other gender, Doane's inconsistency demonstrates how common critical categories are already inflected by the historicity of sexual difference and modern homo/hetero sexual definition.

Popular and scholarly histories of lesbian cinematic representation have tended to focus in a more sustained manner on the figure of the Countess as part of an investment in the political and social value of recuperating representations of marginalized sexualities.[7] These works draw attention to the contradictory terms of the Countess's sexual legibility, whether in terms of her "sickness and decadence" or her same-sex devotion emblematic of the Weimar's progressive sexual politics.[8] Such divergent interpretations register not only the time elapsed between the character's adaptation from play to film, but also the character's intelligibility in terms of competing historical systems and cultures of sexual knowledge. Yet the visual strategies and aesthetics of *Pandora's Box* only further unsettle readings of Geschwitz's character in terms of sexual pathology, personality, orientation, or identity. Situating Geschwitz as a figure representative of a polymorphously perverse Weimar Republic, the film privileges the mobility of desire and the instability and contingency of social and sexual identities.[9] Thus, even at the moment of her screen debut, the Countess's sexual legibility is hard to synchronize to any one historical period or sexual discourse, raising questions about retrospective historiographical procedures of contextualization and periodization. The character's cinematic renovation from stage to screen, and the subsequent restoration and digital archiving of *Pandora's Box*, preserve and amplify the queer temporalities of her sexual modernity.

The Countess's intertwined textual, cultural, and cinematic genealogies function as a "temporal drag" on any claim to be able to identify her retrospectively and definitively as the representation of a new and modern lesbian. Here I am taking up but also reorienting, for historiographical purposes, Elizabeth Freeman's evocative phrase, which describes the anachronisms of sexual identities and politics in the present, in particular the forgotten, foreclosed, or unfinished political possibilities registered by the retrogressive effects that lesbianism and feminism seem to exert in relation to queer political thinking.[10] A consequence of foregrounding the anachronisms of the Countess Geschwitz's sexual modernity is that it becomes increasingly difficult to sustain the more general and seemingly straightforward proposition that lesbian representation in early cinema is consolidated by the early 1930s.[11] This future-oriented claim sustains a continuity with present-day sexual identities that makes less visible the wayward temporal orders governing the sexual intelligiblity of the very same figures that are said to evidence it. What the Countess's trouble with time—or rather her troubling of time—enables is a critically queer troubling of the historiographical protocols that underpin *Pandora's Box* scholarship in order to demonstrate how to do a counter-history of sexuality in early cinema.

In Retrospect

Across the twentieth and twenty-first centuries, a sense of retrospectivity inevitably governs critical assessments of *Pandora's Box*, given its limited success when it was first released, an outcome compounded by the excisions and story line changes ordered by censors. It has been the restoration of the film to the director's original cut, itself a lengthy and deferred accomplishment, that has enabled the film's belated critical reevaluations.[12] While it is a critical commonplace that all historical work is inevitably premised on temporal delay, retrospectivity might be an essential historiographical strategy for evaluating the institutional and cultural contexts for the film. One of Weimar cinema's preeminent critics, Thomas Elsaesser, argues that it "cannot be understood in terms of some essence . . . but as the moment where in retrospect something became apparent."[13] This claim registers—perhaps unintentionally—a temporal paradox. Implicitly valorizing the possibility of a broader, objective historical knowledge of Weimar cinema premised on and enabled by a temporal distance from the past, such retrospectivity is nevertheless awkwardly located in an ambiguous time, "the moment." Does it name Weimar cinema as historical period, or does it gesture toward that peculiar temporal fold in which we view the luminous, restored version? The availability of *Pandora's Box* as a restored cultural object unsettles the idea that a chronological gap is necessary in order to ascertain a clearer view of its significance. Retrospectivity continues to authorize the linear temporalities that underpin conventional historiographical protocols of periodization and contextualization, at the risk of failing to account adequately for the historicity of sexuality. Despite the restoration of the film, and its lavish remediations, interpretations of the Countess Geschwitz's role tend to be supported less by how she is represented on screen than through interpretations that contextualize the film's representation of sexuality in terms of the cultural history of the Weimar era.

Many of the scenes in *Pandora's Box* are set in Germany during the Weimar Republic, a transformative political event understood to have cultural ramifications. It organizes the conceptualization of a period of filmmaking and its institutional frameworks, the Weimar cinema, of which *Pandora's Box* is understood to be an important artifact. While the Weimar era has provided a critical starting point for scholars to contextualize the film, situating *Pandora's Box* in terms of the Weimar's erotic history generates contradictory effects in relation to the Countess character that bear on her historicization as a sexual figure. Thomas Elsaesser and Mary Anne Doane, the most influential commentators on the film, establish the Weimar Republic as an era when earlier sexual prohibitions and silences are visibly and multiply transgressed. In tandem with accounts of the political, economic, and social crises of the period, both critics suggest an abrupt change in sexual morals and behavior, in broad terms a transition from a bourgeois mode of sexual secrecy to an excessive and diverse sexual exhibitionism. Both draw attention to the Weimar's highly public and popular cultures of sexual and gender boundary crossing, of which the Countess signifies but one instance. While Elsaesser suggests that "open homosexuality" and "sexual ambiguity" have fixed the Weimar period in the "popular imagination," he points to all kinds of cultural production—from serious literature to fashion—as evidence for the sexual obsessions of Weimar society.[14] Similarly, Doane notes how other cultural artifacts of the period "evince a fascination with sexual transgression and the violation of traditional taboos through the exploration of pornography, prostitution, androgyny, [and] homosexuality."[15] Leaving aside the question of the commensurability of those terms, in these accounts an apparently self-evident and naturalized homosexuality becomes one of a number of signifiers of the Weimar era's reputation for transgressive and experimental sexualities enabled by new consumer and commodity cultures.[16] Ascribing lesbian sexuality to the figure of the Countess ensures that her cinematic presence in *Pandora's Box* in effect acts as a visual stand-in for the sexual energies and heterogeneity of the Republic's sexual modernity.

The changes in social and cultural formations in Germany of the Weimar period are obviously complex; it is how that history has been deployed in analyses of the representation of sexuality in *Pandora's Box* that tends to undermine the historicity of sexuality itself.[17] In describing homosexuality as breaching the prohibitions of a repressive nineteenth-century past, critics implicitly construct a historical narrative in which a publicly and culturally visible homosexuality emerges fully formed as both an indicator and a cause of paradigmatic shifts in attitudes, aesthetics, and social and legal prohibitions. Such a narrative confirms the essential nature of homosexual desire—and distinguishes it from heterosexual desire—by positing its secret and oppressed existence at precisely the same moment that it is seemingly liberated from constraining prohibitions. As Michel Foucault has demonstrated, this "repressive hypothesis" is not something separate from the deployment of sexuality but is itself folded into an increasingly intensive and multivalent network of power acting on and through the body. Rather than representing a historical rupture, the emergence of discourses of repression and its overcoming represents a continuation in the deployment of sexuality.[18] Not only does the dominant critical version of Weimar sexual history fashion a rhetoric in which a visible homosexuality is one of a number of erotic practices and identities that register a sexual modernity, but, as an analytical tactic, it elides the possibility that sexuality itself might have a longer and more temporally complex history.

The Weimar's history of sexuality and sexual cultures, as it is implanted by critics commenting on *Pandora's Box*, produces an apparently recognizable and modern lesbian subject who in her critical figuration comes to bear the historical weight of the very sexual transformation she is said to symbolize. Both Doane and Elsaesser in their audio commentary to the most recent and lavish DVD of *Pandora's Box* persist in describing the character in terms of her "repression in mannish suits" (figure 1.1) an aphorism first used by

Louise Brooks to describe not the character Geschwitz but the performance of actress Alice Roberts.[19] Rather neatly, the sexual repression that Geschwitz signals the end of is rerouted through her body and transformed into an individualizing, debilitating psychic phenomenon. In a convoluted and contradictory logic, Geschwitz's perversity is signified not only by the apparent public legibility of her sartorial style (her "mannish suits") but also by an internalized homophobic resistance to its fullest expression. This scholarly figuration of the lesbian of Weimar modernity—and Brooks herself should be regarded as one of the commentators involved in this enterprise, even as she is also often positioned as an authoritative historical source—produces a thoroughly un-modern sexual subject, a throwback to the nineteenth century unable to liberate herself from its normative constraints. As a temporally convoluted effect of critical discourse, the Countess becomes a foil necessary to sustain the canonization of the film and its timelessness. Simultaneously crucial and inconsequential to the film's representation of a more exciting, mobile eroticism, the Weimar-era lesbian turns out to be a symptomatically anachronistic figure. The Countess bears—as a means of disavowing—not only the temporal contradictions of the history of lesbian sexuality but also those of other sexualities. While returning to the origins of the film in its adaptation from a stage play might seem on its face a retrograde—because retrospective and chronological—historiographical maneuver, it provides an opportunity to retrace the divergent epistemologies that rendered the figure of the Countess erotically and sexually intelligible.

Out of Date

The aristocratic Geschwitz is an obvious but also in many respects old-fashioned character to appear on screen during the Weimar era. Geschwitz was already a familiar fictional figure in German culture, made famous by the regular performances of the play on which the film is based.[20] Although banned from open performances after playwright Frank Wedekind completed it in 1904, *Pandora's Box* was able to be publicly performed with the lifting of censorship in 1918.[21] Mitchell Morris argues that, by the time of the Weimar Republic, the fin-de-siècle figure of the Countess was the archetype of the lesbian in German drama.[22] In this respect, her initial sexual legibility accrues not in terms of contemporary sexual subcultures or identities, or even relatively new discourses of homosexuality, but rather earlier sexological and class-inflected discourses of sexual inversion, perversion, and erotic deviancy.[23] In other words, even within the contemporary moment of her theatrical debut, the sexual intelligibility of the Countess character was contingent upon and determined by the historical sedimentations of older erotic discourses and newer sexual knowledges. The retention of the character's title in the film, while assuming a different and more ambiguous valence in the context of the Weimar Republic's democratic transition, persists to remind audiences of the associations between the aristocracy and discourses of degeneration, nonproductivity and perverse sexuality.[24] The character's last name, on the other hand, secures her legibility in terms of the pathologizing discourses of sexology. But for the addition of a final *t*, the proper name *Geschwitz* is the past participle of the verb *to sweat*, a textual remnant of her more pathological theatrical characterization.[25] In the play, the character's association with illness is secured in the very first scene when she appears on stage as a vaguely malevolent figure sitting "deep in the cushions with a rug over her knees," suffering from cholera.[26] And in a later scene, Lulu cruelly rejects Geschwitz, calling her a "pervert."[27] The sense that film audiences might think they already "know" the Countess would thus have had a particular cultural and historical resonance and specificity for middle-class audiences in Germany and artistic, high culture audiences within other Anglophone cultures.

Wedekind wrote and rewrote *Pandora's Box* over a long period, 1892 to 1913, a time that coincided with the publication and popularization of several significant sexological works.[28] By the time Wedekind had begun to write, Richard von Krafft-Ebing had already published his *Psychopathia Sexualis* and the enormous popularity of the work ensured its continued publication well into the 1920s.[29] In the same period, Otto Weininger's notoriously racist and misogynistic *Sex and Character* (*Geschlecht und Charakter*) became a best seller in Austria and Germany; its 1906 English translation also continued to be reprinted into the 1920s.[30] Just as Wedekind's texts were influenced by sexological literatures, Wedekind also attempted to shape the theatrical performances and receptions of his plays, including that of the Geschwitz character, through his extratextual writing. In a preface to *Pandora's Box* published in 1906, when public performances of the plays were still forbidden, Wedekind claimed that the Countess, rather than Lulu, was the "tragic central figure of the play," an assertion uncritically repeated by some film scholars.[31] Arguing publicly that Geschwitz has to "summon all her spiritual resources in the attempt to conquer the terrible destiny of abnormality with which she is burdened"—other passages in the English translation of the Preface refer to Geschwitz's "curse" and her "affliction"—Wedekind draws on notions of congenital sexual inversion even as he also exaggerates the character's fate in order to secure the sympathy of his readers.[32] While Wedekind's defensive Preface might suggest his sympathies with German homophile reform movements to decriminalize sex between men and foster more tolerance for male urnings and female urinde, others have argued that it was a subterfuge designed to deflect legal objections to the play's performance.[33] Whatever his motivations, Wedekind draws on the rhetoric of tragedy to describe Geschwitz's "fate," at the same time that he utilizes the scientific terms of sexology to modernize her destiny. These contradictions in Wedekind's characterization of his own fictional creation are also temporal ones: in the former, the story of Geschwitz's life is determined by invisible cosmological forces—to the extent that she accrues a grand, timeless aura—while in the latter she is a temporally and thus sexually bound creature, trapped in a degenerative and irreversible history.

By the time *Pandora's Box* was adapted to film in the late 1920s, another discourse of sexuality was emerging in popular culture in relation to which the character of Geschwitz may have been understood, a discourse whose potentially more fluid understandings of identity and desire nevertheless remained both inflected by and in tension with the retrogressive temporal orders of sexology. The transition from the stage to the film version of the Countess character can be read as a transition from understandings of sexual inversion, which included but were not limited to same-sex desire, to a Freudian notion of homosexuality founded on same-sex object choice. The director of *Pandora's Box*, G. W. Pabst, was familiar with the work of the preeminent psychoanalyst. In 1926, he had directed *Secrets of a Soul* (*Geheimnisse einer Seele*), a film expressly intended to promote psychoanalysis as a treatment for neurotic disorders, and the year before *Pandora's Box*, he directed another film that also drew on psychoanalytic theory, *The Loves of Jeanne Ney*.[34] Characteristics of *Pandora's Box* also suggest Pabst's familiarity with Freudian thinking. The relative neutrality of the film about Geschwitz's desire parallels Freud's ambivalence about same-sex desire and erotic practice. For example, in his famous 1920 case study, "The Psychogenesis of a Case of Homosexuality in a Woman," Freud is anxious to demonstrate that homosexuality is a functional way of being while at the same time characterizing his patient's emotional makeup—"her 'masculinity complex,' with its attendant capacity for courtly love"—as part of her abnormality.[35] Like Freud's patient, the Countess's persistent overtures to Lulu can be read as "extravagantly sensitive and romantic."[36] This and other parallels invite the speculation that Geschwitz might have been read in terms of Freud's so-called masculinity complex, a possibility that nevertheless arises in the context of an already uneven and disparate discursive terrain of earlier erotic models of female same-sex desire, and the persistence of other late-nineteenth-century medical knowledges. Elements of Freud's case study also register the ongoing cultural presence of other modes of understanding same-sex desire, including older romantic traditions of natural feeling, often expressed in the language of intense love and friendship, the latter a term still being used in the names of homophile organizations in Germany in the 1920s.

The story of the film's censorship and later restoration suggests the simultaneous—though never coherent—availability of these contradictory and competing sexual discourses within which same-sex desire might be understood. The representation of desire in *Pandora's Box* impacted significantly on its reception: in most territories outside of Germany it was heavily censored.[37] The *Pandora's Box* we view in the present differs in its coherence and singularity from the different versions of the film released in 1929 and their censorship. The resulting confused and disjointed narrative—the product of several forms of censorship that manifested differently in various locations—often led to poor reviews.[38] Rather than a single, coherent auteur cinematic production, *Pandora's Box* at the time of its first release comprised a contradictory set of multiple texts.[39] While it is difficult to reconstruct a detailed and complete account of the film's censorship, the two most significant aspects are the Nero-Film company's own preemptive strategy in which they produced a significantly different version of the film for the French market, and the editing of Pabst's original version by censors outside of Germany.[40] In the alternative version of *Pandora's Box* released in France, entitled *Loulou*, the central character does not die at the hands of Jack the Ripper; instead, the final scene implies her Christian redemption as she watches the Salvation Army parade through the streets.[41] While important elements of the film's narrative and Lulu's character were either recast by the film's producers for the French version or altered by various censoring bodies, the impacts of these different forms of censorship arguably bore most heavily on the character of the Countess. The French version altered the name of the character to "Anna Kerendt"—a strategy also applied to most of the other main characters—and also nominated, via an inter-title, Kerendt's relation to Loulou as her "compagne de misère," a term intended to evoke their friendship and shared childhood poverty.

The unpredictable and productive capacity of censorship in generating sexual discourse—already amply explored in critical literature in relation to the effects of the Hollywood Production Code in the 1930s and 1940s—is suggested by an account of viewing the French censored version of *Pandora's Box*. Aside from the different relation between Lulu and Geschwitz, *Loulou* also changes the relationship of Dr. Schön and his son Alwa so that the latter becomes Schön's secretary, a transformation that according to one notable source made their on-screen relationship comprehensible in terms of sexual desire rather than familial affection. Rudolph Leonhardt, the screenwriter for another of Pabst's films, *Diary of a Lost Girl* (*Das Tagebuch einer Verlorenen*, 1929), claims in a letter to German critic Lotte Eisner, which she reproduces in her book chapter on *Pandora's Box*, that "the same [paternal] gestures become tainted with homosexuality."[42] This interpretation raises the possibility that the censorship efforts geared to the French market, and its revision of the Geschwitz-Lulu relationship in terms of close female friendship, may have failed to desexualize their on-screen intimacies, a possibility reinforced by the film's censorship and reception in other territories.

In the United Kingdom and the United States, it seems that the German version of *Pandora's Box* was released with cuts that significantly altered the Countess's character and role in the narrative. Elsaesser notes that all references to the Geschwitz's "lesbian attraction" for Lulu, as well as other representations deemed morally inappropriate, were removed by censors in the United States by means of cuts and changes to the inter-titles.[43] In a 1930 article in the British modernist film journal *Close Up*, Robert Herring despairs of the censorship of *Pandora's Box* in which "the Lesbian part . . . is cut out. We mustn't know about them."[44] Herring's sarcastic and violent trope—the excision of a diseased part of the social body—invokes a popular pathological model of the lesbian as a personage of a certain kind who can be identified or diagnosed and then exiled from view. Herring's lament about what was lost in the English censorship of *Pandora's Box* subsumes to some extent the generative complexities of visual representation, of which he was undoubtedly aware in his role as film critic. While he is clearly registering a particular abject view of perverted congenital sexuality, his metaphor also suggests the ways in which censorship attempts to disavow certain knowledges. Thus the paradoxical logic of censorship presumes an ability in the censor to identify objectionable material that might be recognizable as such to audiences, all the while maintaining the fiction that excision of the material in question will ensure a continued public ignorance of the matter in question.

Despite the various means by which Pabst's original version of *Pandora's Box* was censored, the discourse of the film's reception could still draw attention to its representation of sexual deviance and its inclusion of a lesbian character. In the United States, for example, a review in *Variety* considers that the story unwinds "awkwardly" as "Lulu hurls herself at men of all ages and even a possible Lesbian or so." The latter's faux uncertainty is undermined by the initial capitalization of "lesbian" which textually amplifies the significance of this notable on-screen presence while also denoting the character's sexual speciation.[45] Even a mention of the film's exhibition in the regular cinema page of the *New Yorker* does so in terms that invoke sexology as its most cogent frame of reference, referring to the film's "subdued Krafft-Ebing overtone."[46] That the substance of the film's interest could be evoked by merely referring to the name of a sexologist suggests the cultural familiarity with studies of sexual perversion and deviancy, while simultaneously addressing the magazine's readership as a highbrow public. By framing the film in these terms—whether by reference to a specific sexual category or type of person, or to an influential body of sexological knowledge—these examples evidence the context within which the film was already positioned, as well as suggesting that viewers may have already been primed to reading the film, its characters, and narrative in contradictory sexual terms. Assuming that both reviewers had seen only the censored version of *Pandora's Box*, these examples may indicate something more unexpected in terms of the generative effects of the censored film's sexual discourse. It also raises questions about the differently located contemporary receptions of the film, given the cross-border extracinematic circulations of erotic and sexological knowledges that were occurring in the first few decades of the early twentieth century. While the capacity of any film to serve as historical evidence is already compromised by its untimely aesthetic and spectatorial temporal orders, these examples of the promotion and reception of *Pandora's Box* attest to the further complexities of how to frame historically its film-specific sexual discourse. The most recent restored version, now the go-to critical source, evidences the availability to some historical spectators of a filmic discourse that unsettles the Countess's sexual figuration via an innovative cinematic style that draws into its orbit other contemporary social and everyday forms of knowledge and pleasure.

Up-to-the-Minute

Most commentators detect the Countess's modernity—and thus the film's modernity—in terms of a recognizable sexual identity, a retrospective critical maneuver that partially secures a historical narrative of the consolidation and continuity of lesbian representation. Yet the filmic discourse of *Pandora's Box* as we see it now disturbs this easy alignment. The modernity of the celluloid Countess is also discursively constituted by other forms of cultural knowledge beyond those of late-nineteenth-century medical and scientific disciplines in ways that render any one aspect of her identity difficult to fix. One of the first signs of this uncertainty is the character's title. A vestige of the film's adaptation of its theatrical source, Geschwitz's title is likely to have indexed for contemporary German audiences both the official abolition of titles by the Weimar Constitution in 1919 and their ongoing retention and incorporation into their proper names by some former nobles.[47] Geschwitz's title, formerly a precise term designating an aristocratic lineage and its concommitant forms of social power, is rendered more uncertain in its significations of class, marital status, and familial connections. The Countess Geschwitz's name, a small but necessary convention of filmic characterization, thus registers a particular kind of late 1920s Weimar modernity in which social standing is increasingly contingent and mutable.

If a name no longer transparently indicates a person's social standing or the nature of her connections to other people, another important aspect of characterization, costume, intensifies these effects. In narrative terms, costume functions in part to establish that Geschwitz shares an erotic investment in Lulu. The film's opening scenes establish Lulu's male "patrons" as they each arrive, much like prospective sexual clients, at her apartment: the tramplike Schigolch (Carl Goetz), ambiguously positioned as her surrogate father, former pimp, and possibly even her first lover; the respectable Berlin newspaper editor, Dr. Ludwig Schön (Fritz Kortner), to whom Lulu is mistress; and the famous acrobat Rodrigo Quast (Krafft-Raschig), who promises to give Lulu a role in his variety act. If being drawn into Lulu's erotic orbit is the only thing that Geschwitz might have in common with these figures, the first scene in which she belatedly appears visualizes this attraction in terms of her fashionable similitude with yet another character under Lulu's spell, Alwa (Franz Lederer). Depicted as joint spectators of Lulu's magnetizing dancelike entrance to the scene, Pabst frames Geschwitz and Alwa in a two-shot in which the details of their jackets, bowties, and even pocket handkerchiefs are carefully matched (figure 1.2). While framing and costume design combine to evoke the characters' similitude, these elements of mise-en-scène fail to secure a commonality of desire that in turn straightforwardly signifies Geschwitz's lesbianism.

Whether the Countess's masculine presentation had the capacity in 1929 to signify sexual abnormality (to the exclusion of anything else) is already tempered by the uneven circulation of disparate sexual knowledges since, as discussed in the previous section, both older and not always coherent sexological understandings of sexual inversion coexisted with the emergence of the new and equally contradictory psychoanalytic discourse of homosexuality. Considered in terms of the history of early-twentieth-century fashions, the Countess's mannish garb troubles the signifying capacities of masculinity and its relation to sexual difference and sexual identity, and establishes instead a fashionable and playful dissonance between her gendered presentation and her female sex. As Laura Doan argues in relation to English fashions of the 1920s, "The meaning of clothing in the decade after the First World War, a time of unprecedented cultural confusion over constructions of gender and

FIGURE 1.2. Matching suits.

sexual identities, was a good deal more fluid than fixed."[48] While the style of Geschwitz's costume may have been recognizable to some contemporary viewers as a look associated with Berlin's homosexual subcultures, it was not exclusively so; it was a popular style that drew self-consciously and playfully on masculine modes of dress and self-presentation.[49] Masculine fashions generated some anxiety in German culture, though this manifested in a range of different discourses about women's role in the family, female sexuality, work, race, and class.[50] In drawing on the desynchronizing effects of fashion—its ability "to grant social status through the mere display of its attributes"—the film registers a broader unsettling of gendered organizations of public and private life.[51]

If the Countess's up-to-the-minute dress style disturbs the capacity of masculinity to signify a sexual identity, or to secure sexual difference and its attendant social hierarchies and privileges, the film's aesthetic style also works against the hypostatizing of social and sexual identities. Geschwitz's first scene contains an exemplary instance of such formal effects: an abstract shot of Lulu and Alwa that accompanies Lulu's assertion that only Alwa wants nothing from her. Across the brief duration of a single tightly framed close-up, Lulu looks almost directly at the camera—her gaze in narrative terms is directed toward Geschwitz now standing alone—before she pulls back slightly and turns to face Alwa who is standing opposite her, partially visible in the upper-righthand edge of frame. Brooks's action together with the lighting effects and cinematographic composition transform the image from one that evokes the three-dimensionality of volume and the temporality of movement to a stilled two-dimensional plane, resulting in an abstract, genderless image of a romantic couple (figure 1.3). Initially associated with Geschwitz's point of view, the image's quality as derealized spectacle dissolves its narratological function.[52] The nature of the desire evoked by the fragmented twosome of Lulu and Alwa remains ambiguous, its sexuality effects dispersed and open.

Given the formal style by which it establishes the always contingent and changing allegiances of its characters, *Pandora's Box* provides very few moments in which we might read the Countess in terms of any stable identity. Only one image in the film explicitly foregrounds the Countess's identity, although it bears an ambiguous relation to the film's discourse of desire. During the film's sixth Act, Geschwitz engineers Lulu's escape from court and then lends her passport to enable Lulu to travel incognito. The film efficiently segues to the following scene on a train bound for Paris with a cut to a close-up of the cover of Geschwitz's passport, before the unseen border official thumbs through several pages in order to stamp it. Momentarily, Lulu assumes the Countess's identity, a narrative development that confirms the inadequacy of a document premised on the unproblematic visual legibility of photography and the capacity of a proper name, birth date, and place to register a unique identity. The brief image of the passport, a banal legal instrument, also points to another paradoxical logic of the film's discourse of identity and desire. Even as the similitude of the sexed body permits a substitution and deception, the impossibility of Geschwitz's desire for Lulu is figured in terms of the modernity—that is, the mobility and mutability—of identity.

The precarious relations of identity and desire instantiated by the filmic discourse of *Pandora's Box* remain in tension with not only the film's later critical recuperation but also the cultural and historical context of its initial exhibition and reception. The discordant elements of the figure of the Countess that I have elaborated in previous sections—across both her later recuperative scholarly discourse and her contemporaneous receptions—attest to her peculiar anachronicity. By reassembling a film that initially comprised disparate, multiple, and incoherent textual artifacts, embedded in the regulatory practices and constraints of exhibition and spectatorship, the restoration

FIGURE 1.3. The abstract couple.

of *Pandora's Box* has sustained the appealing fantasy of its own timelessness and modernity and their concommitant sexuality effects, figured in the mobile Lulu/Brooks vis-à-vis the static Geschwitz. Registering a historically specific set of incoherent sexual discourses that continue in different ways to inflect modern lesbian sexuality, the temporally burdened figure of the Countess indexes a critical disavowal of the historical accumulations that comprise all representations of modern sexuality in early cinema.

Recalibrations

In the penultimate Act of *Pandora's Box*, the Countess Geschwitz once again arrives belatedly, though this final entrance registers uncannily in terms of the passage of time. The film's abrupt edit makes it seem as though she arrives immediately after Alwa and Lulu, and yet the following inter-title indicates that three months have passed. In narrative terms, the sequences onboard the ominous ship—it doubles as a salubrious casino and hotel—comprise

Geschwitz's second attempt to rescue Lulu. These scenes—overshadowed by the melodramatic horror of the final moments when Jack the Ripper ascends the staircase to Lulu's London garret to kill her—suggest something of the historical legibility of the film's discourses on female sexuality, modernity, and Geschwitz's position in them. While they appear on screen for the first time as a couple, the narrative requires its images of intimacy and friendship to be read again in terms of deception, since Lulu's goal is to trick Geschwitz into sleeping with Quast in order to save herself from being turned in to the police or being sold to the Egyptian brothel owner. The various shots of the two characters together—whether walking to Quast's table with their arms around each other's waists (figure 1.4), or the close two-shot when Lulu touches Geschwitz's face—evoke, even as they also act as a further visual deferment of, the sexual subcultures of Berlin that they have already left. Not only visually registering certain historical and material conditions under which modern sexual cultures are made possible, the Countess Geschwitz's tardy presence in the film at this point in its narrative, read allegorically, also suggests how as a sexual figure she exerts a backwards historical pressure on the intoxicating modernist present film-time of *Pandora's Box*.

The Countess Geschwitz's timely appearance in the film archive has been read in retrospect as a significant instance of the consolidation of lesbian identities across a range of public discourses and visual cultures, and thus the very epitome of what is "modern" about lesbian sexuality and sexual identity. Yet, as a figure, she is marked by numerous temporal and historical contradictions. The legibility of the character's sexuality is contingent and paradoxical, her modernity enabled by the timelessness of the film image even as the circumstances of her literary creation and its proximate sexological discourses temporally desynchronize her from an "always now," wrenching her back into a different nineteenth-century sexual and erotic order. Already a strange anachronism in 1929, the character's temporal discontinuity is redoubled by a scholarly discourse that remains limited by the sexual terms of its retrospectivity. To attempt to "straighten out" these messy temporalities would miss their ideological import, in particular how their accrual to the figure of the Countess ensures that she bears the historicity not only of lesbianism but also that of another "modern" sexuality that always hovers in close proximity, heterosexuality. The inability to synchronize the disparate times that adhere to the figure of the Countess suggests the queerness of sexual historicity in early cinema.

In keeping with the historiographical strategy of suspending our current sexual knowledges in encounters with the archival materials of early cinema, reconsidering the sexual legibility of a canonical figure in the history of

FIGURE 1.4. The deferred couple.

lesbian representation puts pressure on the critical utility of lesbianism as a sexual category and its historical timelines of emergence and consolidation. The following chapter pursues a complementary tactic to the same historiographical end: it considers a selection of early, sometimes obscure, films as ephemeral artifacts whose pertinence to a history of the emergence of lesbian sexuality seems, from a present-day perspective, much less evident. If the Countess Geschwitz of *Pandora's Box* is a transparent effect of sexuality in her anachronistic figurations, the figures and bodies that populate early film as it materializes in the late nineteenth and early twentieth centuries bear a less clearly articulated relation to the regulatory strategies of sexuality itself.

2. Traces, Specks, and Glimmers

Regulating Same-sex Attractions

Ephemera . . . a kind of evidence of what has transpired but certainly not the thing itself.
—José Esteban Muñoz, "Ephemera as Evidence"

THE READY INTELLIGIBILITY of on-screen figures in terms of one sexual category or another is the sign of a remarkable assemblage of strategies of sexuality. It is worth dis-articulating just a few to get a sense of the array of knowledges, practices, and aesthetic forms that may come into play. A sample list would include: certain kinds of knowledge that assume, and thus discursively produce, the body as an already sexual body; practices of interpreting the body that read its surface, movements, gestures, and facial expressions as signs of inner desire; the licensing of men as subjects of the erotic gaze, and women as their objects; contradictory social and scientific understandings of intimacy between women that privilege, alternately, similitude and relationality (romantic friendship), or difference and individuated forms of identity (sapphism, inversion); and the logics of invisibility or impossibility that determine the modes by which knowledge of women's same-sex desire circulates in culture.[1] While such a list is not comprehensive, one of its critical-historical implications is that the lesbian figures that appear on early cinema screens are only the most visible condensations of prior and dispersed strategies of sexuality. This second chapter focused on queer historiography turns back to the early intermedial period in which films are first exhibited commercially in order to trace some of the preceding strategies most pertinent to a counter-history of lesbian representation. In so doing, it also reconsiders some of the concepts, categories, and methods required to make the history of sexuality in early film critically visible.

Given that what remains preserved in archives is only a small fraction of what was produced across the late nineteenth and early twentieth centuries, the potential status of any early film as a representation of nonnormative erotic desire invites a scholarly interest that may seem out of all proportion to its ephemerality. One such short film preserved at the BFI National Archive in London is described in its catalog in the following terms: "COMEDY. Scene from a stage routine. On a stage *a woman dressed as a nobleman* watches another woman dancing, the latter wearing a dress which reveals her thighs. When she rests on a chair the nobleman pays court, fans her with the tails of his coat and finally embraces her (66ft)."[2] As with most early film "attractions," the tentatively titled 1898 film, *Gavotte*, runs for only a minute or so, and the context of its exhibition would have intensified the sense of its brief duration.[3] Likely to have been presented in random if not "illogical succession" with other short entertainments, such as skits, songs, and magic lantern slides, its visual pleasures—taken together with the shocks, sensations, and surprises of the films presented before and after it—would have been short-lived, unpredictable, and difficult for any viewer to "master."[4] Although not "lost" like other early nitrate films that literally went up in smoke or were carelessly discarded, *Gavotte* might still be considered "lost" in the sense that it resists our historical comprehension.[5]

A survey of additional information about the film only further complicates how we might understand its erotic representation and mode of address. The catalog's initial ascriptions of genre (comedy) and intertextuality (a stage routine) are amplified by a note on the film's likely title and provenance: "This may be GAVOTTE, 'dansé par les Cornier-Menesco du Jardin de Paris,' in the Pathé catalog for 1900–01, no. 769."[6] The Archive's note indicates that the film remediates a specific theatrical performance already familiar to French (or at least Parisian) audiences, while the suggestion that the BFI collection's film may be the same as the one listed in the early Pathé catalog further extends its historical genealogy. The tentative title for the film refers to a popular social and theatrical dance with its own specific history of performance, eroticism, and class affiliations. For the purposes of this introductory outline, the following description of a "gavotte" provides a useful summary:

> A lively peasants' kissing dance that became fashionable at the 17th- and 18th-century courts of France and England . . . the gavotte was danced in royal ballrooms as a round with skipping steps adapted from the branle. Couples concluded improvised duet performances by kissing their partners. Later the dance developed more formal figures, and flowers were exchanged instead of kisses.[7]

Thus the catalog note, appended to provide further information about the film's possible title and production history, generates a further question about the effects of filmic remediation on an already eroticized dance performance inflected by social hierarchy. Did the cinematic representation of a stage routine, as part of a broader engendering of new despatialized and detemporalized subjectivities, reframe and reorient its erotic meanings? Did it enable the film to be viewed and experienced as homoerotic? And, if so, how might the terms of that homoeroticism—its relation to more visible gendered forms of embodiment, for example—relate to new categories of sexual identity in cultural circulation?

If this discussion seems like too much critical weight for such a brief and ephemeral film text to bear, an example of how *Gavotte* has been argumentatively deployed raises the historiographical stakes even further. In her discussion of the overlapping erotics of early dance films and cross-dressing comedies, Alison McMahan provides supplementary information in her account of viewing *Gavotte*. Before the final embrace of the film's couple, she notes, "The 'man' kneels at the woman's feet, lays a trail of kisses along her bare arm, and declares his love."[8] Enhancing the spare catalog synopsis, McMahan's description highlights and specifies a further aspect of the film's erotic mise-en-scène, one that for McMahan confirms the purpose of the film as "the eroticism of seeing two women kiss."[9] In this account, the film's seemingly transparent homoeroticism confirms both its generic ascription as an erotic film and its gendered structure of address "designed to heighten the spectacle for masculine eyes."[10] Though only occupying a single paragraph of a monograph that brings together a significant archive of new materials on filmmaker Alice Guy Blaché and her contributions to early filmmaking in France and the United States, McMahan's claim assimilates *Gavotte* to a streamlined account of erotic female spectacle in service to a masculinized gaze.

Even though *Gavotte* is an obscure film, its subject matter and brevity typical of the many ephemeral attractions produced at the turn of the twentieth century, it is already enmeshed in an archival apparatus and scholarly discourse that significantly shapes its erotic and sexual legibility for us "sexual moderns." Rather than smooth over the film's more fugitive erotic effects, this chapter begins from the premise that the sexual legibility of *Gavotte*'s figures and their erotic interactions, and early films more generally, are not immediately intelligible to us in terms of present-day critical concepts, gendered hierarchies of spectatorship, and the sexual subjectivities that they endeavor to sustain. It takes the film as an object lesson in how to trace historically the discursive articulations to one another of the eroticized female body, the sexual intelligibility of homoeroticism and heteroeroticism, and developing cinematic codes that may sustain or reorganize the gendered dimensions of exhibitionist and voyeuristic structures of looking. The chapter situates

Gavotte in terms of the intermedial and unruly erotics of the early cinema of attractions before undertaking a series of close readings of other brief and seemingly unimportant moments of homoeroticism and same-sex intimacy in early films. The aim is to consider how early films may register transformations in the cultural centrality and meanings of homoeroticism as it inflects modes of female visual pleasure, relationality, intimacy, and embodiment. Looping back to *Gavotte* by its end, the chapter reconsiders the film as obscure evidence of the unpredictable effects of modern sexuality.

The Erotics of Attractions

The erotic forms part of the "multivocal field of address" within which, as feminist scholars now recognize, female spectators are differently, and often ambivalently, addressed.[11] In the period of the cinema of attractions, the erotic has tended to be identified with the genre of the erotic film, one that typically involves the partial or full nudity of female figures, whether motivated by social scenarios (such as marriage), the "reproduction" of well-known paintings, or the remediation of stage performances such as burlesque striptease acts.[12] The implied appeal of erotic films to male audience members—and the licensing of their desire—is often figured in the nascent diegesis by the inclusion of one or more male spectators.[13] Yet, in the early period of filmmaking and exhibition, the discursive and institutional systems that might order and normalize heteroerotic film-viewer relations are tenuous. Genre, for example, was a process of negotiation and positioning between producers and exhibitors, the latter exercising far greater influence and control—even in relation to editing shots together and coloration—than in later periods of cinema history.[14] Further, exhibitionist displays of female bodies were not confined to films understood in generic terms as erotic; they occur across other early genres, such as dance and physical culture films and remediations of various vaudeville and circus performances. Even the very process of filmic remediation itself had the capacity to multiply and enhance, rather than homogenize, the diversity of representations that might be considered erotic.[15] The early Edison kinetoscope films on the Black Maria set demonstrate this point with their diversity of styles of female embodied performance, from scenes of gymnastics to precision shooting.[16] The eroticization and display of women's bodies is thus imbricated in a range of performances of movement, intermingled with demonstrations of physical and cultural competency that seem to bear little explicit relation to more overt erotic genres.

The pervasive eroticism of early film, most visibly centered on the female body, can be regarded as part of a broader cultural effort not only to fix the erotically ephemeral but also to organize its spectatorship in accordance with gendered and sexual norms. Yet, the range of sources that early cinema drew on, and the variety format in which early films were programmed, ensured that early cinema's attractions instantiated modes of viewing across which erotic affects could proliferate in often unpredictable ways. The critical exemplar of this process in relation to early female spectatorship is the apparent popularity with women of a famous boxing film, *The Corbett-Fitzsimmons Fight* (Veriscope, U.S., 1897). Noting the reported pattern of female spectators attending the film in large numbers in American cities, Charles Musser suggests several explanations, including the continuation of the habit of moviegoing for women, especially to matinees, and their assertion of independence.[17] Miriam Hansen has argued that the unexpected popularity of the fight film with women was also enabled by the new conditions of a specifically cinematic spectatorship in which "the experience was abstracted into visual terms, removed from the sensuous impact of noise, smell, and audience excitation . . . it afforded women the forbidden sight of male bodies in seminudity, engaged in intimate and intense physical action."[18] For Hansen, underwriting the significance of this example is its apparent violation of a long-standing taboo in patriarchal culture on the active female gaze.[19] In this case, however, it is not just a new visual technology that enables the violation of a taboo but the social context in which it is encountered. This form of cross-sex voyeurism is, as Musser notes, mobilized within a socially acceptable framework of heterosocial spectatorship.[20]

Any claims that can be made for the mode of spectatorship that *The Corbett-Fitzsimmons Fight* seemingly accidentally enables are complicated by a reconsideration of the articles that reported on the film's audiences, and their evidential status. As Dan Streible persuasively argues, news reports of women attending the screenings in the United States need to be read in light of evidence that the fight promoters sought to thwart censorship efforts by generating publicity that characterized the film's appeal to a more genteel, heterosocial crowd, a strategy also calculated to diversify the film's audience in order to maximize profits.[21] Moreover, as Streible reads it, journalistic accounts articulated female interest in the fight film in at least two divergent forms: a staged moral disinterest; and an intense, eroticized focus on the fighters, further accommodated by the matinee idol reputation of Corbett.[22] The difficulty of determining the critical significance of *The Corbett-Fitzsimmons Fight* is amplified further if we focus on its distinctive gendered and sexualized structure of film-viewer relations. As most scholars, including Musser, Hansen, and Streible, have suggested, the fight film registers changes in gendered forms of spectatorship and women's participation in the public sphere. Though the example is constructed in terms of an active female viewer of a male object of visual pleasure, the psychic mechanism of voyeurism that it is taken to instantiate, and the heterosexual subjectivity that it ostensibly constitutes, is complicated by the homosocial and homoerotic scene that it depicts. Alongside its heteroerotic viewing structure, the film also suggests other dimensions to women's viewing pleasures, such as an appreciation of—and perhaps even identification with—masculine forms of embodiment and physical competency. Foregrounding the instability of emergent sexual subjectivities at the fin de siècle, the ambiguous case of *The Corbett-Fitzsimmons Fight* indicates that women's spectatorship is yet to be disciplined more systematically to socially sanctioned forms of heteroerotic visual pleasure.

Blind Spot

The case of *The Corbett-Fitzsimmons Fight* is exceptional in a field in which few feminist film history scholars have addressed, in any sustained manner, the erotic dimensions of women's imbrication in the visual registers of modernity, and cinema in particular, other than as objects of male-looking and erotic desire.[23] In mapping out the contradictory and unstable gendered structures and conventions of representation and spectatorship established in early cinema, scholars have rarely considered the ways in which early erotic films may have reflected and shaped women's varied homoerotic interests and emergent sexual subjectivities. The relative lack of attention to the possibilities of same-sex desire and the discursive transformations of the homoerotic seems all the more surprising given the characterization of early cinema as "deviant" when compared to later institutionalized systems of classical filmmaking, as "lacking" the formal and institutional capacities to interpellate its audiences as "proper," "normal," "adult" spectators.[24] Eroticized images of women in the early film archive occur across a broad range of genres in which diegetic male spectators are often nowhere to be seen, genres likely to have been seen by heterosocial audiences. A few emblematic examples from the thousands of films produced—the titles of which succinctly describe their visual content—might include *Annabelle Butterfly Dance* (Edison, U.S., 1894), *The Physical Culture Girl No. 1* (American Mutoscope & Biograph, U.S., 1903) (part of a series), *A Fight in the Dormitory* (American Mutoscope & Biograph, U.S., 1904), and *Girls Swinging* (American Mutoscope & Biograph, U.S., 1902). Even when voyeuristic male figures are present on screen, their effects cannot be guaranteed by the film text itself. Across early cinema, potentially homoerotic representations appear in a heterogeneous range of diegetic spaces and narrative and exhibitionist scenarios. To give just two more divergent examples: in *The Prima Donna's Understudy* (American Mutoscope & Bioscope, U.S., 1905), according to John Hagan, "an actress' understudy (it might even be her maid) is carried away kicking after she has been discovered trying on the star's stockings."[25] Hagan's description leaves it open as to whether the maid's desires are, as Hagan suggests, for the pleasure of wearing exotic garments or whether those garments act as a fetishlike substitute for the maid's erotic interest in the actress. In *A Busy Day for the Corset Model* (American Mutoscope & Biograph, U.S., 1904), a woman views two other women modeling corsets in a department store fitting room, a setting in which consumerism and fashion can be read as diegetically authorizing—or providing an alibi for—the female customer's erotic gaze.[26] Despite the recognition of the complexities of the early period's forms of address, and the indeterminacy of the film text, such films have most often been assimilated to critical accounts of early cinema's gendered and heterosexual representational modes and spectatorships, either with regard to the implicitly nonsexual socially sanctioned and consumerist modes of film-viewing by female spectators or the constitution of everyday feminine space and its female bodies made publicly available to a putatively masculine erotic scrutiny.[27]

Heteroeroticism, that is an erotics of differently sexed bodies, functions critically as feminist lure to the extent that it obscures the salience of other forms of eroticism, their relation to modes of voyeurism and the historical emergence of modern sexual subjectivities. Innovative models of historically situated, mobile female spectatorships, for example, have tended to envision their utopian and transcendental potential outside of heteroerotic structures of spectatorship, as if the effects of a voyeuristic structural form are only ever directed toward sustaining a male gaze.[28] Catherine Russell claims, for example, that the recuperated figure of the flaneuse—the female version of Baudelaire's modern flaneur—"enables us to think beyond the structures of voyeurism and visibility that have hitherto kept women as the objects of the gaze."[29] In their privileging of the spectatorial agency and mobility of the flaneuse, and their desire to sidestep the voyeuristic, feminist critics miss an opportunity to consider the possibility of the flaneuse's eroticized spectatorship of other female figures or images. A theoretically and historically contested figure, the flaneuse highlights the relative absence of a consideration of the homoerotic in histories of female spectatorship, and draws attention to how women's everyday practices and modes of viewing traversed public and private spheres. They included such activities as the taking and viewing of photographs, the consumption of fashion plates, album-making and viewing, the exchange of cartes-de-visites, and attending more public visual entertainments such as dioramas and panoramas. Even a cursory glance at the literature suggests that homoerotic modes of representation and practices of looking were a significant aspect of a diverse range of visual cultures.[30] One recent study in particular develops a provocative thesis that has the potential to enable a transformative shift in thinking about late-nineteenth-century genealogies of female cinematic spectatorship.

In a book-length study of middle-class female cultures in the decades between 1830 and 1880, *Between Women: Friendship, Desire, and Marriage in Victorian England*, Sharon Marcus demonstrates how homoerotic structures of looking were central to women's engagements with new consumer cultures. With her attention to an archive of imagery and texts drawn from popular magazines, Marcus's work enables a different historical perspective on mass visual media and the development of female spectatorships in light of what was a broader culturally normative tradition of homoerotic representation and voyeuristic practices of looking. Chastising scholars of nineteenth-century culture, Marcus calls on them to "abandon the consistent assumption that erotic interest in femininity can only be masculine" in order to "understand how femininity was objectified and displayed for women as well as men."[31] Consolidating her reading of visual archives through her attention to major literary texts, Marcus persuasively demonstrates her central argument that "[f]emale homoeroticism did not subvert dominant codes of femininity, because female homoeroticism was one of those codes."[32] One of Marcus's more relevant examples that allegorize women's modes of spectatorship are the fashion plates of popular women's magazines. These thematize looking between and at other women while also reinforcing their homoerotic address through motifs of touch and supplementary visual technologies.[33] While Marcus's female viewers presumably consume their fashion plates in the home, the diegetic spaces of the images themselves are more varied. Though they sometimes offer up the space of the drawing room or bedroom as the mise-en-scène of women's intimate glances or touches, at other times single women, pairs, or groups are located in more public spaces, such as the park, the seaside, or the theater. Locating these scenarios of looking in such spaces not only enhances their erotic frisson, but can also be read as an articulation of bourgeois women's experiences and fantasies of the mid-nineteenth-century public sphere. The looks and glances of the women in these scenarios is often further enhanced by optical technologies, such as opera glasses, telescopes, and binoculars. In the imaginary scenarios of the fashion plates, such visual apparatuses supplement ordinary vision, bringing the distant image of the other women closer to the view of the diegetic spectator. Counter to the physical intimacy enforced by the constraining frames of the fashion plates and the sexual valence of motifs of touch to certain body parts, the presence of such optical devices imbues them with a highly charged voyeurism. As a specific nineteenth-century historical phenomenon, women's fashion magazines reinforced and sustained as cultural norm an intense *identification* with and eroticized *desire* for the women represented in that fashion media.

The prominence of such technologies of vision in the mid-nineteenth-century archive of visual cultures, and their place in enabling homoerotic and voyeuristic modes of viewing, is highly suggestive for thinking about how representations of homoeroticism and modes of female spectatorship were further transformed in the late nineteenth and early twentieth centuries. Marcus's archive does not extend into this temporal period, since she argues that by the 1880s sexuality, as well as gender identities and social institutions like marriage, began to change dramatically; one prominent example she cites is the emergence of lesbianism in sexological writings of the 1890s.[34] As I have already argued in the Introduction, such transformations occurred unevenly and in diverse cultural locations, beyond the medical and social sciences, across the last decade of the nineteenth century and the early decades of the twentieth. This gives rise to an important question for this project: to what extent does early cinema function as a site for the intensification and implantation of sexuality at the fin de siècle? The remainder of this chapter considers a sample of instances of forms of female intimacy—a touch, a look, a kiss—in order to consider how early film's emergent aesthetic conventions may have begun to instantiate, however haphazardly or experimentally, new sexual epistemologies, including those codes of knowledge by which forms of same-sex intimacy, and homoerotic modes of looking are rendered impossible, insubstantial, or nugatory. In their experiments with new forms of cinematic syntax, some early films register a desire to reorient the meaning of same-sex erotic action within their frames. The potential sexual meaning of such moments, temporally and historically ephemeral, is bound up in their relation to the attractions or affects generated by, and characteristic of, the very early period of filmmaking. The minute details of physical gesture and the temporal brevity of such visual events bear an inversely disproportionate relation to the effects of the nascent sexual ideology that they index. By adopting this critical perspective, we can then read a film like *A Busy Day for the Corset Model* as performing a kind of discursive labor to reorient and discipline women's homoerotic modes of looking, a strategy related to the emergence of both homo- and heterosexuality. In other words, early cinema's nascent regulation of homoerotic visual pleasure may be the more historically salient transformation for more than one kind of female sexual intelligibility and mode of spectatorship.

How Not to Watch

The single-shot film *Kiss Me* (American Mutoscope & Biograph, U.S., 1904) is one of a number of early films that literalize the viewer in the text, its self-reflexivity offering a mode by which to consider the historical understanding of early film-viewer relations and the potential significance of same-sex eroticism.[35] It re-creates a New York city street scene, the background of which comprises a row of posters advertising various burlesque entertainments.[36] One of the posters is a "live" image of a woman who looks out both at passers-by and toward the camera. This cinematic trick plays on and privileges cinema's superior capacity to animate and attract human bodies.[37] Biograph's in-house publication describes and promotes the main appeal of the film as follows:

> An old farmer and his wife are strolling along, the old gentleman being a little ahead. He looks at the picture of the girl and fancies he sees the eyes winking at him. He puts on his glasses to make sure that he is not dreaming, when the girl leans forward with an expression as if inviting him to have a kiss. The old man is about to take advantage of his delusion when his wife appears on the scene, and taking him by the ears rushes him away.[38]

Such catalog descriptions were often used as cues for film lecturers' accompanying narratives at film screenings. As Maggie Hennefeld points out, "the film plays upon anxieties about the status of risqué female images displayed in public, as well as the pervasive blurring between the cinematic and everyday embodied spaces."[39] *Kiss Me* also depicts—only to render it invisible via mise-en-scène—a related problem: the often indiscriminate appeal of proliferating visual cultures in modern urban spaces. For what is conspicuously missing from the catalog's narrative, and Hennefeld's account, is a description of the action that precedes and sets the scene for the old man's erotic misrecognition. In the first third of the film (totaling only a minute and a half), a female couple first enter from screen right. As they walk swiftly past the "live" poster, they express clearly their distaste, one character even glancing toward the camera to register her disapproval—an example of the kind of action that appeals to the audience directly as members of a shared public. The female couple embody a feminine and bourgeois disapproval of commercial erotic entertainments addressed to male audiences even as their response is briefly made available for visual comparison to another potential same-sex relation involving an erotic gaze. Shortly after the pair's exit, a third woman enters from screen left, trailed by a younger woman who comes to a sharp halt, mesmerized by the poster's liveness (figure 2.1). Realizing that her charge has slipped behind and become distracted by (or attracted to?) the poster, the older woman—a chaperonelike figure—drags the younger woman off-screen right. The young woman's actions mirror, on a smaller temporal scale, those of the older man who follows and dominates the remainder of the film's action. Functioning on one level as a mise en abyme of his ill-disciplined actions, the young woman's presence suggests the juvenile nature of his attraction to the poster even as it fails to distinguish their respective attractions in solely gendered terms.[40] The young woman's presence also renders less stable the interpretation offered above of the preceding action, for it becomes possible to read the disapproval of the first pair of women as encompassing the unpredictable homoerotic pleasures that such visual forms of publicity might provoke.

Kiss Me's male character, the country rube, was a typical foil for representing the film's subject matter, as was its physical comedy—particularly the slapstick punishment of a prurient male spectator. The young woman's presence in *Kiss Me* is significant compared to the cultural currency of the country rube figure if only because she remains relatively unanchored to any socially recognizable female type. The rube, who appeared in a range of contemporary media and theatrical forms, is generally understood to provide a figure through whom the new experience of modernity and the city could be dramatized. The figure of the young woman has no equivalent generic history though she appears, tantalizing, in a number of disparate visual and documentary sources—from etchings to photography—as a more nebulous juvenile figure who finds enjoyment in viewing various early forms of erotic moving imagery.[41] Still dependent on parental figures of authority, she is neither "bachelor girl" nor urban flaneuse, tangential to other more socially visible female figures and modes of spectatorship. While the young woman's attraction acts as an introduction to the country rube's unsophisticated erotic delusion, it also enables the film to construct its own forgetting of the possibility of a homoerotic female gaze. Through the appearance and disappearance of the animated bodies that screen in *Kiss Me*'s short episodic narrative of attraction, the attention of the audience is directed away from any feeling—and any attendant meaning—that might attach to a young girl's wayward look at the eroticized spectacle of a moving female body.

In early film, a female appropriation of the agency of looking remains ambivalent, evidenced in the few "Peeping Tom" films in which women become the subject rather than solely the object of looking, but also present in the

FIGURE 2.1. An accidental attraction in *Kiss Me* (1904). Courtesy of the Library of Congress.

negative form of women's direct look to the camera that often disrupts the fictional world of erotic films.[42] The various discursive efforts of early films to privilege the male look are best read, according to Miriam Hansen, as a "defensive symptom" of masculine anxieties in relation to women's new social and public visibilities and the challenge of cinema to the gendered hierarchy of public and private spheres.[43] *Kiss Me* suggests that the privileging of the male look in early films might also be considered as a defensive counter to the more public and potentially homoerotic pleasures afforded to women by novel forms of cinematic entertainment.

Further implications of the relatively unusual presence of a female spectator in *Kiss Me* are brought to light by comparing the film to the critical exemplar of its type, *Uncle Josh at the Moving Picture Show* (dir. Edwin S. Porter, U.S., 1902). More than *Kiss Me*, *Uncle Josh* dramatizes the spectatorial effects and relations of looking in early cinema. The film comprises three films within a film. Opening in a theatrical space in which a film is about to be projected, a man, Uncle Josh, watches from the seats on screen left. The first film of a woman dancing impels Uncle Josh to leap onto the stage to watch, and to attempt to imitate the dancer's movements. The second film of a train racing toward the camera drives a terrified Uncle Josh back into his box seat. In the final film, a country couple kiss, and Uncle Josh rolls up his sleeves as if to fight the male suitor. Overwhelmed by the illusion, he tears at the screen only to reveal the projectionist whom he proceeds to fight to the ground. Like *Uncle Josh*, the comic appeal of *Kiss Me* rests on a more sophisticated recognition of the illusory capacities of the cinematic trick of the "live" poster. Displacing its own capacities for erotic attraction onto another mass medium (the print poster), and live entertainment form (the burlesque show), *Kiss Me* nevertheless foregrounds cinema's capacity for voyeuristic spectatorial pleasures as well as its superiority in representing a realistic image of the moving female body. While those spectatorial pleasures are visual ones, accessed through looking, they are also made manifest in the body. *Kiss Me* visualizes the physical effects on viewers' bodies by inverting the animating effects of the dancing woman on Uncle Josh: both the young woman and the old man stop walking, and become entranced by the poster and its illusory erotic promise. The haphazard and random attractive effects of the cinema can quite literally lead one off course. The explicit lesson of the film is that such pleasures are naive and disorienting, and inappropriate for its viewers. *Kiss Me* attempts—in a similar vein to *Uncle Josh*—to demonstrate how the erotics of moving images ought not to be enjoyed, without being able to articulate a more positive mode for their proper reception.[44] Despite its negativity, this mode of film-viewing—in which a seemingly crude visual pleasure is entangled with a sense of superior spectatorial knowledge and judgment—contains within it another kind of regulatory potential. Thomas Elsaesser, reconsidering the so-called rube films, asks whether they articulate a "meta-level of self-reference in order to 'discipline' their audience—not by showing them *how not to behave* . . . but rather by a more subtle process of internalized self-control."[45] Though the rube films remain highly gendered, this speculative claim is suggestive for thinking how the treatment of the homoerotic in films like *Kiss Me* indicates the inauguration—albeit in a minor, unsystematized register—of new modes of sexual discipline and normalization.

Editing Sexuality

Certain films in the archive bear the traces of attempts to regulate homoerotic meaning as it emerges in relation to both visual representation and spectatorship by means of new forms of editing and narrating cinematic space.

The attractions of early films are premised on the simple capacity of the cinematograph to record or capture the movement of objects and bodies before the camera lens without any other practical or technological intervention. As a number of cinema scholars have argued, a second order of movement characterizes film narrative or its specific "cinematic" temporality: whether it is the literal movement of the camera and the film editing often necessary to sustain certain kinds of camera repositioning, or the more abstract movement in time and space that such movements may instantiate.[46] It is no accident that early experiments in regulating the homoerotic by means of new forms of editing center on what quickly become two freighted signifiers of sexual meaning: the look and the kiss. Such scenes tend to go unnoticed by critics more invested in determining a film's significance for its demonstration of a development in cinematic syntax, or accounting for the dynamics and structures of early cinema's dominant heteroerotics. Though the films in question sometimes also represent their female characters in terms that emphasize their lack of attainment of a feminine, bourgeois ideal, whether through their portrayal by female impersonators or details of costuming and other elements of mise-en-scène, it is the technological and discursive means by which the relations between female intimacy, homoeroticism, and looking are determined that are most significant for a history of the emergence of lesbian sexuality in early cinema. Such scenes are suggestive of an emerging structural relation between the combined visual suppression of female same-sex intimacy and homoerotic practices of looking, and the cinematic representability of lesbianism—a nascent representational formation that also has implications for the cinematic representability of heterosexuality.

One of the few early films in the archive to represent kisses between female characters—albeit very brief, almost missable ones—*Women's Rights* (Bamforth, United Kingdom, 1899) is more commonly noted as an early experimental attempt to develop the spatial syntax of the 180-degree reverse shot.[47] Based on a magic-lantern slide show, the film begins with two women who stand in front of a fence talking.[48] Leaning toward one another in animated conversation, at one point one of the characters kisses the other, before they discover that their skirts are pinned to the fence, and they are unable to move. The film's denouement literally puts a stop to the women's political ambitions and claims to the public sphere, refiguring their distress in comic terms as the two characters wave their arms frantically and try to run away. The action that we are to understand that the characters do not see but of which the audience has a privileged view—the nailing of their skirts by a man and a boy—is accomplished not by a reverse-angle shot from the other side of the fence but by a jump cut that merely shifts the fence to the foreground of the scene. From the outset, the impropriety of the characters' claim to public space and intimacy is conveyed as a transgression of their sex, since female impersonators are cast for both parts. Yet as the ending demonstrates, the unrestricted occupation of public space by women—and the intimacy that it engenders and makes visible—also requires a spatial resolution. The film's unrealized technological ambition is to represent a comprehensible and unified space across two shots, an experiment in editing intended not only to reveal to the film's viewers a diegetic action unseen by the two characters, but to reinforce the meanings of this narrative event in technological and spatial terms. In seeking to constrain the political and erotic space of its female characters, the film's experimental "edit" paradoxically secures a single cinematic space accessible to all its viewers. Alongside details of mise-en-scène such as costume, casting, and action, the film's failed technological denouement attempts to figure their earlier intimacy in terms of a spatial dead-end or stasis.

While *Women's Rights* represents an early failure to regulate, via cinematic technique, women's political and erotic mobilities, another early film represents the intersection of same-sex intimacies with erotic looking in a moment that dramatizes as incidental the erasure of women's spectatorial agency and visual pleasure. As with *Women's Rights*, this outcome is accomplished by means of a formal device that has become one of the most fundamental of cinematic conventions, the continuity edit. *Come Along, Do!* (dir. R. W. Paul, United Kingdom, 1898) opens with a man and a woman sitting together on a bench outside an art gallery. From their familiarity and age, we are meant to infer that they are an older married couple. A female pair, arm-in-arm, walk into frame and enter through a doorway on the set, marked by a sign that reads "Art Section" (figure 2.2). The man points his walking stick at the sign and, once they have finished eating, the couple get up to go into the gallery, also arm-in-arm, mirroring the familiar actions of the two women. The image that is meant to succeed the exterior view of the art gallery does not survive. Instead, we have to rely on extant still frames to reconstruct the second shot inside the gallery, the action of which seems to involve the man inspecting rather too intently a nude female statue while his wife looks at some paintings on the gallery wall.[49] The comedic denouement involves the man's wife physically pulling him away from the statue that so enamors him, presumably as she echoes the words of the film's title. Although the film is more noted in cinema history for being an early example of more than one shot being used to create continuous action across two different spaces, the gendered and class dimensions of the film's erotic comedy are layered and complex. While the edit marks "the movement of the characters from one

FIGURE 2.2. Moments before the cut in *Come Along, Do!* (1898).

space to another," it is also a barely discernible marker of the elision of the female couple who merely serve as an implicit motivating narrative device for the action on screen.[50] Their tangential visual presence serves a particular function in subtending the heteroerotic comedy of the "main" action. The pair's fleeting presence visually doubles, and suggests in passing, women's moral status as regulators of male erotic pleasure. Their subsequent absence from the gallery scene, an absence moreover accomplished by a splice or cut, ensures that any female visual pleasure in art—and, more specifically, one structured in homoerotic terms—disappears from view. However ambivalent *Come Along, Do!* may be about the inappropriateness of the husband's viewing pleasures, like other earlier films it emerges as part of a discursive field in which the look at the female body is structured as indicatively masculine and overtly erotic. Its particular deployment of its paired female extras to motivate its all-important continuity cut demonstrates one small way in which early cinema renders women's homoerotic viewing practices invisible as it seeks to institute new eroticized relations of looking between men and women.

Rewind, Replay

How might we now reconsider the brief, obscure film that opened this chapter? While the homoerotic potential of its mise-en-scène might seem to guarantee *Gavotte* a certain notoriety in the early cinema archive, its aesthetics and subject matter make it a quite ordinary late-nineteenth-century film. In cinematically remediating a stage-based performance, the film exemplifies the practice of early filmmakers who drew on the visual conventions and performance repertoire of fin-de-siècle entertainments. We should not assume, however, that *Gavotte* comprises either the original performance in its entirety or even a well-known portion of it. The very act of cinematic remediation—of excising, filming, and repeatedly projecting what may be a brief section of a longer stage routine—potentially reinscribes a theatrical form of eroticism as a new cinematic erotic modality. This difference emerges at a very basic level in the film's utilization of a single shot, without an apparent cut. Representing early filmmakers' attempts to maintain a single, unified viewpoint of the action magnified on screen, and its "posture of displaying something to the audience," the space of the single shot contains several elements that compete for the viewer's attention: the erotic spectacle of the female dancer (who ensures that at least one bare leg is displayed throughout her entire performance), the romantic attentions of the gentleman, including his kisses, and the indeterminacy of the gentleman figure in this basic schema.[51] By indeterminacy, I mean whether the gentleman's actions have certain narrative and therefore characterological implications because, for example, he is a woman in disguise, or a woman who takes some pleasure in wearing men's clothing, or whether that figure is another erotic spectacle because he is played by a woman and read as such. By using the movements of the bodies of the actors, their gestures and glances, to direct our attention from one character to the other, without ever settling on or privileging either, the film refuses to determine for the audience which of the figures we should find more erotically appealing.

This sense of erotic oscillation and undecidability is only enhanced by the diverse programs and spaces of exhibition in which *Gavotte* is likely to have been screened.[52] The variety format and viewers' experiences are, of course, closely related. As Miriam Hansen argues, at a very basic level the variety format determined—indeed, overdetermined—not only early films' heterogeneous subject matter and aesthetics, but also early viewers' divergent experiences and responses.[53] It was early cinema's "margin of indeterminacy and alternative interpretations, the public dimension of early exhibition practices, that the implementation of classical modes of narration and address sought to minimize and regulate."[54] While the presence of such a degree of indeterminacy did not foreclose the generation of meaning by spectators who encountered early films, the filmic text itself did not operate to delimit that meaning, and the subjectivities of its viewers, with totalizing effects. Just as Hansen imagines alternative receptions of *The "Teddy" Bears* (dir. Edwin S. Porter, U.S., 1907) in all-black exhibition spaces, with jazz accompaniment and live performances aimed at that particular audience, it is possible to imagine the exhibition of *Gavotte* and its generic sisters in Parisian or London settings frequented by bohemian and sapphic audiences.[55] Framed to suit the erotic interests and tastes of specific crowds, *Gavotte* makes itself available to multiple, albeit transitory, pleasures and recognitions even while its comedic mode also permits those same erotic valences to be framed in more phobic ways.

The eroticism and sexual meanings of the cinematic performance of desire in *Gavotte* are further shaped by its deployment of a theater and ballet convention common to early French dance films: the immensely popular female *travesti*, in which women played the male lead, often in costumes that were more revealing of the shape of the female body than those worn for female roles. Lenard R. Berlanstein's history of the *travesti* tradition suggests that while it initially provided respectable cover for bourgeois audiences to enjoy same-sex eroticism, in the last decade of the nineteenth century the meaning and significance of female cross-dressing began to change.[56] Citing the work of Jann Matlock, he argues that the influence of sexological literatures and medical practice meant that it was increasingly seen as pathological and immoral, though Matlock also points out that the association of cross-dressing with pathologized same-sex behavior was only one of several cultural, social, and political factors influencing attitudes toward, and understandings of, female cross-dressing.[57] While Berlanstein tracks the decline of *travesti* stage performances for bourgeois audiences, the presence of *Gavotte* in the early cinema archive suggests that the filmic representation of *travesti* in French dance films may have briefly sustained this performance tradition, while also diversifying its erotic and sexual possibilities.[58]

Rather than being in collusion with the categorizing and pathologizing impulses of sexology, *Gavotte*'s mode of presentation and likely exhibition can be read as heightening the indeterminacy that the diagnostic rubrics of sexology sought to overcome. While the kisses and embrace between the two characters that concludes *Gavotte* might make the use of *travesti* even more scandalous in the context of the circulation of new sexual knowledges, a small detail of mise-en-scène further complicates matters. Visible within the eighteenth-century-style puffy breeches of the male character, occasionally pressing hard up against them in fact, is the outline of what may be a codpiece. Whether an anachronistic detail of theatrical costuming or a more bawdy signifier of a hard-on is difficult to tell, but its signification of adult maleness rather than feminized youth distinguishes this *travesti* performance from the dominant conventions.[59] Yet another possibility presents itself, however, since, other than signifying the embodied sex of an adult male body, in the late nineteenth century this detail of costuming might more often be taken to signify an internal—but externally embodied—sexual desire.[60] This possibility revises the conventions of the *travesti* tradition while disorienting any attempt to interpret the body and its sexuality through congruent features of sex, gender, and desire.[61]

Gavotte suggests a performance that knowingly draws on the *travesti* tradition even as it reworks it as a more self-conscious performance, one that might be read as both parodying the excesses of male sexual desire as well as satirizing sexological claims about the relation between a masculine style of self-presentation and women's same-sex desires. While the flexibility of the *travesti* tradition was likely to have been enhanced by the prominence of a wide range of performances and representations in fin-de-siècle France that troubled the regulatory norms of gender, *Gavotte* suggests how the gendered practice of *travesti* could also provide a performative conduit for emergent but incoherent discourses of sexuality. It is entirely possible that the actions of *Gavotte*'s protagonist—if we can even call 'him' that—would have been legible to some (but by no means, all) historical audiences as being motivated by sexual desire, or perhaps even a new kind of sexual identity, orientation, or perversion. Such contradictory interpretations would have likely existed alongside other equally plausible understandings of the on-screen erotic action. *Gavotte*'s queer moment of indeterminacy in the early cinema archive is sustained by its single-shot aesthetic. Short enough to be looped, or embedded in a variety program, the film's playful erotics are inherently fleeting and multilayered, countering any effort to resolve or fix them into any one definitive interpretation or experience. No matter how many times we might replay *Gavotte*'s flickering black and white images—whether through the archive's Steinbeck viewer, or its digital remediation—the film's brevity guarantees its own peculiar opacity, its always lost moment.[62] *Gavotte*, I imagine, will remain obscure and unimportant—an accidental trace of the history of sexuality in the archive of early film ephemera.

To claim that early films sustain a certain appealing indeterminacy that makes them available to queer appropriation is a risky enterprise. While insisting on the capacity of early films in their heterogeneity to project alternative experiences and modes of viewing, such a claim may underdescribe the cultural and social forces that endeavor to sustain historically dominant erotic arrangements and norms. It may also miss a more subtle transformation of the ephemeral as evidence of the accidental. Imagining the transitory experience of the erotic as accidental, unintended, or mistaken—as in the case of the homoerotic scenario in *Kiss Me*—represents a small but significant discursive shift. What seems like a chance event is potentially reinscribed as accidental in the Aristotelean sense, as not essential or required to the true nature of something, in this case, human being. Early films, in developing techniques of mise-en-scène and editing to narrate space and time, participate in an ideological project to make heteroeroticism not accidental but rather necessary, coherent, and purposeful—even if they do so through the negative genres of comedy and the popular figure of the rube. Such a history cannot be disentangled from early films' attempts to regulate the erotic toward heteroerotic meaning, and eventually into the consolidation of heterosexuality, a transformation that in its more expansive discursive forms seeks to displace the inherent ephemerality of the erotic onto a deviant "other."

This chapter and the first, "Troubling Sexual History," each pursue a self-reflexive queer historiographical strategy, the suspension of current sexual knowledges, in relation to very different periods of film history. The aim is to dislodge two persistent ideas that animate historical narratives of the emergence of lesbian sexuality in early cinema: the absence of any relevant forms of representation in the very early period in which films are first produced, and the consolidation of recognizably modern forms of lesbian representation by the early 1930s. Each chapter does not simply reverse these positions, but rather offers an alternative account of the emergent sexual intelligibility of on-screen figures and their desires. In such a counter-history, "emergence" accords to queer timelines that register the multiple, contradictory historical temporalities of older erotic idioms that persist even as, in their contingent relations with novel sexual epistemologies, they are transformed and absorbed into new models of sexual identity. In the next part, *Queer Timing* turns to consider the sexuality effects that arise with the institutionalization of film as a distinct medium and entertainment form. While sexuality takes hold and is routed through the body, naturalized as it most potent and obvious site, less easy to track are those cinematic transformations that enable the ascription of erotic intentionality to bodies on screen.

PART II

Bodies

Style, Genre, and Sexual Legibility

FIGURE 3.1. Lillian kisses Bessie goodbye for the second time in *A Florida Enchantment* (1914). Courtesy of the Library of Congress.

FIGURE 3.2. Lillian kisses Mrs. Stella Lovejoy goodbye. Courtesy of the Library of Congress.

3. Queer Character

A Florida Enchantment's Ambivalent Sexual Motivations

A motive, then . . . is more hieroglyphic than we might expect: a mysterious impulse to act, to move.
—Kathryn Bond Stockton, *The Queer Child, or Growing Sideways in the Twentieth Century*

SEXUAL FIGURATION, as the first chapter argued, can be understood as the belated effect of a disparate set of logics, epistemologies, discourses, styles, and practices. While film codes and conventions that eroticize women's bodies make them available to be interpreted in sexual terms—part of broad processes that subject women's bodies to divergent forms of visual scrutiny and objectification—the consequences in relation to sexual legibility are less clear. The inscrutability of the body ensures that sexual identity as a subjective element of sexuality remains difficult to visualize. Construed as internal to the person, sexual identity has been conceptualized in contradictory terms as a permanent psychic orientation or predisposition that may or may not be evidenced by patterns of desire, or forms of behavior (whether intentional or not) that accord with or deviate from dominant social standards. While a fundamental issue for the history of sexuality has concerned the transition from acts to identities as the focus of regulatory energies, the consolidation of sexual identity as a technique of sexuality raises other questions concerning erotic intentionality and its determinative relation to sexual identity and its legibility. United in their attention to how the erotic intentionalities of bodies on screen are rendered cinematically intelligible, the chapters that follow consider the productive sexuality effects of the standardized style and genres of one of cinema's most influential institutions: Hollywood. As ideally systematized conventions geared to maximizing an array of interrelated entertainment pleasures, from narrative intelligibility to eroticized spectacle, style and genre organize the sexual legibility of the female body in unanticipated ways. Structured as case studies focused on single feature films now regarded as important instances of lesbian representation in early cinema, the pair of chapters in this part of *Queer Timing* revises understandings of how the knowability of lesbianism is coded in terms of ambiguity or opacity and the dependency of the representability of heterosexual desire on early cinema's spectacles of homoerotic pleasure.

Though the visual legibility of erotic intentionality is not an uncommon subject in comedy genres, its centrality as theme and problem of narrative articulation in the sex-change comedy, *A Florida Enchantment* (dir. Sydney Drew, Vitagraph, United States, 1914), makes the film a particularly apt case study for this chapter.[1] Its ambivalent place in the history of lesbian cinematic representation, however, indicates something of the difficulty of synchronizing the film to any straightforward timeline of the emergence and consolidation of lesbian cinematic representation.[2] Seeking to contextualize the film's representation of female sexuality and its intelligibility for contemporary audiences, scholars claim that the central sex-swapping character's behavior—which includes same-sex eroticism, a fondness for male clothing, and even smoking—would have been intelligible to some historical audiences in terms of the transgressive sexual typologies of the invert or mannish lesbian. R. Bruce Brasell, for example, suggests that audiences were already familiar with such figures via the widely read work of sexologist Havelock Ellis.[3] Siobhan Somerville argues too that the character's transformation from Lillian Travers (Edith Storey) to the cross-dressed "Lawrence" seems to "embody contemporary constructions of the sexual invert;" she reads the few extant reviews as indicating that audiences would have understood the "lesbian meanings" of the film's "gender play."[4] Acknowledging these historical interpretations, Laura Horak claims that such sexual knowledges, due to their distinctive and uneven circulations in the mid-1910s, were not widely available to the mass audiences of *A Florida Enchantment*.[5] She reads the film as a limit case concerning the sexual intelligibility of female cross-dressing in American cinema in the 1910s. Each of these scholarly perspectives on the film's sexual legibility are the outcome of alternative approaches to historicizing its representation and reception and, more particularly, the question of how to contexualize the film in relation to co-temporaneous sexual discourses, such as sexology and the "new psychology" (as psychoanalysis was often called) or other older but nevertheless still persistent erotic knowledges.[6] In this regard, the ambivalent findings of film scholarship amplify the inherent ambivalence of character and its dependence on extrafilmic "cultural schemata defining the nature of the self."[7]

The ambivalence of character is further amplified by its medium-specificity: as Mary Ann Doane has pointed out, "Because character is *embodied* in the cinema (unlike in the novel where it is the effect of linguistic signals), it is an even more resistant, difficult, intransigent concept than it is in literature."[8] One of the consequences of film character's ambivalence is that critical attention and efforts to historicize representation tend to be directed toward those sexual discourses adjacent to the film text, themselves elements in more extensive and contradictory cultural formations. This approach risks downplaying the differences of sexual categories—such as the lesbian and invert—and their disparate conceptualizations of sexual identity, including the erotic intentionalities that have a double function as their symptom and cause.[9] Redirecting our focus back to film character is an opportunity to consider how film narrative discourse contributes to the intelligibility of sexuality in ways analogous to the contradictory characterological effects of sexology and psychoanalysis. For the most part deliberately eschewing a critical attention to extrafilmic sexual discourses, this chapter pursues a fine-grained reading of the film's form and visual style as a means of tracing the historically specific terms by which the film's narrative strategies endeavor to establish its characters as sexually legible figures.[10]

A Florida Enchantment evidences an affinity with a still relatively novel stylistic transformation in which character increasingly motivates action in order to guarantee narrative legibility—an emergent industrial standard critically recognized in retrospect as the classical Hollywood style.[11] Though the film inaugurates its main plot line with Lillian's ingestion of a magical seed said to be able to transform a person into their "opposite" sex, providing the diegetic physical cause that drives Storey's subtle performance of stop-start masculinity, the film evinces a greater investment in establishing Lillian's sexual character in less corporeal terms.[12] For what more often provokes the film's narrative action are not the contradictory external signs of Lillian's gendered appearance and behaviors—whether the little mustaches she grows overnight, her vigorous wooing of her neighbor and friend, Bessie Horton (Jane Morrow), as well as Mrs. Stella Lovejoy (Ada Gifford), or her final transformation into Bessie's would-be suitor "Lawrence"—but rather other causes less amenable to visual representation: a more nebulous amalgam of the character's traits, wishes, feelings, and desires.[13] More than remediating the characterological elements of new sexual typologies, the development of character in *A Florida Enchantment* represents an instance of a larger discursive effort in which the drive for narrative transparency is bound up in the creation of new forms of sexual legibility and personification.

The relation between the comprehension of *A Florida Enchantment*'s story and the apprehension, however tenuous, of new kinds of sexual persons hinges on the question of causality. Although the main character of Lillian remains the most obviously sexual figure produced by the film's narrative—echoed by the subsequent transformation of her maid, Jane, played in blackface by Ethel Lloyd—it is another critically neglected character, Lillian/"Lawrence's" friend and love interest Bessie, that demonstrates the productive force of the film's uneven narrational energies.[14] Unlike Lillian or Jane, Bessie is not intelligible in terms of sexual inversion. She never takes a magic seed, and—since her style of dress, comportment, and gestures all reinforce her femininity—the character's gender is never in question. Billed in the film's opening credits as "a Florida flower who does not wish to blush unseen," and thus initially typed as a virginal but nevertheless socially adept young woman, Bessie remains an awkward, often reactive figure, whose actions are more often indexed to chance events and the rudimentary informational requirements of narrative design. It is the ambiguity of the character's motivations and wishes that points to the establishment—albeit in nascent form—of another filmic discourse out of which the representation of same-sex desire and lesbian identity becomes possible. As the node at which different orders of narrative and sexual causality accrue, and as the object of various kinds of spectatorial attention, recognition, and identification, psychological character proves to be crucial to the representability of lesbian sexuality in the transition to a standardized, "classical" cinema.[15]

Establishing Character

The sexual effects of character emerge in the transitional era in part as a consequence of new industrial pressures.[16] *A Florida Enchantment* is released during a period in which American industry practice and trade discourse are consolidating the expectation that all events on screen will be motivated; in other words, that films—perhaps with the exception of the most farcical or physical of comedies—will clearly articulate the reasons for or causes of narrative action.[17] This industry expectation becomes focused quite particularly on the development of character, marked by the disappearance of the familiar stock figures of the vaudeville stage and an increasing reliance on representing individuated figures as motivated narrative agents. While the representation of often quite rudimentary or singular character traits and desires was already an important aspect of the development of narrative films by the early 1910s, the longer screen time of *A Florida Enchantment,* together with its ensemble cast and multiple lines of action, presented new problems for articulating a legible narrative and clear temporal relations.[18] With this increasing narrative sophistication, character becomes even more important in sustaining narrative clarity. As Kristin Thompson argues, in her joint history of the development of the classical Hollywood style, "by attaching causality—and hence the spectator's attention to the flow of events—to the characters, the classical film gained a method for insuring a clear temporal progression."[19] This brief quotation depicts each of its key terms as relatively autonomous components whose relations are straightforwardly articulated via the classical style as stable or predictable "method." I do not draw attention to this particular point in order to endorse straightforwardly its broader style of argument, in relation to which there has already been extensive debate.[20] Rather, I think it requires further elaboration, because it suggests something of the discursive space in which arises the possibility of being able to represent sexual desire and identity cinematically. In the transition to classical cinema the representability of sexuality arises in the diffuse nexus of narrative causality and spectator attention embodied by on-screen figures, even as the unpredictability of this dynamic discursive space requires close regulation. The rise of the cross-sex romance subplot, a strategy understood as intended to reinforce the legibility of character motivation and clarify narrative causality, suggests a related social need to discipline the nebulous effects of cinematic character to acceptable forms of erotic relationality.[21] Film character's assurance of narrative transparency is at constant risk of being undermined by less culturally sanctioned schematas of the self, sexual or otherwise.

The sexuality effects of this shift toward an always potentially unstable psychological character are most evident in the film's penultimate scene. In order to sustain its comic story line, *A Florida Enchantment* ensures that, in its late stages, Lillian's fiancé, Dr. Fred Cassadene (played by the film's director Sidney Drew), also takes a magical seed, a narrative action that generates further disruption in the form of a spectacular chase in which Fred tries to elude his pursuers by stealing and donning a woman's dress. While the film incorporates the older generic conventions and narrative logic of the chase film into its longer format, it deploys a prototypical classical editing device in order to establish its heteronormative order.[22] Two shots in close succession, both markedly different in tone and style from the previous long shots of running bodies entering and departing the frame, bring the pursuit to an abrupt close: "Lawrence" looks down from "his" bedroom window with an anxious expression before a cut to a closer, high-angled shot of Fred who—having leaped off a pier in order to evade the chasing crowd—is trying to stay afloat in the water. A key moment in which the film attempts to resolve its story of gender inversion, the shot/reverse-shot sequence indexes a switch from the "primitive" corporeal action of the chase spectacle to the inner workings of character motivation.[23] This relatively new convention of editing evokes "Lawrence's" feeling for the cross-dressed Fred—whether we read it as the alternative or simultaneous possibilities of sympathy, anxiety, and love—and in turn leads directly to the film's final scene, in which Lillian is jolted awake. For as the word *enchantment* in the film's title already indicates, and as contemporary reviews and notices typically pointed out, Lillian's sexual adventure turns out to have been a dream. It is only by yoking spectatorial attention to the reorientation of Lillian's desires and its causal connection to her reunification with Fred that *A Florida Enchantment* is able to guarantee the pair's deferred marriage and the film's heterosexual denouement.[24]

By granting Lillian's look this crucial narrative function, the film's ending demonstrates how the classical style is able to discipline the social and sexual consequences of Lillian's gender-swapping to a heterosexual story line. It also suppresses a central theme of the indeterminate relation between erotic embodied action and sexual meaning that, until these last moments, sustains the film's comic narrative. In the film's opening scenes, it is precisely this thematic problem that establishes the motivation for Lillian's desire to change her sex. Although film comedy is often premised on the unpredictable actions and effects of an unruly character on his or her diegetic world, in keeping with the Vitagraph studio's development from 1909 of "psychologically motivated 'dramatic' comedy," *A Florida Enchantment* takes great care to elaborate a quite specific motivation for Lillian's subsequent transformation and its disruptive consequences: her dissatisfaction with her fiancé Fred.[25] The film efficiently and self-reflexively sets up Lillian's unhappiness as the effect of her own misinterpretation of character in a scene that dramatizes her misunderstanding of Fred's immediate desires, as well as his character's personal qualities, in particular his sexual ethics. While the film establishes Lillian's arrival back at the Florida home of her spinster aunt, Constancia Oglethorpe (Grace Stevens), it delays her reunification with Fred. The other characters keep the news of Lillian's arrival secret—Constancia presses her finger to her lips as Fred enters the frame—so that Lillian can surprise him later, all clearly articulated actions that sustain narrative comprehensibility precisely because they are premised on and support the legibility of Lillian's immediate desire. In a subsequent scene, Lillian, accompanied by Bessie, arrives unannounced at the local resort hotel, the Ponce de Leon, where Fred works as a doctor. What the audience is led to expect will be the scene of their happy reunion is set up through a point-of-view shot structure. As Lillian and Bessie look off screen, the following shot reveals their perspective as a hotel guest, Mrs. Stella Lovejoy—billed in the film's opening credits as "a fashionable New York widow"—is attended to by Fred, who clasps her hand and then moves his free hand along her forearm in an intimate gesture. In the cut back to the previous shot, Lillian's gasp and turn to Bessie convey her character's realization of Fred's apparent infidelity. The audience is not constrained to Lillian's perspective, however, instead understanding that Mrs. Lovejoy is faking her malady in order to solicit Fred's attention. These minor narrative events ascribe to the characters in the scene various faults associated with the interpretability of character, whether of deception and thus a certain order of diegetic illegibility in the case of Mrs. Lovejoy, or the misreading of the embodied signs of character intentionality by both Fred and Lillian. While Lillian's subsequent decision to ingest the transformational seed is immediately motivated by Fred's seeming inadequacies as a doctor and suitor, her desire for what the seed promises in terms of an alternative social and sexual reality is, from the outset, intertwined with a visual discourse concerned with the legibility and meaning of erotic gesture and physical intimacy.

The film's thematization of the unreliable relation between the visual apprehension of erotic action and character intentionality depends on its ability to grant its spectators a more privileged knowledge of its characters' motivations and to mask the parallel—if not identical—difficulty that spectators may encounter in ascribing a singular or definitive meaning to the visual representation of erotic gestures or behaviors. The film registers this symptomatically in the means by which the audience is granted access to the knowledge of Mrs. Lovejoy's nefarious intentions on which the successive deceptions and mistakes of the scene depend. Rather than editing in a shot representing an earlier diegetic moment in the scene, the film resorts to a written inter-title, thus relying on a linguistic description to assure the scene's proper interpretation. This masking tactic positions the film as an early instance of a significant transition in the visual epistemologies of silent cinema comedy. As Lisa Trahair has argued, "cinematic comedy shifts from a straightforward celebration of the deceit of appearances and the negation of the epistemological *connection* between truth and vision . . . to a contemplation and exposition of the ramifications of the *disconnection* between vision and truth."[26] By providing the audience with the most privileged interpretation of the scene witnessed by Lillian, the film draws attention away from the potentially unstable discursive effects of cinematic character that must sustain apparently legible motivations in order to guarantee the clarity of the story unfolding on screen.

While the binding of narrative causality to psychological character was an industrial ideal in the 1910s, in practice—whether because of conditions of production, directorial inexperience, or the demands of certain kinds of stories—the implementation of such narrative strategies was precarious and uneven. *A Florida Enchantment* evinces some of these difficulties in the opening scenes across which Lillian's central motivation is established since, in addition to the need to convey the nature of her relationship to Fred and her disappointments, the film must also introduce the mysterious casket and its supernatural contents. It does so while also introducing its cast of characters: following the first shot that establishes Lillian's imminent arrival back in Florida, the neighbor Major Horton (Charles Kent) and his daughter Bessie arrive to visit Miss Oglethorpe. After greeting Constancia, Bessie is drawn, as if magnetically, to a box sitting on a small table that appears prominently in the lower righthand foreground of the frame. The actress's performance compels us to speculate that the character's action is driven by curiosity, an internal character trait, yet the film's visual composition suggests that it is the enigmatic power of the box itself that motivates her action. On opening the box, Bessie finds a note inside, the details of which are then displayed on screen as an inter-title: "In the duplicate of this casket, whereabouts unknown, lies a secret for all women who suffer. Ha! Ha!" As the note's allusion to suffrage suggests, the political and social empowerment of women remains an implicit theme of the film. Even if it is only a narrative tactic to ensure that the audience has minimal but necessary information about the as-yet-undiscovered duplicate casket, this minor event remains enigmatic when considered in terms of the nature and location of the motivation for Bessie's action. The discovery of the "real" box in a following scene is also secured through random incident, when Bessie and Lillian venture into an old curiosity shop. Rather than reinforce the film's narrative of motivated action—centered on Lillian's dissatisfaction with Fred—the events concerning the nature of the box and its discovery remain contingent, premised on the operations of chance. It is the conjunction of a legible character motivation—Lillian's dissatisfaction—and a random event—the discovery of the casket—that propels Lillian to ingest a sex-change seed, the "initiating event" that generates the remainder of the film's comic action.[27] This combination does not effect a fusion or privileging of one form of narrative causation over another. Instead, their contiguity only amplifies questions about the nature and meaning of Lillian's subsequent sex-change, as well as Bessie's involvement with Lillian and, later on, her male counterpart "Lawrence." The difference between character intentionality and contingency as the "cause" of narrative events is not sustained by their attachment to specific characters but instead persists as a more ambiguous tension that inflects practices of spectatorship and interpretation across the central section of *A Florida En-*

chantment. What is at stake in terms of the film's articulation and regulation of sexual character is whether the pleasures of the erotic and its meanings are somehow organically or psychically determined, or whether they are random effects governed by chance. By absorbing such tensions—indeed by condensing them in corporeal form—the new modes of cinematic character enabled by the prototypical classical style ensured that the body's capacity for sexual signification was increasingly linked to questions of causality and motivation and, in so doing, provided the discursive means for establishing new forms of sexual personification.

Out of Character

How the body is established as the site of more than one kind of sexual sign, and how that might intensify the modes of interpretation, judgment, and speculation required of viewers, is demonstrated by an early scene in which physiological evidence of Lillian's metamorphosis is revealed for the first time to the film's audience. While the effects of the seed that Lillian swallows are immediately apparent, as Storey broadens her gestures and rolls her gait in a subtle parody of physical movement coded as masculine, the following scene shifts significantly the visual terms within which the character's sex-change is figured. Cued by an inter-title that indicates the action has shifted to the next morning, we are presented with a long shot in which Lillian, with her back to us, walks toward her dressing table to get ready for the day. As she sits down, an action that reveals her face in the dresser's oval-shaped mirror, the character and the audience simultaneously discover that overnight Lillian has grown a small mustache. The film's dramatization of the appearance of this facial detail registers not only industrial norms that ban any more explicit depiction of the changes to Lillian's body, but also the adaptation of the Vitagraph screenplay from the 1891 novel of the same name and its references to the dime museum.[28] Lillian's little mustache is a textual remnant that links her to one of the latter's star attractions: the bearded lady.[29]

By removing the context of the dime museum in order to position its film as a middle-class, quality production, Vitagraph's strategy of adaptation displaces and reorients a popular, lower-class–based mode of spectatorship and interpretation. According to Clare Sears, who considers aspects of the original novel in the context of the history of cross-dressing in San Francisco, the dime museum and freak show produced "not only disciplined audiences schooled in gender normativity, but also vigilant audiences trained in the pleasures of suspicion."[30] Cinematic representation alters, however, the relation of viewers to such dissonant figures. In the dime museum, as Sears writes, audiences were encouraged to touch and pull at the costumes and beards of the "exhibits," and to ask questions of the performers about their personal history.[31] In the cinema, such practices of intimate investigation and interrogation are necessarily reoriented so that spectators are required to rely principally on vision in order to evaluate Lillian's transformation and its meaning. Even though *A Florida Enchantment* has already supplied both a physical and psychological cause for the character's sex-change, this paradigmatic shift in the conditions of spectatorship enlarges the domain of embodied visual signs by which spectators might interpret the character and what drives her altered behavior.

The paradoxical impact of the exponential expansion of the sexual signs of the body on the legibility of character motivation is foregrounded in a later scene that relies less on technologies of editing than on other compositional and dramaturgical protocols to ensure narrative legibility. It occurs during a complex cross-cut series of sequences in which Jane is attempting to evade arrest for her assault on the servant Gus Duncan (played in blackface again by Frank O'Neil). As most of the characters gather in the Oglethorpe drawing room, the film's pivotal narrative space, they form a group arranged across the foreground of the shot. Bessie is positioned on the lefthand side of the screen in a swoon, sitting in the chair in which Lillian had earlier swallowed her seed, while the other characters crowd the middle and righthand portions of the frame. The immediate cause of Bessie's condition seems to be the excitement of the intersecting narrative incidents that have led to this late-night gathering. The mise-en-scène, and the already established visual significance of the chair, draw attention to the Bessie figure, and the actions of Lillian who leans over her and seems to comfort and kiss her. This spatial positioning aligns Bessie with Lillian's transformation, even as her near-fainting fit remains indexed to notions of feminine weakness and social decorum. In order to understand the multiple narrative events taking place, spectators also need to observe the actions of the other characters, including the entrance of Constancia's maid, Malvina; the constable; and the return of Jane, now in disguise—but also passing—as a carriage-driver. The shot calls for an intensified form of "topographical reading," one defined by Noël Burch, in relation to earlier "primitive" films, as a reading that can "gather signs from all corners of the screen in their quasi-simultaneity, often without very clear or distinctive indices immediately appearing to hierarchize them, to bring to the fore 'what counts', to relegate to the background 'what doesn't count.'"[32] The attention of spectators and the meaning of Bessie's condition are dependent not only on the composition of the shot and the blocking of the actors within the frame but also on the capacity of the movement of

Bessie's body itself to act as a visual lure. If spectators catch the eroticized action between Bessie and Lillian, the exact nature of the distress that her bodily convulsions signify and their erotic import remain tantalizingly indecipherable. Even as attention is potentially dispersed across the diverse range of embodied characters, requiring viewers to work hard at their task of making narrative sense of the scene and its lines of action, Bessie's embodied performance and its staging underline the interdependent, contradictory dynamic of film character: the intensification of spectatorial interest in the exact nature of a figure's motivation—whether desire, fear, overexcitement or some other unspecified feeling or impulse—which is never answered by, and indeed actually seems to amplify, the opaque signs of the body.

By guiding the attention of spectators to consider the nature and meaning of character embodiment—whether physical appearance, styles of comportment, or forms of attire—the film demonstrates how the classical style establishes the conditions in which viewers might speculate further, not only about the extent to which a character's body and behavior might transgress gender and other social norms but, more importantly, the consequences of such transgressions. In this regard, the historical reception of Storey's cross-dressed performance as Lillian has received more critical attention than other aspects of her performance of female masculinity and homoeroticism.[33] Though Storey's role occurs at a moment when female masculinity is under increasing cultural pressure—in part because of what it might signify in terms of pathologized sexuality—her performance of homoeroticism did not pass without comment either.[34] A brief notice in *The Atlanta Constitution*, for example, makes sure to advise its readers, even within its restricted column space, that after swallowing the magical seed the central character retains her "feminine apparel" while she "makes love to every female in sight."[35] While extant reviews and notices suggest that the cross-dressing licensed by *A Florida Enchantment*'s comic narrative was the subject of both express disapproval and coded subcultural recognition, the film seems especially concerned with elaborating the sexual import of Lillian's transformation in relation to the homoerotic, still a significant cultural norm of middle-class life, and one of its central idioms of relationality, romantic friendship.[36]

In scenes immediately following Lillian's ingestion of the magical seed, the film connects the nascent sexual meanings of her gender-swap to the erotics of middle-class female friendship. Some detailed description is necessary to consider adequately the discursive effects of the film's form, its interrelation with Storey's embodied performance, and their combined effects in terms of the legibility of character motivation. After her partial but private transformation, the now clean-shaven character ventures into the garden where her aunt is hosting Bessie, Mrs. Lovejoy, and Fred. When Lillian enters a wide shot in which all the characters feature, she kisses each woman on the lips but studiously ignores her fiancé. In the second half of the scene—punctuated by an argument with Fred—Lillian again kisses both female visitors farewell (figures 3.1 and 3.2). Storey subtly emphasizes her character's enthusiasm and pleasure by draping an arm around the shoulder of each actress, while the actors' bodies are blocked to ensure that each kiss is fully visible to the audience. At the very moment when Lillian's lips touch Bessie's, the film cuts to a shot of Fred and Miss Oglethorpe, whose looks are directionally matched to the spatial location of the kissing characters. The edit ensures that the kiss becomes the scene's "point of intensity," and underscores the narrative significance of their looks of consternation and puzzlement.[37] Although the cut directs the attention of spectators elsewhere—toward the reactions of Lillian's aunt and husband-to-be—this narrative procedure always remains in tension with the pleasures of the visual spectacle of the same-sex kiss. The visual pleasure and comic effect of the scene also turns on the legibility of subtle differences and visible intensities of Lillian's embodied behavior and what that expansive set of corporeal signs may indicate about the significance of Lillian's actions. As both female friends prepare to depart in an open-topped car, the film shuttles between the Miss Oglethorpe/Fred reaction shot, and successive shots of further kisses with Mrs. Lovejoy—who seems to anticipate enthusiastically her turn in receiving Lillian's intimate attentions—and another final kiss for Bessie. As recognizably inadequate stand-ins for the audience's interpretation of the scene, Miss Oglethorpe and Fred's incomprehension underscores the magnetizing effects of character in the protoclassical style and the satisfaction that the film grants to its spectators as privileged interpreters of the scene. Yet Lillian's actions and what ostensibly motivates her, an impulsive sexual desire, can be apprehended only in dissonant terms: the audience's visual pleasure in a common intimate practice between women, and what that might imply in terms of sexual motivation, relies on a privileged knowledge of the invisible "real" sex of the Lillian character. At the level of film discourse, the ordinary pleasure and everyday social intimacy of two women kissing is subjected to a contradictory sexual regulation.

That Lillian's erotic intimacies with her female friends have a sexual import is consolidated in the next scene in which Bessie stays overnight at the Oglethorpe residence. While the Bessie figure seems particularly eager to share a bed with her female friend, and seeks Lillian's assistance to unzip her dress, Storey's facial expressions and hesitant gestures convey her character's unease. Abruptly stopping herself, the Lillian character's solution is to lock Bessie in a spare room rather than share a bed with her, all actions designed to convey the power of her new libido. In dramatizing such moments when Lillian seems to act out of character, the film ensures that the question of sexual character—considered as the psychological or internal motivating forces directing the character's actions—remains at the center of its narrative discourse and spectatorial attention. In ordinary circumstances, the character's actions would reflect the social conventions of female friendship, but it is the spectatorial knowledge of Lillian's hidden masculinity that allows for the possibility that her actions signify sexual desire. By verifying the sexual meaning of Lillian's earlier kisses—that is, their resignification from friendship to desire—the bedroom scene also confirms the character's gender inversion as a sexual reorientation. The comedy of these homoerotic scenes relies on a judgment about the extent to which, within the diegetic world, Lillian's actions can be recognized as signs of a certain social or sexual type, whether a middle-class young woman or a more deviant or perverted erotic figure, such as a sapphist, invert, or lesbian. If Bessie's comportment seems to indicate her ignorance of the possible sexual import of Lillian's actions, this understanding of a character's practiced forms of behavior, and her failure to scrutinize more closely her friend's actions, relies on the articulation of distinct levels of narrative knowledge and self-reflexive acknowledgment by spectators. As the diacritical effect of narrative and spectatorship, film character thus sustains a fragile interdependency and hierarchization of sexual discourse, of knowledge and ignorance.

Supporting Character

The incipient sexuality effects of the prototypical Hollywood classical style of narrative are most evident in relation to a figure in *A Florida Enchantment* who occupies a significant amount of screen time and yet whose motivations, and thus causal relation to narrative action, remain difficult to ascertain. Bessie is in some respects barely a "character" at all, given the lack of knowledge—or rather certainty of knowledge—that the film grants its audience about her feelings and desires. Although Bessie is a supporting character in the sense that her on-screen presence enables the Lillian-focused narrative, she is certainly not a supporting character as that role later develops in Hollywood classical cinema, particularly because the actress who plays her was not singled out as a well-known actress or "picture personality" at this early point in the development of the Hollywood star system.[38] The Bessie figure is always a tangential character to the main dramatic couple of Lillian and Fred and while she provides opportunities for the film to exploit her status as Fred's rival for Lillian's affections—long after her accidental discovery of the mysterious casket during the film's opening scenes—her ongoing presence as the film's narrative progresses draws attention to the provisional and temporal qualities of cinematic character. Bessie's actions invite spectatorial attention, and sexual interpretation, in the context of the film's narrative and its thematic concerns with erotic legibility and meaning but, as a character, she more often fails to be legible in terms of any certain or specifiable motivation. Perhaps unintentionally at this point in the development of Hollywood classical style, Bessie's enigmatic character only intensifies the discursive operations and sexual effects of connotation and suspicion already established in minimal and comedic terms in relation to the character of Lillian.

By describing Bessie in the initial inter-titles as "a Florida flower who does not wish to blush unseen," the film initially ascribes a minimal set of traits to her character while only cursorily reinforcing them via the actress's subsequent performance and sequencing of narrative events. The perplexing nature of Bessie's character is exacerbated by the seeming intensity of her interest in—and attraction to—not only Lillian but also to other incidental characters.[39] In the scene of Lillian's farewell ball, for example, after Lillian dances with Bessie and then turns her attention to Mrs. Lovejoy, Bessie rejects her former male dance partner with a quick nod of her head, and a clearly mimed "No!" while taking the arm of another man who has entered the frame. Such actions—minor scenes of comic relief—reinforce the sense that the causes of Bessie's behavior are random, even capricious. The effect is to render Bessie as an always receptive figure, while the source of her motivations remains obscure. At a minimum, the accumulation of such on-screen moments establishes a narrative pattern for Bessie's later unaccountable interest in "Lawrence." Repetition itself becomes available to be read as a sign indicative of some hidden order to, or cause of, such behavior. The film's own discourse of the unreliability of vision, and the overdetermined knowledge of Lillian's "true" sex, do not dispel the unknowability of Bessie's motivations but rather amplify their uncertain and paradoxical status within the film's narrative design.

The generation of a speculative and ultimately unsatisfied desire to know that accumulates in relation to the erotic orientations of the Bessie character is further complicated when Lillian, after her physiological and sartorial makeover, returns to her social circle as the mustachioed "Lawrence." Having manufactured a formal introduction—conveyed by a scene in which "Lawrence" writes a note, pockets it, and then, in a following shot, hands it to Constancia to read—"Lawrence" gravitates immediately to Bessie, and they exchange interested looks. The apparent speed of their romance is exacerbated by the film's clumsy handling of temporality, so that the unspecified passage of time between their first meeting and Bessie's acceptance of "Lawrence's" proposal of marriage—a tender scene played in one shot in which "Lawrence" gently kisses Bessie's neck to make her turn around, only then to reveal "his" intentions by proffering a ring—is signified only by a cut to a different shot and a change of costume.[40] Not only for their unseemly swiftness do these scenes seem barely credible. While on the one hand Bessie's attraction to "Lawrence" merely repeats her earlier pattern of seemingly erratic erotic behavior, the audience's understanding that this new character is Lillian/"Lawrence"—ordinarily, and until this moment, a privileged knowledge that has functioned to ensure the audience's enjoyment of the film's comedic story line—fails to secure any greater narrative clarity. An alternative explanation for Bessie's behavior is that she recognizes "Lawrence" as a transformed Lillian, a perspective that would align Bessie's diegetic knowledge with the omniscient perspective of the audience. Such an interpretation may have been further reinforced for those spectators familiar with the novel's story line that ends with the happy marriage of Bessie and Lawrence. The film's inability to reconcile these two possibilities independently of any extratextual knowledge—also simultaneously a failure to articulate clearly the causal relations of its temporally compacted events—condense in the figure of Bessie in terms of the illegibility of her erotic motivations and their potential availability to alternative interpretations.

These ambiguous, amplificatory effects coalesce in a brief image that endeavors to focalize the narrative in terms of Bessie's emotional state. The single-shot scene in which Bessie, Miss Oglethorpe, and the Major absorb the news that "Lawrence" is a murder suspect, while they also await further news of Lillian's possible survival, is intercut with one in which "Lawrence" is confronted by Fred. Just as "Lawrence" snatches the police telegram that Fred has thrust into his face, the film cuts back to the moment when Bessie clasps her left hand and wedding ring, before sinking into a chair in the foreground of the shot, her face guarded and anxious (figure 3.3). The audience is required to read Bessie's feelings as caused by a narrative event, yet there remains considerable doubt as to which one that might be: Lillian's apparent disappearance and suspected murder, or the police investigation to which "Lawrence," Bessie's groom-to-be, is now subject. The film's previous scenes—in which Bessie eagerly greets "Lawrence" and then soon after accepts his engagement ring—have already established the possibility that the cause of Bessie's distress might be both. The obscurity of the cause of Bessie's anxiety is amplified by the twin status of narrative effect as subsequent narrative cause, an expected characteristic of the interlocking chain of events that is characteristic of the Hollywood classical style and its drive for dramatic

FIGURE 3.3. What motivates Bessie? Courtesy of the Library of Congress.

unity. In the turn from effect to cause, we expect that Bessie's emotional display points toward the narrative's future and an indication of her character's desires or perhaps, in this case, erotic ambitions. The Bessie character draws an inquisitive spectatorial attention without offering any clear, unambiguous representation of her desires. It is the very ambiguity of Bessie's motivations, the impossibility of knowing her desires for sure, that registers a new, albeit still amorphous, epistemological matrix out of which emerges the possibility of representing cinematically a nonnormative sexual orientation or identity. The gravitational pull of such persistent characterological opacity indicates the productive potential of the Hollywood classical style of narrative for generating new forms of sexual representation and spectatorship.

A critical attention to the figure of Bessie helps to foreground how in 1914 the processes by which an industry's ambitions to articulate clear character goals or desires in order to generate a legible cinematic narrative produce—however intentionally or accidentally—two related sexuality effects. As the kissing scenes discussed earlier demonstrate, a seemingly transparent heterosexual desire is paradoxically dependent on two different kinds of knowledge and ignorance pertaining to homoerotic forms of intimacy. If, on the one hand, certain motivations are attached unambiguously—albeit in this contradictory manner—to Lillian/"Lawrence," rendering her desires sexually intelligible, they emerge in a generative but much less clear form to the Bessie character. Bessie's actions and expressions repeatedly snag spectators' attentions while failing to provide any further significant characterological or narrative information. By only inviting sexual speculation and supposition, the tantalizing opacity of the Bessie character catalyses and sustains an alternative sexual possibility. As a character unable to satisfy the epistemological demands of emergent protocols of protoclassical narrative and spectatorship, Bessie registers—albeit in nascent form—a discursive shift in which the lack of definition or possibility of ascertaining character motivation opens up a space to which nonnormative sexual meanings might accrue. The character's failure in this sense is a subtle indicator of how the epistemological uncertainties of embodied film character must be displaced in order to guarantee the unmarked presumption and cultural privileging of heterosexuality and the fiction of its legibility and coherence. Even then, however, heterosexuality's legibility loops back rather queerly to the sexual intelligibility of homoeroticism itself. It is only by attending closely to the discursive elaboration of more than one film character that we can understand how Hollywood cinema produces heterosexuality and lesbianism as intimately related sexual formations.

4. Mobilizing Genre

The Wild Party's *Sexual Kinesthetics*

What if the richest junctures weren't the
ones where *everything means the same thing*?
—Eve Kosofsky Sedgwick, *Tendencies*

ORGANIZED AROUND FILM CHARACTER, Hollywood's drive in the mid-1910s for longer-form narrative clarity, as the previous chapter argued, generated queer sexuality effects: the articulation of motivational ambiguity as a potential sign of sexual nonnormativity, and the intelligibility of heterosexual desire dependent on a contradictory epistemological reorganization of homoerotic pleasure. Considered as the hierarchized displacements of the epistemological ambiguity of film character itself, each nascent sexuality effect draws attention to the tenuous conceptual difference between motion and motive.[1] Most basically what the classical style endeavors to render transparent, in terms of intentionality and its causes, are the *movements* of embodied forms of film character, however expansive or minimal they may be. The commonplace question of what animates bodies on screen can thus be understood historically as the effect of complex epistemological fields that both precede and include the emergent Hollywood classical style. This chapter expands on the fine-grained attention to film style in the previous chapter, "Queer Character," to consider how later institutional developments establish the conditions in which the sexual legibility of female bodies can be queerly organized, drawing on the codes and conventions of a popular genre that might otherwise secure a normative relation of embodied sex to erotic orientation and sexual identity.

Like any number of Hollywood films of the 1920s, *The Wild Party* (dir. Dorothy Arzner, Paramount Lasky, 1929) promises to deliver a witty and salacious story of "wild party girls" to its cinema audiences. Story line was not the film's main selling point, however: many contemporary reviews not only

FIGURE 4.1. Publicity photograph for *The Wild Party* (1929). Courtesy of Photofest and NBC Universal.

summarized the film's plot in its entirety but also gave away the film's ending. Though the final scene could not have been a surprise—girl gets boy when Stella Ames (Clara Bow) finally leaves the all-female Winston College with her beau, the new professor of anthropology, James "Gil" Gilmore (Fredric March)—reviewers also cued potential spectators to the pivotal plot event that enabled the formation of the happy couple: Stella's sacrifice of her college place so that her studious friend, Helen Owens (Shirley O'Hara), can win a scholarship. Across the discourse of the film's promotion and reception, these parallel plotlines of heterosexual romance and female friendship appear only as necessary scaffolding for the film's central allure: the moving images of Bow and her scantily clad cohort. In likening the film's characters to flappers and chorus girls, and drawing attention to its "Ziegfeldian atmosphere"—comparisons no doubt prompted by the publicity photos of Bow and her fellow actresses in skimpy fancy dress costumes (figure 4.1)—promoters and critics framed the film's appeals in terms of the kinetic bodies of women on screen.[2] Though *The Wild Party* was promoted as Paramount's first "talkie" and as the unique opportunity to hear Clara Bow speak for the first time on the big screen, the feature was distributed as both sound and silent versions since new audio technologies were still unevenly distributed across exhibition venues.[3] The visual attractions of Bow and her on-screen schoolmates remained pivotal to sustaining audience interest.

Bow's presence was crucial to *The Wild Party*'s screen appeal. Her stardom, measured in box office receipts and fan mail, made her Paramount's most profitable and popular actress, while Arzner was a young, ambitious director and the only woman working in that role in the Hollywood studios.[4] Arzner had already honed her skills on four other Paramount productions and the commercial success of *The Wild Party* marked the beginning of a high point in her Hollywood studio career.[5] Two years earlier, Arzner had directed Bow in *Get Your Man*, but *The Wild Party*, conceived as a low-risk star vehicle, proved to be a more significant production. Reviewers recognized not only Arzner's talent in directing Bow but also her handling of story material variously described as "tedious," "silly," and "impossible."[6] In the wake of Bow's 1927 smash hit *It* (dir. Clarence G. Badger, Famous Players-Lasky), Arzner's direction of Bow in her transition to sound endeavored to sustain the cultural legibility of the star's hypersexualized, kinetic persona. To do so, she deployed the narrative and visual protocols of what was, by the late 1920s, a nearly exhausted genre: the flapper film.[7]

Even today, the sexual legibility of the genre's central figure seems quite transparent. As historian of sexuality George Chauncey demonstrates, it takes few words to encapsulate the significance of the flapper in terms of new sex/gender roles in the early twentieth century: she was "at once both sexually precocious and profoundly heterosexual."[8] In her commodified celluloid form, the flapper's heterosexual excesses are typically disciplined by narratives that recuperate her to the institution of marriage. Despite the genre's conservative ideologies, however, feminist film critics have insisted that the meanings of flapper films regularly exceeded their narrow (hetero)sexualized representations.[9] In her discussion of Joan Crawford's famous wild dancing scenes in *Our Dancing Daughters* (dir. Harry Beaumont, Cosmopolitan Productions, 1928), for example, Mary P. Ryan insists that the images signify her character's "gusto and liveliness," and surpass the sexual objectification that shots of "lustful male faces" attempt to accomplish.[10] This feminist position has been significantly extended, both theoretically and historiographically, by Lori Landay, who argues that the genre afforded opportunities for women to identify with flapper figures via their shared experience of the codified forms of movement represented on screen, whether popular dance forms, physical culture, or more everyday styles of movement.[11] The mode of kinesthetic spectatorship engendered by the flapper film could generate feelings of a "ludic embodiment of femininity" that also surpassed the limitations of any self-commodification determined by the consumer and commodity cultures within which flapper films were embedded.[12] Landay's claim in part reflects a utopian feminist desire to escape the gender ideologies of capitalist forms of mass culture and their repressive effects. Yet it does not quite adequately account for the erotization and objectification of flapper bodies in terms of the contradictory pleasures that such representations offered its predominantly female audiences.[13] William K. Everson's terse description of *The Wild Party* as "a kind of 'Lesbiantics of 1929,'" with its pejorative connotations of grotesque forms of bodily comportment, registers the capacity of the film's kinesthetics to make heterosexuality's "other" cinematically legible.[14] The historian's anxious determination to restore a heterosexual interpretation of the film's visual appeals only provides further proof that *The Wild Party*'s generic erotics remain difficult to explain in terms of one or the other category of a too-familiar sexual binary.

An attention to the place of dance and, more broadly, the choreography of bodily movement in *The Wild Party* of 1929 suggests how the eroticism that underwrites the intense kinesthetic identifications of women's modern spectatorships might bear a close but less acknowledged relation to same-sex desires and sexualities. Arzner was well-positioned to understand the unsettling kinesthetics of flapper films but not only because of the relation of her sexual identity to themes of female friendship and community evident in her work, or her understanding of the role of dance in the flapper genre enabled by her professional and personal relationship with choreographer Marion Morgan.[15] Most importantly, Arzner was already working in an industry whose available genres, representational codes, and modes of spectator address could be readily harnessed to represent, however fleetingly, lesbian desire. As Patricia White has argued, it is precisely in early cinema's mass culture context, one that "encouraged female consumerism and emphasized women's 'to-be-looked-at-ness,'" that new lesbian subjectivities and identities emerged.[16] *The Wild Party* evidences how, in the hands of an astute director, the flapper genre's wayward erotics could be enlisted to refuse the sexual transparency of the female body while mobilizing desire between women as a distributed kinesthetic effect.

Bodies in Motion

Even before the film begins, *The Wild Party* stakes out its generic credentials as the opening credits fade in over a stylized drawing of four slim dancing women, their arms raised in the air like Art Deco statuettes. The sexual potential of these flapper figures is signified by the fringed skirts that draw attention to their boyish hips and "jungle" rhythms.[17] Freezing a party moment in time and space, the flattened graphic style recalls the backlit pool party scene of *Flaming Youth* (dir. John Dillon, Associated First National Pictures, 1923), a film often regarded as the first in the flapper film cycle.[18] More than referencing its cinematic antecedents, however, the opening image should be situated in terms of the wider cultural familiarity of the flapper. The pared-down formal qualities of the image, and the varied repetition of the four dancing women, exemplify the ways in which the flapper is constituted as a reproducible and highly legible mobile figure. The aesthetic simplicity of the image ensures that the figures are instantly recognizable in one glance as representing an already familiar kinetic femininity and precocious sexuality. Yet the reduction of detail and visual signifiers to which meaning might accrue also produces a degree of opacity or blankness. This modernist aesthetic was no doubt one of the flapper's appeals. For example, as Martin Pumphrey points out, in advertising narratives the flapper could become a pliant character able to embody a range of different products and experiences.[19] As a figure discursively constituted not only cinematically but also across other equally ephemeral sites of popular culture, the flapper proved to be a malleable and kinetic body through which new ideas, cultural practices, and ideologies of women's modern mobilities and desires could be articulated.

There is now a considerable body of literature on the flapper, produced across different disciplinary formations—whether history, cultural studies, or modernist studies—often as part of projects oriented more broadly to investigating the relations between gender and modernity.[20] Attuned to the critical implications of such developments, film scholars such as Cynthia Felando, Lori Landay, and Sara Ross have revised and extended earlier work on the flapper film genre and its eponymous figure.[21] Informed by these studies, I briefly highlight the gendered and sexual dimensions of the flapper that emerge as effects of new forms of physical movement, female fashion, and popular dance, before considering the particular role of cinema in animating the flapper as the mobile embodiment of modern femininity.

The flapper's defining quality, her kineticism, would not have been possible but for the development of radically new kinesthetic ideals and practices that emerged out of the late nineteenth century. As Lori Landay remarks in her rich survey of these historical transformations—from the Dress Reform movement to the popularity of Delsartian philosophy and dance classes—"there were social currents that sought to liberate women from the physical and material confines of Victorian ladyhood."[22] Not only did women's modes of presentation become more physically free—athletic even—but their gestures and styles of movement, for instance, swinging the arms while walking briskly, were meant to confirm this new sense of freedom and mobility. New kinesthetic discourses linked rhythmic, spontaneous, and centered bodily movements to psychological health and suggested that a lack of movement, or the lack of responsiveness to the body's need to move, was problematic.[23] Fashion was one site of popular culture integral to reshaping the ways in which women could hold and move their bodies. Contemporary fashion practitioners and later historians discerned in 1920s fashion a fundamental shift to a lithe kinetic form that also intensified and potentially eroticized the body's movement. Historian Anne Hollander argues that the new designs and cuts of skirts and dresses were meant to be best seen "in an instant of walking or dancing, conversing or gesturing"; but even when standing still, the flapper would look "posed as if pausing" before moving again.[24] This "look of possible movement," according to Hollander, signified a new sexual potential: "Immanent sexuality, best expressed in a condition of stasis, was no longer the foundation of feminine allure."[25] These shifts in fashion, premised on the need to visualize women's bodies in motion, were inextricably linked with the expansion and intensification of modern visual cultures. In place of Victorian feminine ideals of quiet poise and restraint emerged a modern dialectic of sexualized stasis and motion premised on the need to be seen to move.

The novel kinetic and spectacular forms of 1920s fashion drew on, and were productively reinforced by, the new kinesthetic vocabulary of popular and social dances such as the Shimmy, the Charleston, and the Black Bottom.[26] Radically different from the slower-paced, formal, and paired dances of the previous century, these new dances enacted a complex shifting pattern of erotic and de-eroticized fragmented movements. Some were sexual, such as overtly suggestive pelvic or hip movements, or gestures that drew attention to erogenous body zones, such as the Black Bottom gesture akin to striking a match on one's hip.[27] Others rendered the limbs as jerky machinelike parts. Dance scholar Elizabeth Kendall emphasizes the quality of the movements of the new popular dances in which the body could reveal something new and unexpected or could be made strange or denaturalized:

> Twenties dance revelled consciously and unconsciously in the general alertness about how the body looked, and its new separation into parts. . . . The

> Charleston, to a jerky syncopation, almost tied the knees together but let the feet twist crazily against the floor and the arms either flap in opposition or make Egyptian-type designs on top. In the black bottom the backside was identified as something that moved; the arms slapped the bobbing backside as if to push the whole person forward through the pelvis. In general the torso, like the geometric dresses that covered it, was seen to contain surprise pieces of itself that promised whimsical expression.[28]

Dance curator Barbara Cohen-Stratyner emphasizes the new dances' mode and style of performance and argues that it was certain elements of performance that made one specific dance, one closely associated with the flapper, more persistent across the decade of the 1920s:

> More than any other dance, [the Charleston] defined the performer as young and willing to take chances on modern life. It managed to be both trendy and individualistic because it was concurrently hard to dance and easy to self-choreograph. In fact, the multiple movements that define the Charleston could be emphasized, deemphasized, or even dropped by different choreographers (for stage) and people (for social situations).[29]

While Cohen-Stratyner goes on to point out the suitability of the Charleston to differently gendered fashions, she also implicitly suggests that the dance moves themselves enabled and enacted a new gendered mobility. There is historical evidence to suggest that certain dances were understood in gendered terms. In the case of the Charleston, dance historians Marshall and Jean Stearns claim that it was the first new popular dance step "taken over generally by men," since the moves that comprised the earlier Shimmy had been seen as too effeminate.[30] The sexual implication of this gendered division is, however, too coarse. If particular moves of the Charleston were regarded as conventionally masculine, performers could also adopt and adapt other moves from the Shimmy and the Black Bottom—moves that might be regarded as more feminine or more sexual—to their own style and personality.[31] It was the built-in flexibility of the dance steps comprising the Charleston that enabled performers to articulate new and complex gendered and sexual identities, identities that were predicated on presenting the spectacle of a body in motion for a watching audience.[32]

This flexible dimension of popular dances and their adaptability to both public spectacle and more intimate social displays meshed with the thematic content and formal structure of the Hollywood flapper film cycle. Since the mid-1910s, popular and other high art forms of dance had been increasingly incorporated into the plotlines of Hollywood films, but, for flapper films, popular dances of the 1920s become one of the primary signifiers of new modern femininities.[33] The opening scene of *Love 'Em and Leave 'Em* (dir. Frank Tuttle, Paramount Famous Lasky, 1926) efficiently encapsulates the social significance of popular dance in an economical series of shots motivated by the movements and looks of Mame Walsh (Evelyn Brent): as she walks across her shared bedroom to close an open window, this action is followed by her sharp glance at a heap of discarded clothes and then at the peaceful sleeping face of her younger sister Janie (Louise Brooks). The reason for Janie's late-night antics is revealed by Mame's point-of-view close-up of Janie's first prize for a Charleston Competition, a doll whose feet whir back and forth. The narrative moment requires the film to condense the flapper's undesirable traits into a single image of an automatonlike windup doll, but the film later capitalizes on the erotic appeal of the dancing flapper when it tilts up and down Brooks's body as she shimmies and shakes at a fancy dress party. The doll's disturbing mechanical movements are rendered visually pleasurable in the spectacular figure of Brooks, a flapper figure animated by another invisible mechanical technology, the cinematograph. In later flapper films, cinema's technological capacity to animate and eroticize the flapper's body is made more explicit. The opening sequence of *Our Dancing Daughters* converts a stilled female body to one in almost constant motion—a spectacular transition reminiscent of proto-cinematic and early projection practices deployed to astound audiences with film's capacity to move the body and a reminder of the mutual imbrication of the cinematograph's technological capacity and the instantiation of sexuality. The transformation from inanimate to animated figure that subjects the feminine flapper to cinema's regime of "visible mechanics" was inseparable from and reliant on popular codified forms of movement—dance, physical culture, everyday practices, and ideals of comportment—those other technologies of the body that co-opted and shaped the frenetic movements of cinema's wild party girl.[34]

Seeing in Motion

As spectacles of unrepressed flapperdom, dance scenes are moments in which the disciplinary power of sexuality is forcefully expressed through moving images of the body. Early in the film, *The Wild Party*'s "Costume" dance scene establishes the terms by which the film sets out to recalibrate the cinematic figure of the dancing flapper.[35] Billed by an inter-title as the "feminine equivalent to the stag," the Costume scene's kinesthetic coordinates are established with a close-up of blurred dancing shoes—moccasins, low-heeled pumps, and boots—tapping out frenetic steps to the syncopated rhythms of the film's theme tune. The heel twists and cross-kicks of these dancing feet mirror those of the kinetic shoes that open *Our Dancing Daughters*, but the tracking shot reveals not a single lone woman performing for herself and the camera but rather an assortment of costumed women—telegraph girls, pirates, cave-girls, and Native Americans—all dancing vigorously in couples. The spectacle and individualistic expressivity of popular dance is reoriented into a same-sex paired set of rhythmic gestures so that the dancers perform for and with each other, as much as for any diegetic or historical film audience. Visually, the performance of the dancers is only visible as several couples dance into the center of the screen, but they quickly circulate away into the crowd, their movements oriented to their partners as well as the inner space of the ballroom as they turn their backs to the camera and the spectator's view. The function of dancing spectacle is instead transferred to the characters who enter the frame next.

While the camera's track back distances the spectator from the space of the ballroom, the scene's first cut establishes a closer, voyeuristic relation to the feminine body. In a disorienting close-up, a satin shoe with sequined brooch and matching glittering heel steps into view. Not only more glamorous than those that opened the scene, the shiny shoe is soon followed by several identical pairs that cross the frame in careful synchronicity. This more overt eroticism accomplished by both camera and costuming is confirmed in the following wide shot, when Stella and her three buddies, wrapped only in sumptuous thigh-length fur coats, emerge at the edge of the lobby area. Rushing across to a coatroom, they fling off their furs to reveal sequined bathing suits. The design itself suggests the metaphorical shock of their apparel, with its white zigzag lightning bolt that threatens to split open the front of each costume. As the group sashays screen right, they strike a pose with their bodies facing the camera, and their interlocutor Faith Morgan (Marceline Day), who has emerged from the ballroom to prevent them from entering it. Their matching movements and costumes heighten their already excessive femininity and sexuality by denying individuality to any one body; their seriality implies a potentially limitless repeatability. The image of Stella and friends as synchronized chorines evokes the famous Tiller Girls dancing troupe, their playful rendering of Tiller-like militaristic precision contrasting starkly with the freer and expressive dancing behind them inside the ballroom.[36] With their coordinated movement across the lobby space and their identical costumes, the fake showgirls transform the lobby into an imaginary dance stage, both diegetically and for the film's spectators.

Although the Costume establishes a narrative ruse for the erotic display of Stella's chorus line, unlike earlier flapper films the visual organization of the scene does not rely on the presence of a diegetic heterosocial audience or male spectator to establish any heterosexual credentials. Though the initial homosocial scene of the ballroom might also suggest a homosexual scene, this possibility is less sexually intelligible than the entry of Stella's girl gang into the lobby space. The dialogue skirts around the problem of the overt sexuality signified by their skimpy costumes and playful showgirl routine: Faith refuses them entry into the ballroom fearing their influence on the "younger and weaker" girls while Stella protests "aren't we all made the same?" (In a playful visual irony, Faith's moralizing stance is reinforced by her costume, a fetching Little Bo Peep outfit complete with shepherdess' crook.) Faith's line ostensibly points to the chorus girls' status as bad heterosexual role models, but Stella's response amplifies Faith's admonition in a more complex way. While jesting about Faith's concerns that their presence in the ballroom may encourage improper identifications if not imitations, in a roundabout way Stella's appeal to a bodily uniformity underneath the costumes ("made the same") implicitly addresses another possible reading of Faith's dialogue, that their visual projection of overt feminine sexuality may incite desire in the young women who see them. Stella's response implies its opposite: that an externally visible and identically embodied femininity may not map so easily onto a corresponding uniformity of interiorized sexual desire. The sexual stakes of the dialogue remain unresolved and are only magnified by the visual organization and kinesthetics of the scene. If it is tempting to assign a greater weight to the chorines and their highly sexualized aesthetics in the formation of feminine heterosexual identities, Arzner refuses such easy divisions. Instead the scene suggests the limits of vision in representing sexuality and the ways in which a kinetic feminine aesthetic and sexualization masks the possibility of lesbian desire.[37]

The uncertainty of knowing what sexual desires and identity the kinetic female body signifies is worked through in the following scene when Stella and friends, denied entry to the ballroom, head off to the local roadhouse. In plot terms, this and the following scenes enable the romance between Gil and Stella, since Gil has to rescue Stella from roadhouse mashers. The roadhouse scene dramatizes the sexual consequences of looking and being looked at in ways that provide a spectatorial alibi for its female audience. In a shot/reverse-shot sequence, a group of older men ogle the young women; to be more specific, the shots establish their gaze as resting on the women's bare legs lined up at the bar. Misreading them as showgirls, the drunken mashers attempt some heavy-handed flirting that soon turns into a melee during which they kidnap Stella. By explicitly constructing the cinematic gaze as gendered (male) and (hetero)sexual, *The Wild Party* grants a privileged knowingness to the audience about the "real" identity of the young women, even as it simultaneously continues to exploit the same visual pleasures of kinetic feminine bodies that animated the previous scene.

Incorporating the sexually rapacious gaze of the roadhouse mashers into the narrative deflects attention from the film's more subtle organization of space and structures of homoerotic looking. The film's very first scene playfully inverts the dance routine imitated by Stella's chorus line while also covertly establishing the central attractions, and distractions, of the moving feminine body for its female audiences. The scene opens with several young women, clad only in their negligées, lounging on a couch eating chocolates, while Babs (Adrienne Doré) sits on the edge of a table putting on her eye makeup. In the foreground, Maisie (Alice Adair), clad only in a tight sleeveless top and short shorts, has her upper back on the floor while moving her raised legs back and forth in a scissoring motion. As Maisie goes through her calisthenic routine, a circuit of glances visually connects all the characters: the girls on the sofa in the background watch Maisie and Babs, while Babs watches herself in the mirror and glances down at Maisie as she performs her upside-down showgirl routine. The off-screen presence of the audience viewing the scene is mirrored diegetically by the out-of-focus young women seated on the couch. Yet, since any clear vision of them is continually interrupted by the oscillations of opening and closing limbs, any on-screen allegorical evidence of the pleasures of a predominantly female audience in watching another woman's body in motion remains obscured. The kinetic female body itself screens from view the identifications and desires that it provokes. Those identifications and desires, intertwined and dynamic, are constituted as part of a restless gaze that is only momentarily short-circuited with a cut to the next part of the scene.

By framing the moving female body in this way, the film builds the broader same-sex kinesthetic identifications of female spectatorship into its dynamic structure of looking, a structure that is predicated on sustaining and amplifying desire without any resolution. In the late 1920s, at the tail end of the flapper film cycle, it is the relation of modern women's shared forms of movement to spectacle and display—both diegetic and cinematic—that opens up the potential for same-sex desire, since women's kinesthetic identifications with one another, secured by similar corporeal expression and kinetic experience, depend on a continual movement between being the subject of looking and its object. Landay's provocative notion of women's kinesthetic spectatorship precludes this possibility, implicitly opposing identification to desire premised on sexual difference, a conceptual move that simultaneously allows Landay to claim identification as a mode of transcendence. The submerged presence of such a counter-directional relation between desire and identity—so that one cannot desire the same 'other' that one also identifies with—is not surprising however. It grounds, even as it also troubles, the work of film theoreticians and the psychoanalytic thinkers on which they rely. As Diana Fuss has argued with respect to a later twentieth-century visual aesthetic and institutional context, "such a symmetrical, rigid, chiasmatic relation between terms may disguise the ways in which any identification *with* an other is secured through a simultaneous and continuing desire *for* that other."[38] The central framing of Maisie's moving bare limbs, together with the length of the shot and the network of glances, institutes a mobile gaze that is guaranteed to return repeatedly to the distracting attractions of her leggy locomotions, even as it is never held long enough to suture the spectator into a more voyeuristic viewing position. As an instance of kinesthetic identification, to reorient Landay's formulation, it does not transcend the sexual objectification of the feminine but rather puts it into mobile play, and thus continually generates the possibility of same-sex desire. Rather than quarantining desire from identification, Arzner's subtle tweaking of the kinesthetics of the flapper genre makes the two difficult to distinguish, the one enfolded within the other, their mutual dependence enabled by new forms of feminine movement.

The Look of Possible Movement

Even though Hollywood could call upon plenty of ambitious starlets to perform flapper roles—indeed part of the pre-publicity for the film included a call for new talent—*The Wild Party*'s appeal, and its kinetic effects, are inseparable from its star. Hollywood's ultimate "wild party girl," Bow was considered to embody the kinetic potential of the flapper at its most extreme. Promoted early on in her career as the "ultra-flapper," Bow was regarded as the most mobile performer of all the flapper actresses of the '20s, even when compared to her contemporaries Colleen Moore and Joan Crawford.[39] Reviewers, fans, and producers, as Cynthia Felando points out, constantly commented on and exaggerated her energetic performances.[40] Landay reminds us that the conception of Bow's acting style in terms of movement extended to her "look," an ambiguous term that referred both to her cultivated image and her dynamic eye movements and facial expressions.[41] While the consolidated conventions of Hollywood classical cinema showcased and reinforced Bow's eye-play and mobile performances, those performances were also read in the context of film promotion, fan stories, and news reports about her hectic and often scandalous love life. In one exemplary story, partly a publicity stunt, it was reported that a football player had tried to commit suicide after Clara rejected him; he had accused her of kissing him so hard that his lips ached for two days.[42] The cinematic exploitation of Bow's kineticism, and extra-cinematic sexual discourse, mutually reinforced one another, often disrupting the conservative sexual ideological terms of the Hollywood films in which Bow appeared. Reading Bow's most well-known film *It* as the quintessential flapper film of the 1920s, critics such as Gaylyn Studlar and Cynthia Felando agree that Bow's "overwhelming dynamic eroticism" problematizes the ideological determinants of the film's plot, including the companionate marriage that is its narrative endpoint.[43] Operating more broadly than the erotic spectacle of dance scenes in flapper films, Bow's physical performances readily functioned as the corporeal location through which other, less ideologically conservative, erotic meanings could emerge.

Bow's disruptive kineticism was reinforced by fan magazine discourse that continued to identify the star as the personification of "it," a flexible and open term whose possible sexual meanings were shaped by the different discursive contexts of its deployment.[44] What is often evident in the discourses of promotion, fanship, and marketing around Bow and her films is the considerable, even excessive, rhetorical labor invested in heterosexualizing "it." In the film *It*, a scene is even included to establish that its gay-coded male character does not have "it." Yet, the potential for "it" to accrue other sexual meanings that might sustain a more ambiguous homoerotic positioning of female readers/spectators is evident in an earlier 1927 image of Bow in which she holds a monocle up to her eye, with a supporting caption that reads: "Clara Bow . . . puts 'It' in front of her eye, and laughs, just to show you she doesn't intend to keep 'It' there. Only a part in 'Get Your Man.'"[45] Capitalizing on the understanding of Bow's mobile gaze, her image incites looking—just as it incites expectations of movement and eroticism—while she also looks out through her monocle at the unseen female reader/spectator. While we might now invariably associate the monocle with lesbian subcultural style, that was only one of its possible associations. As Laura Doan argues, even in the late 1920s, the monocle carried multiple symbolic meanings, "denoting class, Englishness, daring, decay, rebellion, affectation, eccentricity—and possibly, but not necessarily, sexual identity."[46] Nevertheless, in this particular instance, the monocle is directly associated with sexual appeal and desire, even as the caption ultimately redirects any possible implication of same-sex desire by and for Bow. Read allegorically, the transparent technology of the monocle stands in for the cinematic apparatus that structures and enables a new erotics of looking, even as the terms of those new erotics remain seemingly insubstantial and difficult to map. "It"—or sexuality—becomes conflated with, and indivisible from, the invisible cinematic apparatus that enables looking and generates desire. A stand-in for the female spectator as both subject and object of the look, the monocled image of Bow suggests that her kinesthetic "look" (the combination of kinetic fashions, bodily performance, and mobile gaze) was already primed to encompass the possibility of same-sex desire and lesbian identification.

It is the openness of Bow's bodily and facial kineticism, already understood as highly sexual and eroticized, that Arzner harnesses across the narrative and spectacle of *The Wild Party*. Movement motivates Bow's character, and movement generates visual pleasure. Stella's accidental meeting with Gil on the train back to college is the outcome of her stumble in the railway carriage corridor, and her accidental fall against his body. Her rescue of Helen at the later Medford College dance party is effected through movement: she spins the drunken Medford college boy across the dance floor so that the other girls can inflict "the dizzy" on him. Bow's movements catalyze the other characters around her, who take up and repeat her moves in countless variations: the tap-dancing duo in the busy gym locker room, Babs's showgirl-like high kick for a dollar bill at the Medford College party, the darting young women in the hallways and corridors trying to avert Helen's scholarship disaster. All these scenes confirm the observation of *New York Times* reviewer Mordaunt Hall that, in *The Wild Party*, everyone dashes "hither and thither."[47] The repertoire of movement, gesture, and bodily comportment shared by the film's different female characters—a repertoire that inevitably revolves, with centripetal force, around the figure of Bow—is exaggerated and eroticized by the film's multiplication of bodies. While this effect is literalized in the Costume dance scene with its repetition of Bow's body across the identical figures of her female companions, the film ramps up this effect across its other, more everyday, scenes. It repeatedly offers scenes of female bodies en masse, whether the tangled and initially anonymous bodies pressed into the back seat of the car after the roadhouse brawl or the fire drill toward the end of the film that provides another opportunity to squeeze umpteen barely clad young moving bodies into the space of the Academy ratio frame. The comic effect of such scenes only intensifies the homoeroticism of the image, while often only offering the flimsiest support to the heterosexual plotline.

While the flapper genre in its ideal forms required the aesthetic exploitation of movement across all its scenes, new production conditions in the transition to sound had the potential to significantly undermine its kinesthetics and the performance of the star most often identified with it.[48] Earlier films starring Bow could more freely change camera positions (both as complex camera movements and new shot setups) and edit rapid montages in order to build complex kinetic sequences. During the making of *The Wild Party*, in scenes where synchronized sound was required, new technological constraints limited the degree to which cinematography and editing could enhance movement.[49] The advent of sound posed a problem for Bow in ways less related to the expected qualities of her voice than to her physical performance. One of the most significant changes was the new immobility of the camera and microphone when synchronized sound was required, a production environment that impacted on Bow since she had to deliver clearly enunciated lines from a rigid, static position. As is well-known, Arzner collaborated with the sound operator to design a sound boom, the very first, to remove this impediment to Bow's way of working. This practical solution suggests that Arzner was acutely aware of the importance of Bow's kineticism to the success of her performance. More than her behind-the-scenes intervention on Bow's behalf, however, it is Arzner's approach to mise-en-scène that suggests that she understood the importance of Bow's style to the broader feminine kinesthetic configuration of *The Wild Party*.

Attuned to the cultural imagery of the flapper, and the already established framework within which Bow's kinetic performances were read, one of Arzner's significant aesthetic solutions is to block the actors' actions as static poses in order to suggest their potential for movement. The counterintuitive impact of the transition to sound in *The Wild Party* is that the arrangement of the body, rather than the sound of the voice and its dialogue, becomes more privileged.[50] In Bow's initial entrance, for example, the arrangement of her body for the camera suggests the potential for movement. When Maisie helps Stella open her suitcase, the two characters pose one behind the other in profile, a doubled image in which Maisie visually repeats Stella's stance; both are positioned so that the soon-to-be-opened suitcase will reveal its contents most fully to the audience. The angularity and visual rhythms of their posed limbs echo the opening credits image of dancing flappers in the way that the bold diagonal lines of their bodies signify movement. When the case finally opens, they tumble over each other, an explosive shift from stasis to motion. The overall effect is to invest the pose, and stasis, with a kinetic potency.

Whether considered a pause between other movement or the physical stance of a character in a scene, the pose might be seen as merely part of the dramatic exigencies of Hollywood narrative production. But in the context of the flapper genre, the pose assumes a more freighted relation to the feminine kinesthetics that the genre both mediates and constitutes. The pose has a complex history. Its cinematic genealogy extends back to the practice of tableau or "living pictures" as forms of erotic theatrical presentation. As a performance technique, a pose presents and displays the body in a certain arrangement of costume, posture, and gesture in order to signify specific attitudes, emotions, and ideas.[51] At the same time, the stillness of the body ensures that it is available to the spectator as erotic spectacle, able to be contemplated at leisure. By the 1920s, the pose had assumed an important kinetic dimension, as seen earlier in relation to the example of women's fashions: it was part of a dialectic of stasis and motion in which the holding of a "pose as if pausing" signified the possibility of past and future movement, a possibility that could also be read in sexual terms.

The imbrication of movement and eroticism was further intensified by production conditions that often required actors to hold their bodies in too still a pose, for slightly too long, intensifying the anticipation of movement. This is first apparent near the end of the opening scene where the young women in Stella's dormitory room surge toward the window to see the arrival of Gil, the new professor of anthropology. The rush of bodies is part of the activation of the romance plot (since it connects Stella again to Gil), and their movement across the plane of the screen simultaneously expresses and secures the heterosexual orientation of their desires. But their bodies, and the frilly details of nightgowns and undergarments, visually overwhelm and outnumber the unsuspecting Gil. At the same time, as they come to a stop to look down upon the new professor, the camera offers a tightly framed image of the posed profiles of the women's bodies. Their erotic kineticism is only accentuated by their momentary pause. They become both the active subjects and objects of looking: diegetically at Gil and extra-diegetically in their commodified presentation for view by the film's spectators. The duration and static nature of the poses of the other characters in *The Wild Party* complement the film's already eroticized dynamics of motion centered on Bow, not only in terms of suspense as we wait for their next move, but because the slightest extension of the duration of their poses beyond the typical performance conventions of the period makes their poses more available to an audience's appraisal. Such photographic-like moments of stillness briefly arrest the narrative flow and invite—indeed, incite—an eroticized reading of the looks, glances, touches, and bodily presentations of and between the characters on screen. The "look of possible movement" embodied by über-flapper Clara Bow and her cinematic cohort stages the ephemerality of erotic experience even as it also plays a part in constituting the always in-process sexual subjectivities of its cinematic audiences.

Going Through the Motions

It is within this rich and densely textured visual schema that the possibility arises of representing and decoding lesbian desire. Read in kinesthetic and historical terms, the sexual intelligibility of scenes between Stella and Helen become more than a function of their friendship (the other major plotline of the film) or visual proximity in the frame. With the proliferation of all kinds of movement across the scenes of the film, movement that accumulates and saturates the image, all its female characters come to be invested with the capacity for heightened sexual desire, even at moments of stasis, moments which might seem to be the antithesis of the film's and the flapper's kinesthetic design. In signifying the potential for movement in those moments when bodies on screen are only minimally animated or "live," the erotics of stasis reinforce the notion that sexual desire always emanates from bodies, obscuring its genesis as a sexuality effect of the intertwined corporeal technologies of new physical cultures—including dance—and cinema.

It is a scene between the two main female characters that occurs in a space of shared intimacy that provides perhaps the most poignant illustration of this effect. After the fire drill, Stella and Helen meet up again in their dorm room and Helen laments the loss of her incriminating love letters to her new boyfriend, George, letters that reveal her transgression of strict college curfew rules. Toward the end of the scene, the characters perch on the edge of a recently vacated and rumpled bed. A site at the very least of an easy physical familiarity between two girls who have already spooned together in a railway car sleeping berth, the bed remains in the background for the entire scene. With a cut to a tighter mid-shot, the camera focuses attention on their two poised and static bodies as Stella listens sympathetically to Helen's plight while looking intently at her, occasionally caressing her cheek. The erotic legibility of the scene, the possibility that it might represent lesbian desire on the Hollywood screen in 1929, is paradoxically articulated via the characters' stillness, and their mutual embodiment of a "look of possible movement." The brevity of the moment on screen not only testifies to its charged capacity for erotic meaning, but ultimately works to secure it.

The bedroom scene (and other similar ones) points to Arzner's interest in creating a lesbian couple who become visually legible within the terms of the film's overall aesthetic design. While it is also possible to read this scene as signifying an institutional homophobia—as establishing the representational boundary of a Hollywood cinema increasingly invested in relatively new heterosexual ideologies—when interpreted in terms of historical kinesthetic femininities, the scene offers no clear-cut sexual distinctions. Like other scenes in the film, the bedroom scene resists a straightforward analysis in terms of sexual binaries that might neatly match onto either visual form or incipient narrative.[52] This indeterminacy and potential for movement—between the characters, between different plotlines, between narrative and image—allows the bedroom scene to perform a double purpose, advancing the film's heterosexual and homosocial twinned story lines, even as it also makes the scene available to homosexual interpretation. The scene's function as both sexual and narrative switchpoint evidences Arzner's recognition of the transformational possibilities of modern kinesthetics that become available through the moving body of the cinematic flapper. The epistemological ambiguities of embodied film character, considered in the previous chapter, are here amplified and repurposed. In Arzner's capable hands, the variable momentum of new femininities can momentarily register same-sex desire at the same time that it confounds a system of sexuality predicated on fixing erotic preferences into hetero- or homosexual taxonomies.

The steady and regular mechanical rhythm of the train that begins the final sequence of *The Wild Party* contrasts markedly with the playful rhythms of the film's cast of characters. Subordinating individual bodily movements to movement in a larger spatial register, the ultimate scene relies on a vehicle symbolic of linearity and forward movement to shift the romance story characters away from the College and to guarantee its ending. For a film all about the body and its kinesthetics, the relative spareness of the ending incites a reading back—even as the train drives relentlessly forward into the future—not only to those earlier visually rhythmic images but also to their generic context and the images of flappers that enabled them: complex discursive figures whose cultural currency, vibrancy, and potential for feminine and sexual freedoms were shortly to be eclipsed by a new and less generous sexual culture. If, as Patricia White has convincingly argued, the representation of female homosexuality in Hollywood film is more often veiled by "the public sexualization of the female body," then in the case of *The Wild Party* it is excessively kinetic female bodies that screen—that is, both project and hide from view—lesbian desire as a new form of cinematic knowledge and pleasure.[53] The possibility of desire between women is not signified by the external signs that might be employed to distinguish some bodies from others as particular kinds of sexual bodies. Rather, lesbian desire is coded in terms of embodied movement, directionality, and time—as a possible erotic orientation toward another that might arise in an evanescent moment. *The Wild Party* demonstrates how the centrality of the eroticized female body to a historical genre sustains a complex dynamic of desire and identification in which the pleasures of homoeroticism are never definitively welded to any one specific sexual identity or subjectivity.

The two chapters that comprise this middle part of the book have each considered how the representation of lesbian desire is articulated to the development of film-specific styles and genres and made legible in terms of a motivational ambiguity, or a more elusive, switchpointlike erotic orientation. These ways of "knowing" lesbian desire comprise part of a more expansive history of the cinematic representability of homosexuality in terms of connotation, a paradoxical epistemological structure that permits the ready denial of the existence of what it purports to represent.[54] Such contradictory and culturally devalued codes of knowing lesbian desire cannot be understood in isolation from concomitant efforts to render cross-sex relations in early cinema intelligible as always—or always potentially—heterosexual. That all it takes is an eye-line match or two-shot to suggest the existence of an erotic motivation drawing one sexed body to its "opposite" is evidence of an extraordinary ongoing labor at the level of film discourse and the fragility of its normative effects.

PART III

Bonds

Spectatorship and Queer Subjectivities

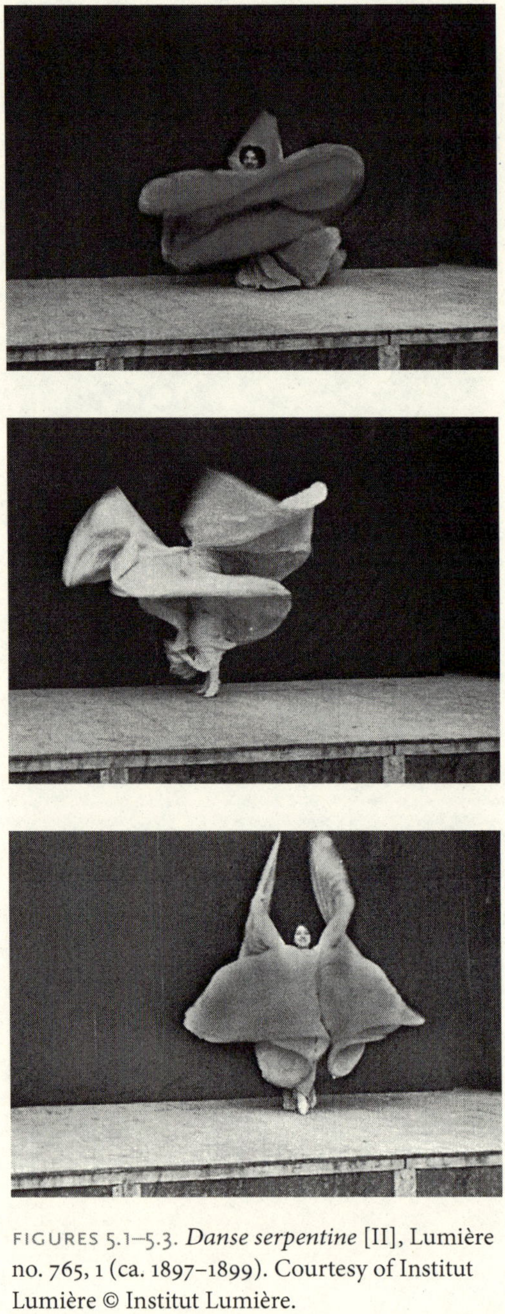

FIGURES 5.1–5.3. *Danse serpentine* [II], Lumière no. 765, 1 (ca. 1897–1899). Courtesy of Institut Lumière © Institut Lumière.

5. Looking Backward

Loïe Fuller and the Virtual Erotics of Spectatorship

> What happens to the energy of attachment when it has no designated place? To the glances, gestures, encounters, collaborations, or fantasies that have no canon?
>
> —Lauren Berlant, "Intimacy"

THIS FINAL PART OF *Queer Timing* turns to consider the queer effects of sexuality itself, that is, how various strategies of sexuality as they manifest in early cinema might have unexpected, nonnormative effects. This chapter and the next demonstrate possible modes of artistic and erotic agency within very different though equally complex institutional and cultural fields, and the potential for leveraging, in counterintuitive fashions, the effects of modern sexuality. Each chapter is also reliant on methods that de-center any single film or performative text in order to recover alternative modes of early cinema spectatorship. While the final chapter recovers the queer effects of Hollywood spectatorship as it is organized by one of its most potent cult stars, this penultimate chapter returns to the late-nineteenth-century intermedial period and one of its most privileged archives: the spectacular performances and contemporaneous film imitations of dancer Loïe Fuller.[1]

Approaching Fuller's archive—her on-stage performances and her filmic imitations—from the perspective of the history of sexuality is an opportunity to reconsider the extent to which culturally normative same-sex erotic spectatorial relations may have been subtly inflected and reorganized via moving image practices and technologies that preceded, overlapped with, and were appropriated by early films. As historiographical strategy, this turning back to consider the implications of Fuller's archive in terms of spectatorship and sexual subjectivity follows the work of other film and visual culture historians who have increasingly looked to early cinema's immediate "prehistory" in order to resist teleological accounts of cinema's future development. Leading early cinema historian, André Gaudreault, has called for scholars to go "against the grain of chronology," by undertaking a retrospective rather than progressive point of view.[2] Retrospectivity is deployed strategically against the tendency to always read early film in terms of what it anticipates—or fails to anticipate—a historiographical strategy akin to the one pursued in Part I of this book, in that it requires suspending what we now know of what was then cinema's only imagined future-present. In this regard, we might redefine the prefix in the term now often used to describe Fuller's performances, *proto-cinematic*, that encapsulates Tom Gunning's appealing claim that they prepared audiences for future encounters with film.[3] *Proto-* can indicate a point of origin in a future-looking chronology but a strategic retrospectivity instead emphasizes its meaning as only one potential, or incipient quality, among many. Thinking more specifically of the historical development of cinema spectatorship, and implicitly taking a less linear and more synchronic view, Vanessa Schwartz has argued that it is essential "to locate cinema in the field of cultural forms and practices associated with the burgeoning mass culture of the late nineteenth century."[4] Along with a strategic retrospectivity, such an approach has the critical advantage of situating Fuller's archive, and its specific forms of spectatorship, in the context of a late-nineteenth-century mass culture that is fundamentally diverse and heterogeneous.[5]

Considered from this historiographical perspective, Fuller's archive unsettles relatively unexamined assumptions about the erotics of female cinematic spectatorship. Her proto-cinematic performances multiplied the orientations toward and desires for her performing body in order to maximize pleasure for a broad range of audiences, whether in mixed heterosocial venues, or the time-bound and gender-specific space of the matinee. In so doing, they also sustained and reoriented seemingly outdated but culturally normative nineteenth-century modes of female homoerotic spectatorship (see the earlier discussion in Chapter 2 "Traces, Specks, and Glimmers"). The regulation of women's homoerotic viewing pleasures is one of the discursive practices by which sexuality penetrates and intensifies bodies, both of spectators and bodies represented on stage or screen. Fuller's performances draw on only to reorient such modes of power through a paradoxically disembodied form of visual entertainment. Her moving image archive, broadly construed as both Fuller's "live" dances and her screen imitations, suggests how at the fin de siècle the emergent sexual subjectivities of female spectators—just as much as male spectators—were implicated in forms of visual pleasure centered on the moving female body.

Unfixable

Fuller first performs her novel dances in 1891, and by the late 1890s a particular dance in her repertoire, the serpentine dance, had become one of the more popular of early film subjects.[6] Yet one of the paradoxes of Fuller's early career, given her interests in and use of electric light and image projection on stage, is her apparent lack of interest in utilizing, in a more systematic fashion, film—the one innovative form of visual technology that likely did the most to enhance her popular appeal and international recognition.[7] Though a number of performers move back and forth between stage and screen when films are first produced, so that their embodied performances could be experienced by audiences at the same time as their virtual ones, Fuller herself was rarely filmed, if at all.[8] Instead, early filmmakers in the United States, France, and Germany recorded the performances of an increasing number of Fuller imitators. By the late 1890s, her proper name was such a recognizable and potent signifier that film producers used it to title their dance films and to market them to potential exhibitors.[9] As these appropriations of Fuller's name and signature performance attest, early film emerges initially as part of established nineteenth-century performance and visual cultures and draws on its already established content and forms, including what Laurent Guido calls its "para-cinematographic spectacles and kaleidoscopic dances."[10]

Unable to reproduce the dramatic conditions of darkness in which an ethereal Loïe Fuller would materialize on stage, nor the temporal duration of her performances, which often comprised a series of dances, the serpentine dance films provide the only moving image record of what is now an obscure genre of stage entertainment.[11] Though serpentine dance films record a range of styles of movement and costume, *Danse serpentine [II]*, Lumière no. 765, 1 (ca. 1897–1899) archives a particularly skilful demonstration and approximation of Fuller's signature dance (figures 5.1–5.3).[12] In the surviving print, the action starts midperformance with the dancer, encased in a gigantic flowing robe, manipulating its material with unseen rods that extend the length of her arms. Even as it might be tempting to fix the dancer's rapid movements back and forth across the stage in terms of a coherent representational project—an exotic orchid, a butterfly—other transmogrifications defy any exact mimetic relation. As the thick, undulating layers of dress material arc across the dancer's torso, different colored tints wash across the twirling fabric. The variable result of hand-painting, these pulsations of color only seem to animate further the swirling material, making it seem almost alive and indivisible from the dancer's body and her movements. As one of the earliest color experiments, the film attempts to replicate Fuller's use of multihued electric lights projected onto her mobile costume while she performed.[13] Offering only the briefest of cinematic experiences, *Danse serpentine* manages to convey in proximate terms the serpentine's interdependent visual pleasures: brief glimpses of the dancer's body that are more often obscured by a sensual floating fabric; the magical possibility of transforming a human body into other objects and kinds of bodies; and a highly abstract spectacle of moving form and color that nevertheless conveys a vital sense of energy and life.

As these ineluctably intertwined but subtly different visual pleasures suggest, serpentine dance films and their pleasures have always been difficult to categorize, a difficulty that seems inevitably to converge on the question of their erotic appeal. The films have not been easily accommodated within feminist theorizations of film spectatorship predicated on the narrative inscription of a spectacularized female body and concomitant gendered structures of voyeurism. The visual dialectic of concealment and revelation that would typically eroticize and objectify the serpentine dancer's body is, as Judith Mayne has pointed out, disrupted by a sheer "excess" of fabric, undermining the ability of spectators to distinguish adequately between material and body.[14] Even at the historical moment of their production, serpentine dance films occupy an uncertain position within early film's organizations of genre, often classed as dance films but also cataloged in close proximity to other more overtly erotic productions, such as films depicting women undressing and getting into bed.[15] Such uncertain generic ascriptions are not only an effect of the conditions of early film production but also of disparate programming and exhibition practices. When serpentine dance films were exhibited, they could appear alongside a diverse range of other film subjects, including films with more explicit erotic subject matter. In the British colony of New Zealand, for example, a serpentine dance film was a regular feature of a vaudeville show starring illusionist Carl Hertz, touring in 1897, that included scenic views and *The May Irwin Kiss* (Edison, United States, 1896).[16] The stage performance of the serpentine dance could be subject to similar programming practices. Fuller's performances in her second season at the Folies-Bergère in Paris, for example, were framed by other highly sexualized, even bawdy, performances by women.[17] The late-nineteenth-century variety mode of entertainment programming only reinforced the uncertain generic status of both the serpentine dance films and their onstage performances.

The difficulty in categorizing the serpentine dance was compounded by the particular forms and content out of which it was assembled. As is well-known, in developing a new type of theatrical performance, Fuller drew on established stage and visual entertainment practices in order to fabricate a novel show that could not be easily contained within or understood in terms of any one of its antecedent forms. Early reviews, for example, questioned whether the serpentine dance was a form of dancing or posing.[18] Though the latter term was sometimes used to suggest the serpentine dance's originality, the association of "posing" with different forms of nineteenth-century popular culture—from the risqué theater entertainment of erotic tableaux vivants or "living pictures" to the Delsartian physical culture poses and movements promoted to and practiced by women—could imply anything from overt eroticism and crass popular appeal to amateurism and triviality.[19] Descriptions of the serpentine dance as "posing" not only hinted at its links with new forms of physical culture for women but also drew attention to the difference of Fuller's physical steps and gestures from the more familiar stage conventions of both formal and popular forms of dance such as ballet or burlesque. While some commentators framed the dance as appealing to both men and women because it did not deploy the usual movements of popular erotic dances—it had "no leg show"—others emphasized the erotic appeal to a male audience of seeing the outline of Fuller's body, backlit through the transparent material of her costume.[20] Interpretations of Fuller's style of bodily movement as natural and spontaneous, predicated on the knowledge that she danced uncorseted and the rumor that she also performed naked under her costume, registered in both political and erotic terms. Implicitly associated with the feminist dress reform movement and new physical freedoms for women, even as it was understood and experienced in terms of the titillating mode of more conventionalized erotic stage performances, the novelty and modernity of the serpentine dance remained contradictory. The disparate meanings and erotic effects of Fuller's onstage comportment and style of dance movement, together with the uncertain generic categorization of their stage performances and filmic imitations, sustained the ambiguous and contingent erotics of her novel assemblage. Yet what significantly augments the enigmatic erotic quality of Fuller's performances is the use of what we now recognize as proto-cinematic technologies that further unsettle the meanings and spectatorial experience of her moving body.

The history of Fuller's "screen," and the particular ways in which it reorganizes the visibility of Fuller's body and her movements, demonstrates how the erotics of the serpentine dance and its proto-cinematic qualities come to be mutually imbricated. Fuller's novel costume is the outcome of her appropriation and reworking of the constitutive eroticized elements of the serpentine dance's antecedent form, the skirt dance. Though initially popularized as a swaying, gentle form of dancing in England in the 1870s—a form of posing and movement that was considered the ideal of middle-class feminine grace and bodily comportment—the skirt dance by the early 1890s had been modified and explicitly eroticized with the addition of high kicks and the lifting of skirts to reveal the dancer's pantaloons.[21] One of Fuller's most significant renovations of the skirt dance is her alteration of its typical costume into a much larger, free-flowing form of dress—exaggerating the skirt, as Carl Van Vechten put it, to "insane proportions."[22] Fuller's redesigned serpentine costume, which she refined throughout her career, required a different kind of manipulation to the lifts and drops of the theatrical skirt dress, bodily movements, and gestures that also transformed the relation of the costume to the body of the dancer. In becoming something more like "drapery," as one contemporary commentator put it, the volume and movement of the costume not only overwhelmed and obscured the body of the dancer from the uninterrupted vision of the spectator, but—as *Danse serpentine* suggests—gave a different, and displaced, expression to her bodily movements and gestures.[23]

Fuller's renovation of established practices of theater stagecraft further altered the significance of her body and its relation to her costume, enhancing the sense of mobility already embodied and visualized by her "screen." During her early stage career, Fuller had encountered a range of theatrical genres and stagecraft, including the practice of indicating scene transitions by means of projecting colored lights and magic lantern slides onto gauzy curtains or fabrics.[24] In taking up this practice but projecting changing colored lights and photographic slides—of landscapes, people, and even microscopic views—onto her costume, Fuller revised the transformational functions of such elements of stagecraft from indicating movements in space and time to projecting those virtual mobilities onto an equivalent curtain or screen and a body that was already in motion.[25] Fuller's innovations destabilized the relation between different visual, theatrical, and performative practices and their established meanings and experiences in ways that not only sustained an ambiguous relation to her body but also suggested a transformation of her body into a less corporealized, abstract form. It remains an open question as to whether, in this newly technologized and visualized form, Fuller's costume was regarded as equivalent to the curtain that portended a scene transition—implying the drama of it being drawn aside to reveal the spectacle or entertainment proper—or a screen that was itself the visual entertainment—functioning as a two-dimensional framed space of illusionistic projection and focus of a virtual gaze.[26] Foreclosing neither possibility, the place and function of Fuller's body in her serpentine dance performance remains contradictory and dynamic, both a material and virtual focal point of spectatorship. Part of what early films appropriated from Fuller's performances was this disembodied, semivirtual aspect of her dance, a quality that inflected their spectacle and eroticism.

As a further sign of the virtual gaze instantiated by Fuller's performances, the practice of darkening the auditorium aligned Fuller's performance not with theater, where the practice was still relatively new, but visual entertainments such as the diorama and magic lantern slide shows where a darkened viewing space was commonplace.[27] Contemporary accounts of this practice suggest that darkness "cancelled the visual distance and made the viewer feel that he [*sic*] was right inside the picture."[28] The effect of the electric lighting on stage potentially inflected this sense of intimacy with a more objectifying visual relation to Fuller's performance. As Felicia McCarren points out, the electric light of Fuller's performances reinforced the impression that she was performing under hypnosis: "the light falling on Fuller makes her unable to see her audience; she seems 'withdrawn,' or 'unconscious,' before their gaze."[29] While McCarren—elaborating on symbolist poet Stéphane Mallarmé's brief but highly influential account of Fuller's performances—emphasizes the effect of the electric light on the Fuller's mode of performance, her description also alludes to the possibility that these same conditions produce a voyeuristic mode of spectatorship, in which the audience observes and enjoys Fuller's dance while she is unable to reciprocate their gaze.[30] As a consequence of these lighting practices, the serpentine dance performance shuttles between two different modes of visuality, never settling definitively on one or the other but instead establishing an experience of spectatorship that is at once mobile and constrained, proximate and distanced.

By reconfiguring the more conventional manipulation of costume that characterized the skirt dance, and adapting practices of the fin-de-siècle stage in ways that further mobilized her body and its movement as the virtual focal point of the serpentine dance, Fuller recalibrated its experience as erotic. Rather than the concealment of the dancer's body disrupting, diminishing, or even closing down an erotic spectatorial experience of the serpentine dance, early reviews suggest that the erotic is instead melded with the visual pleasures of abstract form and motion. This experience of the serpentine dance as a both highly erotic and disembodied performance is suggested by an 1892 review of Fuller's debut in New York:

> Suddenly the stage is darkened, and Loïe Fuller appears in a white light which makes her radiant and a white robe which surrounds her like a cloud. She floats around the stage, her figure now revealed, now concealed by the exquisite drapery which takes forms of its own and seems instinct with her life. The surprised and delighted spectators do not know what to call her performance. It is not a skirt dance, although she dances and waves a skirt. It is unique, ethereal, delicious. . . . Again she emerges from the darkness,

> her airy evolutions now tinted blue and purple and crimson, and again the audience rise at her and insist on seeing her pretty, piquant face before they can believe that the lovely apparition is really a woman.[31]

While the reviewer notes how the movement of Fuller's costume conceals and reveals her "figure," these effects are not simple moments in which Fuller's body is offered and withdrawn from the view of the spectator. Rather the experience of viewing the "drapery" through which these moments are effected is described in terms of its contradictory relation to Fuller's body, at once separate to ("takes forms of its own") and indistinguishable from it ("seems instinct with her life"). The latter observation points to the transformative capacity of the serpentine costume, so that the dancer's body becomes less a body than a kind of force or energy ("her life").[32] It is this quality of Fuller's performance that early cinema historian Tom Gunning identifies as Fuller's most modern and proto-cinematic:

> Like the modern experience of shock that violently disarranged concepts of solidity and objectivity and conveyed the seeming insubstantiality of modern experience, Fuller's dance displayed motion as a matrix from which form was born, a possibility of continuous transformation.[33]

Gunning's interpretation of Fuller's performance in terms of its aestheticization and sublimation of the traumas of modern experience points to the utopian appeal of the serpentine dance, even as it displaces and obscures the ambiguous relation of the dancer's body to her costume. While the body dematerializes in this particular valorization of modern forms of fluidity, it rematerializes in more corporeal and gendered terms in discussions of the sensual appeal and sexual nature of Fuller's performances.

Recent interpretations of Fuller's performances in terms of sexuality pivot on the particular terms in which Fuller's unstable body is made available to the visual apprehension of the spectator. Claiming that "one would be blind not to note the strong sexuality of [Fuller's] sensual appeal and [her] heavily gendered form of attraction," Tom Gunning argues that these qualities of Fuller's performances elicited even as they also confounded a "male gaze."[34] Making this gendered and hierarchical structure of spectatorship central to his broader claim that Fuller is emblematic of the gendered ideologies underpinning modernity's crisis of representation, Gunning foregrounds the different orders and functions of Fuller's corporealization: "a hidden yet evident source of rhythm, an imagined attraction glimpsed through veils, the active manipulator of the fabric, and a site for the projection of images and colors."[35] Yet the same dynamic—predicated on the disappearance of Fuller's body and the unknowability of what lay behind Fuller's mobile costume—is interpreted differently by critics invested in recuperating Fuller to a history of lesbian performance. Tirza True Latimer writes, for example: "Audiences were never sure, in all the lights and swirls of fabric, exactly what her body was doing, where it was, or even exactly how many bodies were on stage."[36] De-emphasizing the promise of the revelation of the body, Latimer reads Fuller's veiled and disappearing body as analogous to Fuller's own experience of "fugitive" attractions to other women, affairs that had to be conducted with discretion and coded language.[37] Unlike Gunning's recuperation of Fuller to a high culture modernism, Latimer seeks to ground her reading of Fuller's performance in a social experience of lesbian sexuality. Though their perspectives and projects differ, Gunning and Latimer's readings each register the persistent and retrospective force of modern sexuality, and the homo/hetero sexual binary in particular, organizations of erotic desire and identity in relation to which Fuller's performances are much less clearly organized.

The modes by which Fuller's body is represented and apprehended are key to both homo- and heterosexual interpretations of her electric light performances, yet such interpretations necessarily work against the intertwined erotic and virtual aesthetics of the serpentine performances that I outlined above, stabilizing and resolving their inherently unsettling corporeal logics, or what French journalist Yvon Novy called their "un-fixable errancy."[38] Critical efforts to bring Fuller's body back into view, to make it sexually legible in terms of either a heterosexually structured spectatorship or a form of late-nineteenth-century lesbian artistic expression, foreground the ways in the body itself is required to appear as the necessary and seemingly neutral ground of sex and sexual identity. Dance scholar Rhonda Garelick's criticism of lesbian interpretations of Fuller's performances such as Latimer's draws attention to this discursive effect of sexuality. Garelick claims that sexual interpretations of Fuller's oeuvre that depend on the ways in which her body disappears, or is de-eroticized, paradoxically undermine their critical perspective by absenting the body as the site of erotic expression and sexuality: "These queering readings of Fuller seem to subtract the body in order to see it, reading lesbian sexuality as an absence or refusal of Eros rather than as an alternative expression of it."[39] Garelick's objection helpfully points up the ways in which the visible female body is naturalized as the ground or site of sexuality. The multiplication of sexual interpretations of Fuller's performances is indicative of the dependency of sexuality on modes of interpretation of the body as an apparently privileged site of sexual knowledge. Hetero- and homosexual interpretations of Fuller's oeuvre reflect the specific twentieth-century transformations and consolidations of the fin-de-siècle impulse to fix, define, and interpret ephemeral erotic experience, an impulse that Fuller's performances more often unsettled and displaced.

Retrospective claims about Fuller's lesbian sexuality—ostensibly progressive interventions in scholarship that has ignored her erotic interests—manifest the tensions and contradictions comprising these sexuality effects. The limitations of this recuperative strategy are evident in the difficulties that two leading dance scholars have in accounting for Fuller's public and private sexuality. Ann Cooper Albright asserts that Fuller was "known publicly as a lesbian," immediately following this claim with an important parenthetic qualification: "(although she didn't use that terminology)."[40] Rhonda Garelick notes how Fuller was "openly lesbian," and cites the historical discourse on Fuller's personal life (describing her as "chaste" and "correct") as evidence of her ability to do this without public disapproval.[41] In contrast, Albright deploys the very same historical discourse, one that she argues repeatedly frames Fuller as being "sans coquetterie érotique," as evidence of public anxieties about the sexual dimensions of her persona.[42] Rather than confirming Fuller's sexuality, these kinds of critical jostlings about her public erotic identity suggest the trouble with the critical deployment of an incoherent sexual category that was at this cultural moment in the process of uneven emergence.[43] Paradoxically, affirming Fuller's sexual identity as a lesbian obscures the historical processes by which public lesbian identities come to be possible, processes that are implicated in the very same public/private topoi that govern critical discussion of Fuller's sexuality. Critics are caught in a double-bind in their desire to delineate and acknowledge the erotic truth of Fuller's life and public performances, since to do so retrospectively installs a modern sexual identity that anachronistically registers the force of an intensifying regime of sexuality. Fuller's erotic identity and the public experience of her performances are not exactly intelligible in terms of contemporary concepts of sexuality, such as gender inversion, and they are not easily understood in terms of contemporary sapphic cultures or styles of female masculinity. One symptom of this is the use that critics make of the masculine sartorial style of Gabrielle Bloch, Fuller's partner from the late 1890s. Most commentators on Fuller mention that Bloch "dressed only in men's suits," as if this terse (and possibly inaccurate) description of Bloch's masculine sartorial style were enough—and obvious enough—to summarize her sexual identity and erotic preferences, in a way that also confirms Fuller's.[44] Further troubling discussions of Fuller's sexuality and the erotic appeal of her performances is her relation to and production of modern forms of femininity. It is the increasing visualization and sexualization of the female body in late-nineteenth-century popular culture that provide the conditions within which Fuller's serpentine shows register even as they also reorient the meanings of contemporary female dance performance, physical culture, public feminine identities, and same-sex eroticism.

Sexuality Effects

Fuller's bricolage of modern movement, costuming, and stagecraft emerges within a complex and contradictory field of discourses and institutional practices in which the body, and the female body in particular—its every movement, attitude, and gesture—is increasingly thought of as the external, visible sign of internal, psychological, or pathological states, including new forms of sexual personality. The attraction of Fuller's performance depends on, even as it also reworks—and even resists—the logics of these new forms of body-centered scientific and medical knowledges. One experimental technique assumes particular prominence in Fuller's performance: hypnotism. One of the stories of the origin of the serpentine dance recounted by Fuller in her autobiography—several different accounts circulated in the years during which the dance was popular—establishes its accidental discovery as the outcome of Fuller's rehearsals of a scene in a play that required her to act as a young woman under hypnosis.[45] According to the play's narrative, Fuller was required to demonstrate her character's hypnotic state, her movements understood as generated by, and expressive of, her character's unconscious, determined by and performed under the aegis of a male doctor. Less a reliable text than Fuller's articulation of and influence on her own celebrity discourse, this autobiographical account retrospectively highlights the connections of the serpentine performance to psychiatric techniques and the visible manifestation of the unconscious.[46] It also demonstrates Fuller's awareness of hypnosis as a popular subject of entertainment and literature, and its potential appeal in shaping her particular brand of celebrity.[47] By reiterating and privileging this story in her autobiography, Fuller articulates and reinforces hypnosis as a key term within which her performance could be understood.

Hypnosis, as it was updated by late-nineteenth-century medical discourse, provided a term through which audiences could make sense of the movements of Fuller's body, its ability to express unconscious states, thoughts, and ideas, and a mode of spectatorship in which an embodied connection was established between the performer and her audience.[48] The visual and gendered iconography of hypnosis—often conflated with and sometimes indistinguishable from that of hysteria—is recognizable in one of the most well-known posters that advertised Fuller's Parisian shows in the early 1890s (figure 5.4).[49] The poster portrays Fuller as a young, lithe dancer, her head

FIGURE 5.4. Folies-Bergère/Loïe Fuller poster by Jules Chéret, 1893. Courtesy Minneapolis College of Art and Design Collection.

thrown back with eyes glazed open, her back arched, and the outlines of her body visible through the translucent fabric wrapped around her. Figuring Fuller's body and the serpentine dance performance in terms of an eroticized loss of self-control, it implies the sexual nature of the woman's body in particular terms, as revealed through bodily expression in an unguarded moment. This form of representation of Fuller's body is already imbricated in the visual discourses and institutional practices of the late nineteenth century, whereby the female body is rapidly becoming the central node through which "a machinery for [the] incitement" of sexuality is organized.[50] It also illustrates Foucault's argument that, by the late nineteenth century, "sex" is no longer a question of "sensation and pleasure, of law and taboo, but also of truth and falsehood."[51] Just as Chéret's poster makes the form of Fuller's body and its movement available to an eroticized gaze, it can also be understood to articulate visually the truth of the body's inner state.

Even as it is entangled with these sexuality effects, the visual iconography of hypnosis on which the promotional imagery of Fuller draws also enables her body to be figured in terms other than an eroticized loss of self-control. Most simply, Fuller's hypnotic style of dance is a conscious, creative performance. When read alongside other accounts of Fuller's self-invention and ingenuity, the story of the theatrical context within which the dance was allegedly invented and its gendered narrative of medical intervention become elements of a broader narrative of female independence. One article published about Fuller and her serpentine dance, for example, purports to convey the "strange" story of the dance's invention by relating it to the inability of a "stage-struck" Fuller to settle down to "domestic life" with a husband whose relationship to Fuller was more complicated than the article implies.[52] The short narrative economically establishes an implicit interdependency between Fuller's ambition, her capacity for artistic invention, and her freedom from marriage. While the story suggests that Fuller was herself mesmerized by the prospect of performing, hypnosis also provided a discourse through which Fuller could emphasize her own artistic agency and power. Contemporary accounts of Fuller's stage performances also suggest that they were experienced in a hypnotic register, as absorbing and mesmerizing.[53] Reorganizing the typical gendered structure of hypnosis, Fuller becomes akin to the medical practitioner or mesmerist putting the audience under her spell.[54] Construed as an unstable and flexible practice, hypnosis also partly refigures the relation between the audience and Fuller in homoerotic terms, one in which the dancer mesmerizes and seduces her audience as part of a shared, embodied, and unconscious experience.[55]

The same iconography of the body and its movements was also increasingly encountered in relation to another significant visual discourse, that arising out of the scientific study of the human body in motion. Representations of Fuller from the 1890s, whether the promotional poster illustrations produced in Paris or the range of photographic postcards that represented her midperformance, bear a more specific resemblance to one of the most prominent examples of this new scientific discourse, Eadweard Muybridge's photographic motion studies first published and popularized in the 1880s.

While Muybridge photographed a vast range of scenarios of movement, one of Muybridge's more famous series features a dancing female figure who manipulates a gauzy fabric across her naked body.[56] The woman in this particular image series may have been a well-known skirt dance performer in the United States, and this generic connection to the serpentine dance draws attention to the close links between the generation of new forms of scientific knowledge of the body and the erotic iconography and visual pleasures of popular entertainments.[57] Muybridge drew on the conventions of the popular stage in order to motivate the movement and visual analysis of his female subject, subjecting the skirt dance and its conventional performance of female eroticism to an elaborate scientific scrutiny.[58] In setting the dancer's body against a background of grids, and subjecting the performing female body to the "objective" analysis of instantaneous photography, the Muybridge photographs generate a sequence of images in which the body is able to be read in relation to its different positions in time and space, the temporal minutiae of poses and gestures that typically remain unavailable to ordinary human vision. Such modes of visualizing the body and its movement anticipate the force by which sexuality is embedded in and reinforced by later forms of cinematic representation. As Linda Williams argues, "this very machinery of observation and measurement turns out to be, even at this early stage, less an impartial instrument than a crucial mechanism in the power established over that body, constituting it as an object or subject of desire, offering up an image of the body *as mechanism* that is in many ways a reflection of the mechanical nature of the [film] medium itself."[59] This forensic imperative to visualize human movement, and its attendant but initially unexpected visual pleasures, are what make such images "cinematic," according to Williams, even before the invention of the cinematograph.[60] The popularization of the skirt and serpentine dance forms thus occurs within a dense visual field in which the female body is increasingly constituted as both a sexual and proto-cinematic effect.

At a time when bodies are becoming ever more subject to the visual scrutiny of medical and scientific disciplines, Fuller's covering and visual transformation of her body deflect and reorient this optical will-to-know. The same visual technology that makes previously unseen moments of the body's movement available to scientific investigation also provides an opportunity to consider how Fuller's performance destabilizes the body as emergent sexual and proto-cinematic signifier. One of the more striking visual artifacts of Fuller's career is a Samuel Joshua Beckett photograph of her dancing, taken around 1900 (figure 5.5).[61] Against what were by the turn of the twentieth century already highly conventionalized representations of serpentine danc-

FIGURE 5.5. Loïe Fuller dancing photographed by Samuel Joshua Beckett (ca. 1900). Metropolitan Museum of Art Gilman Collection, Purchase, Mrs. Walter Annenberg and The Annenberg Foundation Gift, 2005.

ers as delicate, feminine objects of eroticized visual pleasure, Beckett's photograph stresses the opacity of Fuller's costume and its gravity-defying form. Drawing on the iconography and instantaneous photographic techniques of scientific motion studies, this particular Beckett image foregrounds the capacity of Fuller's performance to erase the body from view, rendering her exact mechanics of movement invisible to spectators, while substituting in their stead a blank, unreadable surface. The startling nature of the image, not of Fuller herself but of bandagelike reams of white fabric frozen mid-motion, is only further compounded by its everyday metropolitan setting: a park lawn crisscrossed by gravel paths, in broad daylight. Considered as an effect of sexual discourse, the photograph demonstrates how Fuller's performance resists the conventional eroticization of women's bodies by removing the body from view, obscuring its mechanics, while also problematizing the very fixity of the body's surface and its visual intelligibility. The photograph highlights a dynamic and irresolvable tension: a concealed body is rendered invisible by a fabric that seems at once to obliterate the body while making its animating forces visible as abstract form and motion. The photograph also relies on a new practice of looking centered on the body, even as it also refuses an interpretation of the body in terms of a recognizable personality or interiorized sense of identity. The Beckett photograph suggests how the notion of a legible bodily surface is destabilized and displaced through Fuller's manipulation of costume and movement while opening that surface up to the subjective views and enjoyment of spectators. It is this aspect of Fuller's performances that the Beckett photograph both enacts and evidences, a mode of viewing not wholly regulated or disciplined by the regime of sexuality yet paradoxically enabled by it. In this respect, Fuller's performances represent a novel form of eroticized, proto-cinematic spectatorship that comprises part of the prehistory of the "eclectic and ambivalent makeup of early cinema's scopic relations," a mode of viewing, moreover, that potentially enables the revision of aspects of current understandings of the historical development of cinematic spectatorship and its gendered and sexual modes of address.[62]

Then in Now

Fuller invents her electric light dance shows during a period in the late nineteenth century when public and private cultures of female spectatorship and practices of viewing are undergoing significant transformation. In this final section of the chapter, I consider how Fuller's performances, and imitations of her signature serpentine dance in early films, drew their energies from, and transformed in proto-cinematic and sexual terms, already established modes of female homoerotic spectatorship. It is important to note that at the end of the nineteenth century there was an already developing female spectatorship for dance. There were specific sapphic subcultures for which dance—in particular, Oriental dance forms—provided a performative repertoire for visualizing same-sex erotic styles and tastes.[63] Yet, while some of Fuller's performances at times intersected with Orientalist styles, her electric light dances comprised a different kind of aesthetic and perceptual experience. Although Fuller's serpentine dances do not represent an explicit homoerotic performance between two dancers on stage or any form of homoerotic narrative, they emerge in a cultural space that makes them available to be experienced in homoerotic terms. As I have already alluded to, various elements of Fuller's performance and its cultural context establish the conditions for homoerotic modes of spectatorship, such as her hypnotic mode of performance and its contemporary medical and celebrity discourses. In what follows, I risk privileging accounts of Fuller's female audiences in order to recover a significant aspect of the spectatorship and reception of the serpentine dance and its filmic remediations, a critical move that has the potential to revise current understandings of the regulation of gendered forms of film-viewer relations in early cinema.

The new pressures on, and regulations of previously dominant nineteenth-century codes of homoeroticism and voyeuristic modes of female spectatorship are evident in a review of one of Fuller's very first shows early in 1892, in which the writer makes sure to point out to readers the shared heterosocial pleasures of the performance:

> Men and women are both enthusiastic over the dance. This is one time when the ladies are permitted to express their admiration; they don't have to confine their gaze to peeps from behind their fans, for there is no leg show in this.[64]

Despite its brevity, the review manages to position the eroticism of the dance in complex gendered terms, distinguishing Fuller's performance from its more overtly eroticized stage precedents aimed at soliciting the enjoyment of male spectators, while suppressing its other connections to the 1890s skirt dance craze, and its acceptability as a form of classroom instruction and domestic entertainment for young middle-class women.[65] Predicating the lack of an overt eroticization of the dancer's body on the absence of movements and revelations of a specific body part, the review also economically draws attention to the socially acceptable ways in which middle-class women might enjoy the performance.[66] It suggests that female spectators watching Fuller's shows are not required—by social etiquette or decorum—to demonstrate their alleged indifference or disapproval by physically shielding their eyes. While such gestures enable a covert enjoyment by intermittent "peeps," the review makes an explicit connection between the apparent lack of eroticism in Fuller's performances and the implication that women were able to watch her dance with more open, overt gazes. Following the paradoxical logic of this gendered discourse, the alleged lack of erotic *content* enables a *form* of attentive and engaged spectatorship by women that mirrors the culturally sanctioned modes by which male spectators may enjoy and view more explicit erotic entertainments. What remains unclear, at least from this textual remnant of Fuller's reception, is the extent to which female viewers' modes of spectatorship continued to be cathected to a homoerotic and voyeuristic enjoyment of Fuller's complex visual spectacle.

The implication that women's experiences of Fuller's performances were erotically benign, their spectatorship of the serpentine dance and dancer uninflected by a same-sex voyeurism, tended to be reinforced by the contemporary receptions of one of the more significant events in Fuller's early career, her first season at the Folies-Bergère in Paris, 1892–1893.[67] Fuller's dance shows are credited with changing the reputation of the music hall by expanding and diversifying its audience to include not only the aristocracy and upper classes, but also significant numbers of women.[68] After her first two weeks, Fuller expanded her number of performances to afternoon shows aimed at attracting women and children to the Folies-Bergère. While these new matinees created an additional albeit regulated public and largely homosocial space for women's spectatorship, they continued to be framed as acceptable entertainment for bourgeois women; as one contemporary reviewer noted, "Mothers can now take their daughters, even their granddaughters to see Fuller."[69] Fuller also broadened her female audience in other ways, for example by performing at private gatherings and salons, and contemporary commentators were similarly concerned to emphasize the chasteness of such semiprivate performances. According to one report, "the most prudish American ladies see no harm in her serpentine dance."[70] The uncritical repetition of such commentary tends to buttress further the implication that any eroticism associated with Fuller's performances was harmless, unregistered within the phallocentric heteroerotic economy within which other performances of the Folies-Bergère were framed.

In contrast to the public discourse about the lack of eroticism of Fuller's performances for her female spectators, a highly suggestive anecdote in Fuller's 1913 memoir suggests that Fuller not only sought to sustain the possibility of women's erotic interest in her novel dances but that she understood the significance of the place of her body in those performances for her audience's visual pleasure. Fuller's story, worth quoting in full, seems designed to demonstrate not only her ability to attract women's eroticized attentions, but also their capacity for voyeurism:

> I was once at the Swedish gymnasium at Carlsbad, where machines with electrical vibrations shock you from head to foot. I was just about to dress myself when one of the women of the place came to me, and said:
>
> "Won't you please return to the hall, and pretend to take the electric treatment again in order that the archduchesses, who are there, with a whole crowd of court ladies, may see you?"
>
> I replied: "Tell the archduchesses that they can see me this evening at the theatre."

> The poor woman then declared to me that she had been forbidden to mention their Royal Highnesses, and that they had bidden her get me back into the hall on some pretext or other.
>
> She was so grieved at not having succeeded that I returned to the machines, and had my back massaged, in order that the noble company might look at me at their ease, as they would survey an interesting animal.
>
> They looked at me, all of them, smiling, and while they viewed me I never turned my eyes away from them.
>
> The odd thing was that they did not know that I knew them. I was, therefore, as much amused by them, and without their perceiving it, as they were amused by me.[71]

This ending emphatically reinstates Fuller's agency within a voyeuristic scenario that threatens to render her body an unflattering object of spectacle—a possibility registered in Fuller's aside that the royals look at her as they might "survey an interesting animal." While, as Ann Cooper Albright, observes, "Clearly Loïe Fuller did not mind being naked in front of a group of ladies," the anecdote also represents an instance—as Albright also recognizes—in which Fuller acknowledges the intense interest of female spectators in her body as an object of both curiosity and visual pleasure.[72] Their scrutiny of Fuller's body is also enmeshed within the broad cultural shifts discussed earlier, in which women's bodies are more and more produced as the site of sexual meaning and interiority.[73] Whether their erotic interest in Fuller enfolds a more explicit sexual interest or desire persists as a productive possibility, even as it remains untethered to any recognizable late-nineteenth-century discourse of modern sexual identity.

While the Swedish anecdote centers on the spectacle of Fuller's corporeality—a voyeuristic desire perhaps also incited by public discourse about the difference between Fuller's physicality and the ethereal "body" enacted in her performances—Fuller's performances themselves interweave such voyeuristic modes of looking with more confounding abstract, motion effects.[74] As discussed earlier, various elements of Fuller's show—such as the practice of darkening the theater, and her visual and performative references to hypnosis—generated forms of spectatorship that shuttled between a distanced and proximate sense of engagement with the spectacle that she generated on stage. While such dynamic modes of viewing remain always in tension, they are also imbricated in the dance's contradictory novel erotics, the latter predicated on the ability of spectators to apprehend her body even as such visual attentions are deflected and reoriented to the surface effects of her mobile costume.[75] Fuller's innovative assemblage—including physical culture styles of movement not ordinarily seen on stage, the renovation and transformation of a costume typically deployed to expose parts of the body for the audience's erotic pleasure, the appropriation of technologies that had up until then been used to suggest transitions in time and space—enacts a particular form of spectatorship that potentially rewrites female spectators' memories and experiences of the serpentine dance's constituent elements of performance and visual culture.[76] While the electric light performance connects audience bodies to the body on stage through shared modes of movement, and sensational and affective experience, it remains implicated in new visual practices and discourses that increasingly sexualize the female body as the visible sign of personality or even pathology. The constant flux of the serpentine dance brokers women's voyeuristic modes of spectatorship and late-nineteenth-century forensic productions of the sexual body, establishing an ambivalent and unstable space that sustains the possibility of a homoerotic structure of viewing even as that is also implicated in new understandings of the female body as the source and sign of sexual desire.

One intriguing possibility that arises out of Fuller's novel visual spectacle is that its depersonalized register enabled the expression and experience of an alternative and modern form of homoerotic relation. In a perceptive reading of Fuller's biography and its account of her relationship with Gabrielle Bloch, dance scholar Peggy Phelan suggests that it expresses an unusual erotic ethic in which Fuller and Bloch understood their relationship in "liberatingly impersonal" terms.[77] As Phelan points out, Bloch is, in many ways, Fuller's ideal spectator and the dancer includes in her memoir Bloch's brief essay written after first seeing the serpentine and other dances performed at the Folies-Bergère in Paris.[78] Fuller follows this reproduced passage with her own memory of what Bloch says to her one day fifteen years later—"I never see you exactly as you are . . . but as you seemed to me on that day"—before concluding:

> I wonder if her friendship, so well founded and positive, is not intimately mingled with the love of form, of color and of light, which I interpreted synthetically before her eyes when I appeared before her for the first time.[79]

In a highly suggestive turn in her argument, Phelan claims that Fuller and Bloch "seemed to have felt that erotic love is indeed theatrical, an exchange that involves, above all, a heightened sensitivity to form and structure, rather than to the personality of one's lover."[80] Phelan's observation about the nature of the bond between Fuller and Bloch might be usefully extended to the historical context of Fuller's performances and the discursive conditions that make personality—and sexual personality in particular—one of the more pressing "problems" of the late nineteenth century, manifest in the proliferation of sexualized representations of the female body and new sexological writings. Though it might seem strange to us sexual moderns now, Fuller's performances sustained the homoerotic possibilities of spectatorship in a virtual disembodied and depersonalized register.

No longer a lost figure, yet one who strangely resists being pulled into a history of modern sexuality, Fuller is part of a broader cultural transformation that popularizes and consolidates practices of reading the body that simultaneously produce the body as sexuality-effect. In an era in which the female body in particular was being constituted in new visual forms—not only as the model for and bearer of erotic sensation but also as legible evidence of an interiorized sexual personality—Fuller's performances take up and reorient the visual discourses and pleasures through which the regime of sexuality is partly organized. Considered in terms of spectatorship, her performances and the serpentine dance films demonstrate that the eroticized female body of the intermedial period of early cinema functions as a complex and unstable representational site implicated in reconfigurations not only of male sexual subjectivity but also of female sexual subjectivity and erotic identity. A strategic look backward at Fuller's semivirtual performances and their filmic appropriations enables the critical perception of a homoerotic mode of spectatorship engendered by—but also resistant to—the personifying forces of modern sexuality.

6. Valentino's Lesbianism

Stardom, Spectatorship, and Queer Recognition

> The demand for the recognition of queer history as a viable practice is charged with a long history of similar claims for the viability of certain "hard to believe" modes of existence and desire.
>
> —Heather Love, *Feeling Backward*

OF ALL THE CHAPTER TITLES in this book, this last one might seem to invoke a fantasy in the sense of a whimsical historical fiction or even an unconscious critical wish—possibilities that haunt much queer history and historiography—since the 1920s matinee idol Rudolph Valentino is most commonly identified not with lesbianism but with a hyperbolical heterosexuality. By this point in the book, however, readers should be quite alive to one of its central claims, that any counter-history of the emergence of lesbian sexuality in early cinema cannot be undertaken without also considering its relation to the developing intelligibility of heterosexuality as an always related, albeit privileged, sexual discourse. The most well-known films that book-end Valentino's brief but volatile Hollywood career—the Orientalist romances *The Sheik* (dir. George Melford, Famous Players-Lasky, 1921), and *The Son of the Sheik* (dir. George Fitzmaurice, Feature Productions, 1926)—are often considered key film texts that first establish and then systematically sustain the male actor as heterosexual erotic spectacle. This reading of Valentino's stardom is frequently buttressed by evidence of his extraordinary capacity to mobilize an audience seemingly dominated by women, a phenomenon of central interest to feminist film scholars concerned with the historical and gendered dimensions of cinema spectatorship.[1] Miriam Hansen summarizes concisely the gendered aspects of Valentino's stardom and spectatorship and its significance in the history of Hollywood cinema: "Never before was the discourse on fan behavior so strongly marked by the terms of gender and sexuality, and never again was spectatorship so explicitly linked to the discourse on female desire."[2] The overdetermined quality of those discourses that Hansen draws attention to indicates the extent to which Valentino's disparate star image—both dominant and submissive screen lover, hypermasculine and androgynous erotic spectacle, alternately sadistic and masochistic romantic lead—disturbed normative, predominantly white, middle-class conceptualizations and ideals of sexual difference and desire. While as a potent fantasy figure, Valentino often confounded certain structural differences organizing dominant cross-gendered sexual culture, his heterogeneous image also made other forms of desire and erotic identification visually legible. Kenneth Anger, the author of the now classic camp text *Hollywood Babylon*, was perhaps the first to reclaim Valentino as a gay icon and to recuperate the possibility of gay men's historical receptions of the star.[3] Recently, Anger's suggestive fan-based perspective has been extended and more explicitly historicized by Mark Lynn Anderson, who recuperates for Valentino spectatorship the fairies and queer men of urban working class same-sex cultures.[4] But the multifaceted nature of Valentino's stardom is not just a matter of acknowledging the historical context of his erotic appeal for male audiences and its difference from present cultural architectures of homosexuality. Valentino's stardom also generated a specific queer appeal for his female audiences, one that permitted the recognition not only of desire between women but also of an interest in same-sex eroticism that could be shared by both women and men, manifest as a sexual identity held in common.

One of the more productive interventions in recent film studies scholarship that has enabled thinking about the possibility of such spectatorships has been the recourse to psychoanalytic theories of fantasy, which in turn permit more nuanced readings of the historical materials of reception. As Patricia White notes in her study, *Uninvited: Classical Hollywood Cinema and Lesbian Representability*, fantasy "allows us to detach processes of identification and desire—which are both involved but which are not collapsed—from an assumed correspondence between spectator and like-gendered character, an ideology of sexual difference governed by a heterosexual teleology even more relentless than that of Hollywood."[5] While fantasy in its everyday manifestations as daydreams or gossip can offer forms of "homo life support" for queers living in often hostile cultures, fantasy as it has been elucidated in queer film studies has proved to be a useful mode of analysis for considering how cinema—and Hollywood cinema in particular—enables lesbian and gay spectatorships.[6] By loosening the determinative hold of what have tended to be totalizing and heteronormative accounts of identification, sexual desire, and subject formation, fantasy theory is able to preserve a sense of contingency, variability, and contradiction in the formation of modern sexual subjectivities. Fantasy theory, both generally and in relation to what I'm calling the lesbian dimension of Valentino's 1920s spectatorship, does not authorize an open-ended, playful field of desire and identity formation, however.[7] As Brett Farmer points out in relation to his theorization of gay male spectatorship, any cinematic fantasmatic is "produced in and by the determinate relations of culture and history."[8]

The responsiveness of fantasy theory to specific cultural and historical contexts can be traced back to the influential extension of Freud's ambiguous thinking on the subject of fantasy by Jean Laplanche and Jean-Betrand Pontalis, on which much film scholarship relies.[9] The authors famously reconceptualize fantasy in spatial terms not as the object of desire but as its setting.[10] This much-cited articulation of fantasy as, in more specifically cinematic terms, the mise-en-scène of desire, foregrounds the claim that fantasy shapes and orders—or disorders—a range of sometimes contradictory sexual identifications and trajectories of desire. Though clinically oriented, the critical advantage of fantasy for thinking about the relation between film spectatorship and sexual subjectivity arises in terms of how it relates psychic processes to historical conditions and experiences. In Laplanche and Pontalis's account, fantasy is the effect of two sets of historical forces: those that preexist the subject, and those in the particular moment in which the subject is constituted through fantasy.[11] In order to foreground the structuring action of fantasy, Laplanche and Pontalis adopt the term *fantasmatic*, a term that Brett Farmer also takes up in order to emphasize the constitutive force of fantasy as it may manifest for particular gay spectators, in specific contexts, at certain moments in time.[12] Though Farmer is concerned to acknowledge the limits of theorizing gay male spectatorship in his study—"The most that can be targeted . . . is a theoretical imaging of certain potentialities of gay sexualities/subjectivities and their effects on cinematic reception"—his shift to the term *fantasmatic* permits a critical recognition of the historically specific effects of the institutional and discursive formations that comprise Hollywood cinema.[13]

In related work that extends the intertwined historical and temporal complexities of spectatorship, Patricia White argues persuasively that spectatorship is inherently retrospective. Drawing on Freud's concept of deferred action or retrospection (*Nachträglichkeit*), White suggests, "All spectatorship, insofar as it engages subjective fantasy, revises memory traces and experiences, some of which are memories and experiences of other movies."[14] White's concept of retrospectatorship draws attention to the generative effects of historically situated institutional practices, whether cable reruns of Hollywood classical films or the rerelease of early Valentino films across the course of his brief, interrupted career. To attend to Valentino's "lesbianism" in this context is to acknowledge the everyday potency of fantasy's variable and heterogeneous effects while diverting critical attention to the cinema-specific historical discourses and institutional forms and practices by which such a lesbian fantasmatic is, in part, produced.

While I draw upon these enabling aspects of queer theorizations of spectatorship—in particular, the absence of a requirement of similitude between on-screen character or star and off-screen spectator, and a finely tuned awareness of the potentially determinative effects of historical institutions and social conditions—I take up the notion of the fantasmatic across this chapter not strictly as a psychoanalytic concept but rather as a flexible historiographical paradigm that allows for a more complex relation to the Hollywood cinema archive. Like White's work in *Uninvited*, this chapter extends beyond a single scene, narrative, or text to delineate broader institutional contexts of consumption and reception. The fantasmatic as the spectatorial scene that (dis)orders desire and identification can then be approached more expansively, more genealogically: not only as the multiple scenes of Hollywood films and extra-filmic texts and images, such as those in fan magazines but as those elements comprising a complex set of discursive fields that make certain forms of subjectivity possible, such as historically emergent queer or same-sex–identified sexual subjects. While certain prohibitions on the representation of same-sex desire operate in the period of Hollywood cinema under consideration, even prior to the advent and consolidation of the Production Code, I am not claiming that a prohibition on lesbian representation—that is, the representation of a specific, already intelligible and coherent sexual category—manifests as a range of fantasmatic cinematic and extra-cinematic effects. Rather, I am suggesting that Valentino is one figure or site where elements of a novel same-sex–oriented female spectatorship become possible. Pressed into the service of an alternative history of the emergence of lesbian sexuality, this historiographical version of the fanstasmatic readily accommodates ephemera and the ephemeral as historical evidence even as it also registers the historical subjection of the erotic to regulation and normalization.

Read primarily through the archive of extant films, fan magazines, and newspapers, Valentino's lesbian fantasmatic is in part generated by two contradictory aspects of his star image: his frequent failure to conform to the normative requirements of masculine cross-sex desire, and his ongoing proximity to and alignment with various similarly "deviant" female figures, whether the excessively desiring vamp figures that populate a number of his films, the sapphic women who sometimes played those parts and who were part of his professional and personal networks, and the spinsterish or mannish women with whom he was occasionally paired on screen. Combined with the various elements of Valentino's star discourse that underscored his femininity—whether registered by his passivity and capacity for domination, the cinematographic styles that rendered him an object of erotic contemplation, or his often extravagant costuming—such on-screen couples offered alternative points of identification and desire for female spectators, whether with Valentino or his female counterpart. The entangled spectatorial relations catalyzed by Valentino enable not only an unpredictable set of identifications with the feminized star but also register the possibility of his own identifications with the various "lesbian"-like figures with whom he was associated. In other words, Valentino's stardom encompasses the potential for imagining that he shares with those female figures an erotic or sexual identity, whether understood in the quite different, if not contradictory, terms of same-sex erotic taste or preference, sexual inversion, or homosexuality.[15] Extending Mark Lynn Anderson's claim that Valentino opened up "a queer space for the reception of mass culture," this chapter argues that Valentino makes available to a range of spectators a novel form of sexual identity shared across sexes, as well as the possibility of recognizing new forms of same-sex and cross-sex queer affiliation and relationality.[16]

Setting the Scene

In her pioneering and magisterial work *Babel and Babylon: Spectatorship in American Silent Film*, Miriam Hansen analyzes the lesbian elements of Valentino's fantasy formation as part of her consideration of Hollywood cinema's cultivation of a female audience and the development of an alternative public sphere, a model of feminist film historical scholarship to which this chapter—indeed this book—is clearly indebted. Hansen acknowledges that the Valentino cult would have had different implications for viewers, depending on their sexual orientation, among other differences such as ethnicity and social class, yet lesbianism in Hansen's critical discourse occupies an ambivalent position.[17] It is at once external to Valentino's film texts and thus outside the primary field of his cinematic spectatorship, even as it also subtends the more perverse elements of his filmic representations. For example, what Hansen calls the "peculiar configuration of Valentino's relationship with women" comprises both its "homosocial dimensions"—that is, of the relations between women in Valentino's audience—and "the star's affiliation with lesbians."[18] For Hansen, Valentino's second wife Natacha Rambova most strongly secures Valentino's associations with "deviant" sexualities, both through her well-known gift to him of a slave bracelet—implying Valentino's pleasure in passivity and domination in heterosexual relations—and her connection with Alla Nazimova, whom Hansen describes as "the famous lesbian actress and spiritualist."[19] While I consider in more detail these affiliations and the terms of their sexual legibility in the next section, Hansen repeats her reference to the star's associations with lesbians in her argument about the development of Valentino's masochistic reputation, conjoining the former discourse on the star's "private" life to the more systematic development of Valentino's masochistic image in certain of his later films and the corresponding sadistic positioning of his spectators.[20] Despite Hansen's careful attention to the multiple identificatory positions that Valentino, as a fantasy figure, enables for his female spectators, lesbianism is enlisted to her argument as a kind of sexual supplement, a necessary though submerged component of Valentino's fascinating and threatening ethnic and sexual mobility that in Hansen's larger claim is ultimately in the service of a new form of "erotic reciprocity" between men and women.[21] Yet, ironically, what makes Valentino's utopian guarantee of sexual compatibility possible is the sidelined presence of female homosexuality, a new form of sexual discourse dependent on notions of "sameness and mutuality."[22] Thus, Hansen's argument about the progressive heterosexuality instantiated by Valentino, however precarious and uncertain that might be, implicitly sustains in retrospect the oppositional force of homo/hetero definition while occluding the possibility that some female viewers might have had an alternative film-viewer relation to the Valentino phenomenon.

Another figure connected to Valentino illustrates both the implications of this critical blind spot for thinking about the development of modern lesbian spectatorships as well as the kind of considered historical work involved in revising them. Prior to her Hollywood directorial career, Dorothy Arzner was the film editor (and also uncredited director of the bullfight sequences) for Valentino's *Blood and Sand* (dir. Fred Niblo, Famous Players-Lasky, 1922), a film in which the actor plays a Spanish matador, Juan Gallardo, torn between his childhood sweetheart—who eventually becomes his wife—and a seductive vamplike figure, Doña Sol, played by Nita Naldi.[23] While Arzner remains a tangential figure in the public discourse concerning Valentino's circle of female friends and professional colleagues, her behind-the-scenes presence in the Valentino film archive offers an opportunity for rethinking the relations that some female spectators may have had to the star, relations premised less on desire than on the different forms of erotic recognition that his stardom enables. Albeit in the different context of film authorship, Jane

Gaines puzzles over the possible connection between the erotic content and pleasures of *Blood and Sand* and Arzner's sexual interests and identity:

> Do we overlook the fact that this was a Rudolph Valentino vehicle when we focus on Dorothy Arzner or do we relish the apparent contradiction in her role in the production of heterosexual excess, in the creation of a matinee idol for female fans?[24]

Precisely because this passage is only a brief rhetorical aside, it demonstrates the ease with which heterosexuality and lesbianism are often thought of in oppositional terms, as ostensibly unrelated sexual formations. While it is possible to consider Arzner's involvement in *Blood and Sand* from a range of critical perspectives, considered in terms of spectatorship her historical presence in the archive represents the possibility that cross-gendered identifications with Valentino's character could be mobilized by female audience members as a means of enabling the recognition of same-sex desire. Indeed, such a prospect is supported by evidence of Arzner's own identification with the male protagonist in one of her later films.[25] The puzzle posed by Gaines also implicitly draws attention to the imbrication of the historical formations of sexuality and stardom, the specific conditions of which inflect the identificatory possibilities that Valentino's films might have instantiated for certain of his female spectators—whether friends, colleagues, and collaborators, or anonymous fans.

Valentino's availability as an identificatory figure in a lesbian spectatorial fantasmatic is contingent upon the ways in which film character is transformed by the discursive operations of the Hollywood star system. While the productive, albeit tenuous, sexual effects of character in articulating new forms of interiority and psychological motivation are evident in a feature film like *A Florida Enchantment* (1914), considered in Chapter 3, the emergence of a film-specific star system complicates the sexual logics of character via its central organizing paradigm: the distinction between an actor's on-screen professional performance and his or her off-screen personal life. A singular consequence of this shift, as Richard deCordova has argued, is that "the private lives of the stars emerged as a new site of knowledge and truth."[26] With its dialectic of concealment and revelation—also conceptualized in terms of a star's surface image and his or her real identity beyond this surface—the star system produces the star's personality or persona as an intense site of conjecture and scrutiny. The volatile, generative effects of the dissemination, circulation, and regulation of different orders of knowledge of Valentino's public and private life are best demonstrated by the central issue that biographies of the star are inevitably compelled to address: his sexual identity.[27] Though scholars of Valentino may claim to have resolved this issue, the persistent interest in this sexual question testifies to the powerful epistemological effects of both the apparatus of modern sexuality and the Hollywood star system. As deCordova points out, "the very modes of knowing the star, of investigating the truth of his or her identity, are linked to and a part of a broader strategy of deploying sexuality in modern times."[28] Valentino's peculiarly magnetizing stardom is one potent manifestation of these developments, and while this aspect of Valentino's star discourse may seem to take us some way from the central argument of this chapter, it is the historical discursive forms through which his "sexuality" is constituted by the Hollywood star system that also enable a lesbian fantasmatic.

Identifications

The institutional context for Valentino's "lesbianism" is his ability to attract not only a diverse mass audience but also a predominantly female one. Evidence on women's filmgoing in America in the 1920s is scanty yet it does suggest that the proportion of women in movie audiences increased throughout the decade. It seems clear too that the Hollywood industry itself operated on the assumption that the majority of audience members—however slender a majority that might be—were female.[29] Although at the time of his breakthrough film, the World War I epic *The Four Horsemen of the Apocalypse* (dir. Rex Ingram, Metro Pictures Corporation, 1921), Valentino was not promoted to a specifically female audience, this gendered element of Valentino's film career—along with the sexual reputation that he developed as an emergent star figure—shifted with the production and release of *The Sheik* later in the same year.[30] Hansen traces in detail this complex and turbulent terrain of reception, including the meanings and erotic exploitation of Valentino's Italian ethnicity, arguing that *The Sheik* "locked [Valentino] into a discursive economy that haunted him for the remainder of his career—by dividing viewers and reviewers along the lines of gender and sexual orientation."[31] As Hansen reads the archive of public discourse, one of the significant aspects of the reception of *The Sheik* was the emphasis on the female spectator enthralled with the moving image of Valentino while "real" men in the audience remained indifferent to Valentino's screen charms. This dominant discourse of reception endeavors to obscure not only the diverse identificatory relations of men to the star, but also the possibility that the intense pleasures of female spectators might include a lesbian fantasmatic. The latter emerges in the context of the "aura of notoriety" that accrues to Valentino across several of his films, augmented by two public scandals concerning his relationships with women, and sustained by elements of fan magazine print and visual discourse.[32] The lesbian fantasmatic that emerges in relation to Valentino is not the product of a linear development or straightforward reciprocal relation between successive film releases and their accompanying extrafilmic discourses, but is instead shaped by the episodic and recursive nature of the production and exhibition of Valentino's films.[33]

Though it is now a minor film, *Camille* (dir. Ray C. Smallwood, Nazimova Productions, 1921) provides a starting point for considering how Valentino's sexual reputation develops, and its impact on his emergent stardom and spectatorship. Released the same year as *The Four Horsemen of the Apocalypse*, *Camille* stars the actress and director, Alla Nazimova, and in retrospect seems an aesthetic rehearsal for her more famous cult film, *Salome* (1922). Based on the novel by Alexandre Dumas fils, Nazimova plays the role of Marguerite Gautier as a hedonistic and consumptive antiheroine, against Valentino's Armand Duval, a young law student from the provinces. The actress' idiosyncratic performance and the Aubrey-Beardsley inspired costumes and sets—designed by Natacha Rambova, the stage name of Winifred Hudnut—convey an aura of decadence and perversity. As Patricia White argues, Nazimova's image as it was generated across various fan magazine profiles and interviews at the time of *Camille*'s release, and just before she was to go into production on *Salome*, figured her in contradictory terms: "the aesthete qua femme fatale meets the new woman qua lesbian."[34] Nazimova's complicated sexual reputation moderates, and to some extent undermines, the heterosexual meanings of the film's central romance between Gautier and Duval, while inflecting Valentino's developing star image—a process sustained by public discourse about his post-*Camille* associations with the star and his eventual marriage to Rambova. Two minor scenes in particular make themselves available to a lesbian reading: one in which Nazimova embraces and kisses the young woman Nichette (Patsy Ruth Miller), a friend from Gautier's days working in a dressmaking shop, and another that takes place in Gautier's bedroom early in the film, when she says to Duval, in dialogue conveyed by an intertitle, "You know who—or what I am? Go home—forget that we have ever met."[35] Gautier's ambiguous line—"what I am"—encompasses the possibility of an alternative and implicitly deviant sexuality, one that Nazimova's complex star image readily enabled, even as its potentially contradictory sexual meanings are not easily assimilated to the contrasting scene of friendship and intimacy between Gautier and Nichette. While the film is primarily a vehicle for Nazimova—billed in the opening credits by her last name only, in a distinctive slanted cursive script that resembles a signature—there is some evidence to suggest that Valentino's ascendant stardom also influenced

FIGURE 6.1. Publicity photograph for *Camille* (1921). From the core collection, production files of the Margaret Herrick Library, Academy of Motion Picture Arts and Sciences.

the film's promotion and reception during the course of its exhibition.[36] As one of Valentino's first roles cast opposite a more dominant vamplike female figure, *Camille* also augurs the feminization of Valentino as a component of his multivalent image—one of the series of publicity photographs for the film has Valentino kneeling on the ground at Nazimova's feet in a setting that film-viewers would recognize as Gautier's bedroom (figure 6.1). This process becomes bound up in the interlinked possibilities of identifying with the star even as he also acts as a legitimating conduit for a homoerotic spectatorship centered on the female characters with whom he is romantically coupled.

The sexual meanings of Valentino's image—a heteroerotic passivity that also registers the possibility of the star's homosexuality—are inflected by a discourse that highlights his continued intimacy with female figures who are themselves associated with same-sex desire. This public knowledge emerges in the context of Valentino's marriage scandals that occurred around the same time as *Camille* and Valentino's other early films were released—including *Blood and Sand* (1922), *The Young Rajah* (dir. Phil Rosen, Famous Players-Lasky, 1922), and *Moran of the Lady Letty* (dir. George Melford, Famous Players-Lasky, 1922). In relation to the function of sexual scandal in the emergent Hollywood star system, deCordova argues that, in promising an increasingly intimate revelation of an actor's identity, scandal created a "more elaborate grid through which the actor's identity could be specified and differentiated."[37] Yet this work of specification and differentiation could be disturbed by those very same discursive processes, as the tensions and contradictions in the public discourse of Valentino's second marriage scandal indicate. In 1922 Valentino was arrested and charged with bigamy, since he and Rambova had married before his divorce decree from his first wife, Jean Acker, had been made final. Valentino's divorce had been widely reported in newspapers, and included details that hinted at Acker's affair with a female friend, and the lack of consummation of the marriage on their wedding night.[38] The second scandal continued Valentino's public association with female figures who were not sexually interested in the star—and most prominent again was Nazimova who was included in the wedding party. Elements of the newspaper coverage of the trial, and eyewitness testimony of the whereabouts of the various actors in the event, exploited the sexual valence of this relationship through a narrative of misrecognition and substitutability centered on the sightings of its three main figures—Nazimova, Rambova, and Valentino—all reportedly wearing purple silk pajamas.[39] Such public discourse drew on and reinforced the mobility and uncertainty of Valentino's sexual and ethnic identity, while consolidating the implication that Valentino was somehow like Nazimova and Rambova. This particular aspect of the story of Valentino's bigamy scandal rests on a paradox: while purporting to identify Valentino's sexual interests and therefore his sexual personality, the narrative demonstrates instead the impossibility of distinguishing between Valentino and his female intimates. The position that Valentino occupies in his relation to women in public scandal was also buttressed by, among other things, a varied discourse that characterized the film star as feminine and effeminate, as "the male orchid" or "the masculine counterpart of Sappho, Lais, Phryne, and Aspasia."[40] As examples of elements of discourse that circulated around and thus also constituted Valentino's image, they figure the star as, among other things, a passive spectacle of beauty, a lover of women, a prostitute, and as both sexually receptive and assertive.[41] Countering the apparently specifying forces of sexual scandal, these forms of star discourse enabled the further proliferation of disparate and unpredictable sexual meanings associated with Valentino.

The queer possibilities that develop for identifying with a feminine Valentino were bolstered by another form of extra-cinematic homoerotic discourse that cohered to the star, as suggested by a particularly notable fan magazine article entitled "Are Wives of Screen Lovers Jealous?" Purporting to survey the wives of stars, the article begins its section on the Valentinos by first describing the role of Rambova in the direction of Rudolph's love scenes, a professional role that immediately distinguishes her from the other "wives" and their relation to their husbands' screen performances. The article appears to report the precise terms of her direction to Valentino in a rehearsal for a scene from *Monsieur Beaucaire* (1924): "'Try brushing your lips along her neck,' she suggested, 'and then—it should be more of a bite than a kiss!'" It then quotes Rambova in terms that claim to explain why Valentino relies on her judgment: "'A woman,' says Natacha Rambova, smiling her heavy-lidded, scarlet-lipped smile, 'knows more about what other women want.'"[42] Read in light of the erotic specificity of her reported directorial advice to Valentino, Rambova's double entendre suggests an identification with the "other women" in her husband's life, not only the film actresses who play opposite him but also his female spectators; at the same time, the ambiguity of her response, and the vampish characterization of her facial expression in delivering it—"her heavy-lidded, scarlet-lipped smile"—suggest her own knowing and superior sexual experience with, and understanding of, women. The article evidences Gaylyn Studlar's critical observation that fan magazine discourse channeled women into nominally normative models of female subjectivity while at the same time they "attempted to satisfy sexually and socially transgressive aspects of women's desire."[43] The apparent ease with which Rambova is able to invoke the possibility of same-sex desire in this instance is also premised on the familiarity of magazine readers with the scandals in which Rambova and Valentino were both implicated.[44] Rambova's double entendre suggests not only that she was quite willing to exploit the notoriety of her highly publicized professional connections with Nazimova—as well as rumored erotic ones—but that she understood their multiple appeals to magazine readers, as did the writers and editors of those magazines. As a more prominent figure in fan magazine discourse after she married Valentino, Rambova also modeled for readers a certain knowing mode of spectatorship in relation to the star.

FIGURE 6.2. "No—Guess Again!" *Motion Picture*, February 1924. Library of Congress National Audio Visual Conservation Center; digital access coordinated by the Media History Digital Library.

These elements of Valentino's lesbian fantasmatic—the male star as "lesbian"-identified and as conduit of female same-sex desire, and the particular relation of Rambova to those functions—provide some of the context for the likely appeal for fan magazine readers of a series of photographs that appeared in early 1924, of Viola Dana and Shirley Mason impersonating Valentino and Rambova on their Mineralava dance tour (figure 6.2). According to newspaper reports and trade and fan magazine articles, the two well-known actresses "travestied" the couple in at least two stage performances, one for the Los Angeles Actors' Fund Benefit in late October 1923 and the other for a Hollywood star variety revue sponsored by Western Motion Pictures Advertisers (WAMPAS) in late December in San Francisco.[45] Different photographs of the pair were published in several fan magazines, including *Photoplay*, *Motion Picture*, *Screenland*, and *Picture-Play Magazine*, across January and February of the following year, while the continued currency of the impersonation for fan magazine readers is suggested by references in articles published across issues in April and May 1924.[46] While newspaper reports characterized the performance as a "novelty" and "satire," trade papers and fan magazines emphasized the actresses' skills of impersonation.[47] A sign of ability for the film industry, the capacity to impersonate Valentino and Rambova can also be understood as an everyday aspiration and practice for fans of the star and his wife. The captions and bylines to the photographs published in *Photoplay* and *Motion Picture*—"Natacha and Rudie! Well, Almost, At Any Rate," "No—Guess Again!"—each play on the possibilities of performance, imitation, and sexual similitude that were already important aspects of Valentino's star image and Rambova's public profile. Though the captions attempted to dispel the photographs' erotic dimensions by reminding readers that the actress-impersonators were, in real life, sisters, the images in circulation offered multivalent pleasures for fan magazine reader/viewers: as Hollywood satire, a blend of professional and fanlike impersonation, and homoerotic fantasy.

The range of heterogeneous interests for female viewers sustained by Valentino's queer persona manifests in a film produced toward the end of Valentino's short career. *The Eagle* (dir. Clarence Brown, Art Finance Corporation, Photoplay Productions, 1925) demonstrates, and also understands its audience to share, a certain knowingness about Valentino's contradictory star persona and, in particular, his sexual reputation as it had developed since the early 1920s.[48] From its opening scenes, and in a more systematized manner than some of the star's earlier films, *The Eagle* aligns the spectator's gaze at Valentino with that of a "deviant" female figure: a hypersexual, masculine, and powerful older woman, the Russian Czarina (Louise Dresser). As the Czarina descends a staircase to mount her favorite horse, in order—the inter-titles inform us—to inspect her favorite and handsomest regiment, the rifle shots from a line of soldiers practicing at a firing range startle both her horse and a carriage just outside the grounds of the Czarina's palace. An unknown soldier (played by Valentino, as the yet-to-be-introduced Vladimir Doubrovski) catches the Czarina's horse, and rides it away to stop the runaway carriage. It is the editing together of the Czarina's look, in a close-up, with the shots of

FIGURE 6.3. *The Eagle* (1925) publicity still. Clarence Brown Collection MS.0702, University of Tennessee, Knoxville—Libraries.

Valentino riding to catch the carriage, that directly aligns the Czarina's line of vision with that of the camera—and thus of the audience—to the extent of straining the credibility of the Czarina's diegetic point of view of the action. While the Czarina's desires are not sanctioned by the film, her relation to Valentino is resolved in a way that evokes the possibility of alternative erotic practices and sexual identities even as the film forecloses any potential for their more explicit expression.

The cinematic pleasures that result from the visual alignment between the Czarina's look and the audience's view of Valentino are considerably complicated by the following scene. Having recalled the soldier to her apartment, the Czarina erotically appraises the nervous Doubrovski before announcing that she will gift him her horse. As the astonished Valentino character kneels and kisses the Czarina's hand in thanks, the camera cuts in to a close-up where her hand presses the top of his head as he attempts to regain his feet, forcing him to remain kneeling at her waist; the cut to the following close-up, tightly framing the Czarina's face, smiling, her eyes closed, not only conveys the character's enjoyment but also eroticizes Doubrovski's submission. A publicity photograph for the film (figure 6.3)—it has no exact visual analog within the film itself—evidences the saliency of this moment for the film's producers and their solicitation of an audience.[49] With its configuration of bodies, and the Czarina's arched back when the film returns to its wide shot at the end of the sequence, the visual mise-en-scène evokes a scene of oral sex.[50] Given the Czarina's figuration as a spectatorial stand-in, the moment can be read as a calculated visual representation of the imaginary pleasures that Valentino galvanizes in his female fans. Later, after the Czarina briefly presses her lips to Valentino's, the latter wipes his lips—more precisely, he brushes his white-gloved forefinger across the edge of his tongue—a gesture that economically and emphatically signifies his character's distaste for her sexual interest in him.[51] This gesture of disgust only reinforces the sexual connotations of the earlier part of the scene and its aura of perversity, with its compactions of male submissiveness, female masculinity, domination, and nonpenetrative, intergenerational sex. In playfully alluding to a sexual practice that fails to signify securely any one particular sexual identity, the scene also sustains the possibility of viewing Valentino queerly—not only as a gay figure but also as a visual substitute for those sapphic women with whom he is so closely associated. The possibility of an unalloyed pleasure in this scene for female spectators, whether their erotic identifications veer toward the Czarina or Valentino's character, is undercut by the film's negative, albeit comedic, characterization of the Czarina's erotic enthusiasms. Yet the shame or humiliation that Valentino's disgust might engender is never reinforced by any parallel diegetic representation of the Czarina's response (since she never sees his gesture) but remains a possible feeling for spectators only.

The ambivalent affect of these elements of the scene, and the sexual incompatibility that it partially registers, contrasts with other elements that visually reinforce the similarities between the Valentino character and the Czarina: each wears a military uniform, the length and swish of Doubrovski's long dress coat mirroring the skirts of the Czarina; each mirrors the actions of the other in their comic drinking game, tossing the alcoholic contents of their glasses into conveniently placed plant pots, a mirroring emphasized by their frontal framing and the sequence's shot/reverse-shot structure. Finally, the ending of the film revisits and confirms their connection to one another. While they are paired off with more age- and gender-suitable mates, this double-date ending is secured and extended through their on-screen farewell in which the characters cannot stop waving goodbye to each other. This lengthy exchange is brought to a close when Doubrovski's partner uses her parasol to obscure the Valentino character from the sightline of the Czarina, and thus the audience who is aligned with her point of view. The final scene confirms the transformation of the initially perverse erotic encounter between Doubrovski and the Czarina, and her expression of desire—one explicitly aligned with the audience's mode of looking—into an encounter that connotes the possibility of friendship. Read in light of Valentino's star discourse, the final scene rehearses the possibility of another kind of identificatory relation between the two characters, a sexual commonality that is ambivalently foreclosed by their respective cross-sex couplings. *The Eagle* suggests that the possibility of same-sex desire might be recognized by spectators not only in terms of the desire expressed by the embodied characters portrayed by Valentino and his female counterparts but also as a form of fragmented or distributed sexuality, registered in moments that symbolize or connote queer sexual practices or that represent Valentino's erotic relations as moments of potential identification for female spectators.

Queer Bonds

The fantasmatic possibilities of Valentino's gendered and sexual identifications with the female characters in his films are most evident—albeit in a sexual register different from the examples discussed so far—in the early Valentino film *Moran of the Lady Letty* (1922), a seafaring adventure based on the 1898 novel of the same name by Frank Norris. The film features Valentino playing the dandy city-boy love interest, Ramon Laredo, to the eponymous mannish sailor (played by Dorothy Dalton), who works on the Norwegian ship the Lady Letty under the captaincy of her father. Considered in terms of box office and genre, *Moran of the Lady Letty* is a relatively unsuccessful and minor film in Valentino's oeuvre. Most scholars rarely consider it in any detail. Gaylyn Studlar, for example, points out that the film's narrative is a generic variant of the "ideologically normative transformation" from mollycoddle to man that never became a significant element of Valentino's stardom.[52] Yet, framing the film in these generic terms not only directs critical attention away from its female character but also fails to recognize the film's queer effects. In contrast, Anderson undertakes a detailed reading of

Moran of the Lady Letty as one of two significant examples (the other being *Cobra*) of both the textual inscription of Valentino's queerness, and the textual insufficiency of the film to resolve questions of gender and sexual identity.[53] While Anderson focuses on the intelligibility of the star's deviance in terms of concurrent discourses of sexual inversion, and the film's related representation of a cross-sex coupling founded on "perverse narcissistic desire," in what follows I argue that Valentino's textual effects include the possibility of recognizing, in less embodied terms, relatively novel modes of (homo)sexual identification and queer relationality.[54]

The initial incompatibility of the two central characters of *Moran of the Lady Letty* is established early on in the film, with their chance meeting as they pass each other on the docks in San Francisco. This brief scene establishes their difference in terms of masculinity and seamanship—in an aside to her father, Moran belittles "the softy in his minstrel clothes," in a reference to Ramon's pristine yachting suit. Despite this inauspicious encounter, the entire film is from the beginning geared to the inevitability of their union. Most prominently, before establishing through parallel editing the different lives of each character, the film begins with an inter-title that excerpts lines from a popular American poem about fate: "Two shall be born the whole wide world apart . . . / And bend each wandering step to this one end / That, one day, out of darkness, they shall meet / And read life's meaning in each other's eyes."[55] Before Ramon and Moran meet again, Ramon is shanghaied by some pirates to work on their boat. The scene on the pirate ship, The Heart of China, places Valentino's character in a treacherous and submissive position surrounded by a group of menacing men on deck, a position reinforced by the leader of the pirates, Kitchell (Walter Long), who insists on referring to the Valentino character as "Angel child," "dearie," and "Lillee of the Vallee." Across these early scenes, the film persists in deploying gender as the rubric that governs Moran and Ramon's romance. As Anderson points out, the film's parallel editing between the scenes of Ramon learning how to be a sailor on The Heart of China and Moran on the Lady Letty constructs their similarity in terms of a successful attainment of masculinity: "each is able to find his or her place at sea by performing a tough and self-confident version of masculinity."[56] At this point in the narrative, the future compatibility of the characters is figured in terms of a gendered convergence.

Other elements of the film's representation of Ramon and Moran, however, run counter to this effect. Instead of registering their affiliation to one another in terms of a gendered similitude, both characters are represented in terms of their inversion of normative gender in ways that also inflect their class status—whether Ramon's effete dress, and clean, cultivated appearance in contrast to the weather-beaten, bearded faces of the pirates, or Moran's seamanship, and the rough, baggy trousers that she wears on board the Lady Letty. These gendered inversions, and what they promise about their future romance, are also reinforced by the characters' names, each an anagram of the other. As such, their names—like their respective femininities and masculinities—lack a priority or ordered hierarchy: neither precedes nor succeeds the other, but each is configurable in terms of the other. Aside from suggesting the complementarity of Ramon and Moran, it also suggests their potential interchangeability. They even repeatedly signal their affection by addressing each other in terms of a genderless noun: "mate." After various adventures, the film ends with the reunion between Ramon and Moran on the deck of the Lady Letty, and a final two-shot in which the characters kiss. The conventional ending, and the heterosexual romance that it attempts to secure, is belied by almost all of the preceding narrative. Less erotically charged than the decadent aesthetic linked to Nazimova, the anodyne Hollywood style of sexual inversion that *Moran* in part instantiates ensures that the sexual effects the romance narrative seeks to anchor remain unsettled.

It is an earlier ostensibly romantic scene between the pair that demonstrates most the queerness of the relationship between Ramon and Moran, the terms of its sexual legibility, and what it potentially offered its female audiences. This scene occurs on an isolated rocky beach, while Kitchell meets a band of smugglers. It begins with a conventional romantic shot of the pair, hand in hand, running along a beach, though the romantic implications of the image are tempered by its composition, in which the action is framed ominously by the dark outline of a rock arch. While the characters rest on an outcrop of rocks, Ramon exclaims: "Moran—I never knew a girl could be like you—I had no idea what life was until I met you" (figure 6.4).[57] For Valentino aficionados, the apparent meaning of this line is readily undercut by the discourse about Valentino's "private life," since it was public knowledge that Valentino had possibly known girls "like" Moran, if what her gendered inversion signifies is an erotic interest in other women. While the film frames the pair in mid-shot profile, Moran's next line rejects the erotic import of Ramon's statement: "I don't like that kind of talk. I never could care for a man—I'm not made for men." While Ramon only clasps her arm more fervently, Moran reinforces her rejection by stating: "I ought to have been born a boy."[58] Moran's gender identity seems to be confirmed when they descend from the rocks, and she slaps Ramon on the back, in a friendly, masculine gesture. While the scene registers the difficulties in making sexuality—whether hetero- or homosexuality—cinematically legible, its chaste effect also paradoxically implies the possibility of alternative sexual identities.[59]

FIGURE 6.4. "I had no idea what life was until I met you." Rudolph Valentino as Ramon and Dorothy Dalton as Moran, in *Moran of the Lady Letty* (1922).

As one instance of the interlinking of filmic and extrafilmic discourse that constitutes Valentino's contradictory star image, *Moran of the Lady Letty* makes their relationship legible in terms of queer friendship, even a kind of sexual solidarity. The film foregrounds the possibility of the recognition of the Valentino character and his female counterpart not only as a same-sex couple—their near-identical costumes in the scene on the beach renders Moran quite boylike—but also as a pair of differently sexed queer characters whose bond rests on another kind of sexual similitude, their shared same-sex erotic interests. While *Moran of the Lady Letty* establishes the sexual terms of its queer romance in relation to a couple of characters with whom viewers might potentially cathect to in varying degrees, there is also a sense that the sexual effects of the film are less easily attached to either figure. The sexual legibility of cinematic figures, as argued in Chapter 1, can be understood as the belated effect of a complex assemblage of discourses and practices of sexuality itself. In this case, it presupposes the presence of a more nebulous, discursive visual and affective field within which such figures might be recognized.

More than the sexual legibility of the female figures or cinematic characters associated with Valentino, or the heterogeneous sexual image of the star himself, Valentino indicates the presence of—and provides access to—an alternative discursive space for the recognition and expression of women's same-sex desires. Such desires are never consolidated as those of any one particular figure or character but rather their manifestation, recognition, or experience are made possible by the modes of performance, imagined queer affiliations, and relations that Valentino's stardom instantiates.[60] Unattached to specific bodies yet paradoxically generated as an outcome of their visual and filmic representation, this Valentino effect might be extrapolated in relation to Raymond Williams's evocative notion of a "structure of feeling."[61] It registers the historical presence and lesbian specificities of a modern sexual discourse, homosexuality, and its disruptive and resistant—that is, its queer—potentialities. In a film like *Moran of the Lady Letty*, for example, it manifests less in the gendered inversions, parallels, and convergences of the film's two main characters than in the feelings engendered by the film's queer romance, whether the sense of unease that subtends their possible sexual liaison, or the friendship evidenced by their later easy familiarity and comradeship. In this aspect of Valentino's lesbian fantasmatic, the star functions not only as a figure with whom spectators might identify—or who enables a homoerotic spectatorship in relation to the female figures he is associated with—but also as a particularly generative node in a cinematic discursive field enabling the production and experience of other shared ideas or emotions, or emotions as ideas (to paraphrase Williams), less amenable to explicit representation in dominant culture yet enabled by its cinematic institutions and discursive practices.

Several striking images from the fan magazine archive—their significance registered in their placement on the covers of the magazines rather than between their pages—evidence Valentino's alternative spectatorial role. Gaylyn Studlar has argued that fan magazines are "a crucial index of the ideological and historical dimensions of the cinematic field of the 1920s and a neglected source for assessing how women were positioned as viewers/readers/consumers within discourses specifically aimed at influencing women's reception of Hollywood film."[62] Drawing on the extensive fan magazine archive of the 1920s, Studlar demonstrates that the female subjectivity inscribed in those magazines "is hardly over-identificatory, passive and mindlessly consumerist, but distanced, skeptical and active as well as being relational, intimate and empathetic."[63] While the contradictory sexual and relational elements

FIGURE 6.5. Valentino as Juan Gallardo in *Blood and Sand* (1922) on the cover of *Screenland from Hollywood*, March 1923.

of Valentino's early star discourse provide a context for similarly complex female reader/spectator relations to Valentino and the female characters he appeared alongside, the heterogeneous imagery of the star in his film roles and public/private life reproduced in fan magazines also comprises a diverse visual field that partly sustains Valentino's more dispersed lesbian fantasmatic. Valentino's queerness in this sense is evident in one of the more unusual magazine covers promoting the film *Blood and Sand* (1922), discussed earlier in relation to Dorothy Arzner's behind-the-scenes participation in the film's production. Portrayed in his role as the Spanish bullfighter Juan Gallardo, the cover illustration of *Screenland from Hollywood* in March 1923 (figure 6.5) draws on a mix of graphic visual patternings and colors to render Valentino's character somewhere between cartoonish caricature and a more perverse male exoticism.[64] Valentino's appearance on the magazine cover, a placeholder more typically reserved for images of actresses and female film stars, only reinforces the illustration's potentially dissonant gendered and sexual effects. While the thick lines and clashing colors tend to accentuate the latter interpretation, the curved accents of the Valentino character's brilliantined hair and curls together with the signature pigtail of the Spanish bullfighter, the curvy lines of which are mirrored in the obscure background decoration, suggest an allusion to a decadent visual aesthetic, a coded extra-cinematic reference to Valentino's role in *Camille* and his associations with Nazimova's public persona—a connection that the visual motif of the round frame further reinforces. Just as such interpretations of the *Blood and Sand* magazine cover depend on knowledge of Valentino's scandalous queer affiliations and networks, as well as a mode of viewing attuned to the visual logics by which sexual identity is signified, it also suggests that the complexities of Valentino's appeal for his female audiences could encompass less a desire for the star than dynamics of sexual recognition and identification.

While the *Blood and Sand* illustration makes Valentino's queerness recognizable in terms of a partially anachronistic visual aesthetic—the outmoded late-nineteenth-century decadent styles renovated for *Camille*'s film design—that manifests as a contradictory amalgam of masculine embodiment and feminine style, other images of the star register his erotic appeal and his place in a lesbian spectatorial fantasmatic in more fashionably androgynous terms. One of the more prominent images of Valentino and Rambova that appeared in 1923 is the illustrated portrait of the couple published on the cover of the fan magazine *Motion Picture*, one of the two dominant publications of this period (figure 6.6).[65] The image redeploys the visual conventions for representing royalty typically found on coinage—the profile and flattened perspective of kings and queens—to suggest the prominence and status of the couple in a different realm: Hollywood industry and society. It is Rambova who is visually privileged through her placement in the foreground of the image, while Valentino's profile in the background plane of the drawing echoes her profile, at the same time that it is also partially obscured by it.[66] Efficiently establishing the reputed power dynamics of their relationship, the only significant formal difference between the two figures is Rambova's turban, secured by a pearl brooch. This Oriental fashion not only alludes to her role in designing Valentino's exotic and elaborate costumes in *The Young Rajah* (1922),

FIGURE 6.6. "The Valentinos" on the cover of *Motion Picture*, September 1923.

but it also mimics Valentino's costuming in that role, acting as both a visual reminder and replication of Valentino's cinematic character.[67] The caption, "The Valentinos," by adopting the pluralized convention of referring to the couple to signify their marital unity, further defers any distinction between them. Even as the image evokes the prior scandalous history of Valentino's personal and professional relations, and his substitutability with the deviant women in his life, it also makes both Rambova and Valentino the conduits for an imagined set of queer affiliations in Hollywood.[68] The image is composed in almost oppositional terms to the promotional iconography of clinches between Valentino and his female leads; its composition, with their identical poses facing screen left instead of toward each other, tempers the image's ability to signify their relationship as conventionally romantic or sexual. This visual protocol references a certain style of portraiture fashionable in the 1920s and 1930s, a visual aesthetic that Terry Castle argues "often turned upon an implicitly 'homosexual' confounding of traditional sex roles."[69] The availability of such a reading is premised on a "*homo*-style homosexuality," as Eve Kosofsky Sedgwick puts it, in which "an erotic discourse comes into existence that makes available a continuing possibility for symbolizing slippages between identification and desire."[70] Such slippages are on display in these images of Valentino and Rambova, as viewers/readers are invited to speculate on the gendered and sexual identities of both figures and their relation to each other through a fashionable visual aesthetic with its own specific relation to 1920s queer sexual culture.

Another cover portrait of Valentino, published around the same time as "The Valentinos," suggests how the star's androgynous image might further enable specifically lesbian fantasmatic effects. The cover of the August 11, 1923, issue of *Movie Weekly*, purportedly edited by Valentino himself, features a photographic portrait of the star with slicked back hair and a simple open-necked shirt, a style of personal grooming and attire increasingly fashionable for both men and women (figure 6.7).[71] The optical-illusion–like effect of the cover photograph—it is possible both to recognize the portrait as one of the heterogeneous images of the star even as it is equally possible to read it as an image of a fashionably handsome, and anonymous, woman—is accentuated by Valentino's relatively neutral expression, a sense of blankness reinforced by the pale color of his skin, itself an effect of the high contrast between the photograph and the cover's dark background. While such gradations of color register the relation of constructions of the star's ethnicity to his multivalent eroticism, it also works to diminish the distinguishing characteristics that make Valentino recognizable in terms of any specific gender or other personal, individualizing features. More than "The Valentinos," this frontal but nevertheless still enigmatic head-and-shoulder shot invites the viewer both to fantasize and project onto the visual surface—or screen—of Valentino's face the possibility of an alternative spectatorial and sexual relation to the star. These particular fan magazine images of Valentino suggest how the star system's surface-depth dialectic—in which notions of depth are aligned with sexual "truth" and the "real" persona of a star—is reoriented to make available to viewers/spectators new sexual possibilities, including the possibility of homoerotic interests or sexual identities shared by both men and women.

FIGURE 6.7. Valentino on the cover of *Movie Weekly*, August 11, 1923.

In sustaining the possibility of alternative forms of desire, whether through Valentino's on-screen relationships with mannish or asexual female figures or his off-screen relationships with women known or rumored to have sexual interests in other women, Valentino's star discourse afforded female spectators the opportunity for queer identifications with not only the actor himself but also a diverse range of female figures with whom he was associated. Made visually legible through images that accentuate Valentino's femininity or androgyny, this aspect of his public persona can also be seen as an alternative figuration of, and working through, women's different relations to femininity—in contrast to the spectatorial relations enabled by the ostensibly more uniform kinesthetic femininities of the *The Wild Party* considered in Chapter 4. The prominence and saliency of gender in the discourse that constructs the contradictory figure of Valentino—his problematic femininity, the feminine desires of his fans—might also be read as symptomatic of the ways in which Valentino signifies sexuality in terms that are not fully captured or articulated in terms of normative genders and their differences. Although constitutive of his sexual ambiguity, these and other contradictory elements of Valentino's image comprise a historically contingent fantasmatic that supports female erotic recognition of, and identification with, other nonnormative on-screen and off-screen characters, without ever consolidating those desires and identifications into a single sexual figure. In this latter sense, Valentino's lesbianism is not a discursive sexuality or sexual identity that attaches to the film star but is rather a dynamic set of cultural signifiers and discourses marshaled by, and in proximity to, the figure of Valentino. Valentino's lesbianism thus names a historically contingent set of conditions that arise at the intersection of Valentino's film texts, the star system, and public discourses in relation to which women's same-sex–oriented erotic identities and desires are productively enabled by the tensions and contradictions inherent in the dynamic institution of Hollywood cinema. It foregrounds, too, some of the instances whereby a new kind of not always coherent sexuality—homosexuality—also enables queer effects, registered in certain modes of visual representation, styles, and the feelings that they engender. The lesbian fantasmatic possibilities that Valentino indexes remain dispersed and fragmented, suggesting both how a particular mode of spectatorship develops for female film-goers whose sexual interests and erotic identities are oriented toward other women and the conditions under which a certain sexuality is rendered seemingly impossible or invisible—or, indeed, fantastic.

While early cinema develops, as Part II argues, medium-specific styles and genres that aim to render figures and bodies on screen intelligible in terms of novel sexual identities and desires, its particular aesthetic and entertainment-oriented institutional forms also enable the deflection and rearticulation of those same specifying discourses. Two figures that each are understood to enact and be subject to highly gendered and heterosexual forms of erotic spectatorship turn out to enable other kinds of queer and lesbian-positive modes of erotic recognition, acknowledgment and valuation. Loïe Fuller's virtual homoerotics and Rudolph Valentino's lesbian fantasmatic are each shorthand for complex structures of spectatorship that emerge out of distinct historical, institutional, and cultural conditions. They would not have been possible but for the advent of modern sexuality.

Coda

Out of Time

> The opacity of sexuality means that the relations between the material and the metaphoric, reality and representation, will remain inextricable and shifting, subject to temporary stasis only through the discursive and disciplinary framing imposed upon it.
>
> —Valerie Traub, *Thinking Sex with the Early Moderns*

THE POSSIBILITIES FOR REMEDIATION afforded by digitization now ensure that early cinema's representations of sexuality are increasingly accessible outside of public archives or private collections, whether we search for them diligently or they appear, as if by magic, in our algorithmically determined social or news-media feeds. One such silent film artifact circulating online is the acclaimed tracking shot from the Folies Bergère scene in the American film *Wings* (dir. William A. Wellman, Paramount, 1927).[1] Sliced out from a longer sequence set in the famous music hall, the shot initially frames a man and woman, sitting across from one another at a table, conversing and drinking. Barely visible behind them are other couples—including one same-sex couple—similarly positioned, lined up as if an identical series. The initial image that I have described lasts only a moment as the camera flies over the café tables and through the seated couples, heading toward its final destination, a young soldier who looks longingly at his glass of champagne being filled before taking a greedy gulp.[2] The camera framing and linear perspective establish the likeness of the couples, but the dynamic mise-en-scène—of longing looks, the exchange of money, tender caresses, frightened or suspicious glances, and angry gestures—emphasizes the fraught affective terrain of erotic relationality. The fragility of the couple form is reinforced cinematographically, as the camera visually breaks each pair apart as it heads missilelike for its main character target.

Aside from its technical virtuosity, the shot is notable because it represents an instance in which, very fleetingly, a lesbian couple is represented on screen. In her close reading of the shot's mise-en-scène in terms of cross-dressing and the representability of lesbianism in American cinema, Laura Horak writes that "positioning the two women analogously to heterosexual couples makes it clear that they are a romantic couple."[3] In this account, the couple's relation to each other, and its sexual legibility, depends on the already assumed sexual identities and erotic relations of the male and female pairs. Why must these cross-sex couples be read this way and not, say, in terms of kinship or some other social, or even commercial, relation? Such an obstinate question, which willfully ignores the scene's dominant meaning in light of its narrative and diegetic location, seeks to denaturalize processes of sexual representation and their interpretation in order to consider their imbrications in sexuality itself. We might then consider the shot as evidence that, by 1927, the intelligibility of a novel sexual category—however momentarily visualized on screen—already depends on a logic of derivation, the sheer obviousness of which suggests something of the discursive labor that Hollywood cinema has already invested in ensuring that any visual coupling of a male and female figure on screen seems always already charged with erotic potential.

Despite the force of these institutional effects, the logic of derivation is not analogous to the temporal duration and direction of the one-way tracking shot. Its logics move in another way: the legibility of desire between men and women as (hetero)sexual desire, outside of its more conventional and institutional forms, such as the family or marriage, is in part derived from the visual representation of the same-sex couple. This possibility indicates the tight, interleaved relation of homo- and heterosexual discourse, and the presence of another potentially disruptive logic of homo/heterosexuality that the film seeks to manage in this scene: sexual similitude. Evident in the visual composition of the couples as a linear but variant series, the logic of sexual similitude—as it inflects embodied sex and sexual identity, both lesbian and straight—is playfully deployed in an earlier shot that introduces the Folies Bergère to the film's audience. In a cut from a wide shot of the crowded venue, the film frames in close-up the derrières of two figures, the one on the left dressed in a military jacket and tartan kilt, the one on the right in a dark-colored, tightly fitting silk dress. Read in gendered terms without any knowledge of national culture or military history, the deliberate composition connotes a female couple, though the camera soon tilts up to reveal a male figure on the left and a female figure on the right. A joke about the visual misapprehension of gender, embodied sex, and sexual identity, the shot deploys a same-sex visual discourse to convey the erotic deviancy of the Folies Bergère venue while seeming to render the figures' heterosexuality momentarily visible. Yet even this interpretation fails to resolve one way or another: if the pair share a sexual identity, it remains an open question as to which one.

The simultaneous sexual transparency and opacity of such digital fragments in the present foregrounds the ongoing value of an interdisciplinary film history while also sharpening the need to make explicit our perspectives, disciplinary frameworks, and historiographical approaches. The project of *Queer Timing* has been to challenge approaches to the study of representations of sexuality in the early cinema archive, initially by reframing the emergence of lesbian figures in early film as the belated visible condensation of nascent and disparate strategies of "sexuality itself" that arise as part of the formation of cinema. Rather than seek to adjust the periodization of the emergence of lesbian cinematic representation, this book has sought to complicate the linearity of its chronological narrative and the legibility of an emergent sexual identity that it supports. It traces the stuttering, looping, and even regressive timelines by which same-sex eroticism is made to signify, or not, in the first decades of cinema. In this tumultuous period, new but not always coherent sexual knowledges and categories emerge, even as older erotic modalities persist. *Queer Timing* articulates some of the discursive and institutional processes by which women's same-sex desires and identities have been reorganized as impossible, marginal or—perhaps not so surprisingly—central to new forms of cinematic representation and spectatorship. Revising feminist perspectives on the gendered structures of cinematic representation and spectatorship, *Queer Timing* foregrounds the centrality of homoeroticism to historically distinct cinematic discourses of both homo- and heterosexuality. The larger historiographical point is that a counter-history of the emergence of lesbian sexuality in early cinema cannot ignore its contradictory and obscure connections to the establishment of another perhaps even more hard-to-detect sexual discourse, that of heterosexuality.

Queer Timing articulates across its chapters the emergence of lesbian sexuality—and that of its intimate "other," heterosexuality—as the effect of diverse discursive operations of early cinema, considered as a complex assemblage of film texts, exhibition practices, modes of spectatorship, and reception. As with the reading of the queer couple in *Wings*, this has required a heuristic approach that seeks to question even the most obvious kinds of sexual intelligibilities—not to deny the historical presence of same-sex desire but to approach critically the historical transformations of sexuality itself and to try to apprehend some of those queer forms of sexual knowledge, relationality, and culture that we may no longer recognize. If some of the chapters in the book risk an attention to too much detail—from the gendered specificities of star discourse and filmic representations to the homoerotics of selected scenes and film magazine articles—this is not to overvalue such minor, ephemeral materials or moments but rather to attend to their imbrication in broader visual and sexual discursive fields, while retaining a sense of the contingency of their sexual meanings and disciplinary effects.

For all its claims about the disparate temporalities and fugitive effects of the emergence of lesbian sexuality in the early cinema archive, *Queer Timing* accomplishes its project through a kind of discursive and disciplinary freeze-frame. As Valerie Traub suggests in this Coda's epigraph, sexuality is not only opaque but complexly ordered across multiple, dynamic registers.[4] Film's fugitive effects may be often hard to discern or describe even on repeated viewings, but cinema's contributions to novel transformations in modern life remain with us in the present. Sexuality, like the effects of cinema, can seem hard to pin down or put into order. Rather than replicate its regulatory and disciplinary effects, a more productive, queer critical enterprise—as pursued in *Queer Timing*—is to trace its nebulous logics, structures, and effects. Mapping out sexuality's contradictory, multiple chronologies as they are inflected by film's own paradoxical temporal effects promises to reshape our histories of sexuality in early cinema into a different form of historical time: an always queer time.

Notes

Introduction

1. The studies that have inspired and informed this book, in order of original publication, include B. Ruby Rich "From Repressive Tolerance to Erotic Liberation: *Maedchen in Uniform*," in *Chick Flicks*, 179–206; Dyer, *Now You See It*; Weiss, *Vampires and Violets*; White, *Uninvited*; Kuzniar, *Queer German Cinema*; White, "Nazimova's Veils," 60–87; and Horak, *Girls Will Be Boys*.

2. It is impossible to cite here all the relevant scholarship, including work published in new journals such as *Feminist Media Histories*, edited by Shelley Stamp. Most influential for this project has been Miriam Hansen's work on early cinema, including *Babel and Babylon*, and the still standout collection of essays published in Bean and Negra, eds., *A Feminist Reader in Early Cinema*.

3. As Eve Kosofsky Sedgwick writes: "The making historically visible of heterosexuality is difficult because, under its institutional pseudonyms such as Inheritance, Marriage, Dynasty, Family, Domesticity, and Population, heterosexuality has been permitted to masquerade so fully as History itself—when it has not presumed itself as the totality of Romance." See Sedgwick, "Queer and Now," 10–11.

4. Even the periods indicated here are provisional, in part because they are still subject to some debate, but also because they are determined by a focus on North American and European cinemas.

5. For an astute summary of the disciplinary value of periodization for history, see Blackbourn, "Horologe of Time," 301–307.

6. For an extended argument in this regard, see Bean, "Introduction," 6–11. Bean and Negra situate their discussion in terms of historical time, citing Annette Kuhn and Jackie Stacey, who remind film historians that "rather than being simply 'about the past' in any straightforward way, screen histories are of necessity concerned with past-present relations with a view to the future": Kuhn and Stacey, "Screen Histories," 9.

7. Bean, "Introduction," 8.

8. The modernity of sexuality is also premised on the establishment of a conceptual space for thinking sexuality: see Davidson, *Emergence of Sexuality*, 30–65.

9. Foucault, *History of Sexuality*. While this volume remains a foundational if sometimes vexing text from historical and feminist perspectives, it is also important to remember that other critics before and contemporary with Foucault contributed to theories of sexuality and its history. See, for example, the work cited by Gayle Rubin in "Thinking Sex: Notes for a Radical Theory of the Politics of Sexuality," 38n28, not to mention Rubin's seminal essay, "Traffic in Women," 157–210. The queer temporalities of the history of sexuality as disciplinary field may only be amplified with the recent publication, as this book manuscript was being completed, of *Les aveux de la chair* (Paris: Éditions Gallimard, 2018), Foucault's fourth volume in *History of Sexuality*, written just after he completed *Will to Knowledge, Volume 1*.

10. Halperin, *How to Do the History*, 88, my emphases.

11. For an in-depth consideration of the opacity of sexual knowledges, see Traub, "Thinking Sex: Knowledge, Opacity, History," in *Thinking Sex with the Early Moderns*, 1–34. The methodological implications are considered later in this Introduction.

12. For a now canonical queer theoretical discussion of this final point, see Berlant and Warner, "Sex in Public". Their examples include banal visual representations of immigration and city rezoning laws.

13. For a recent collection of essays that consider how historians of sexuality can move beyond Foucault, while also returning to reconsider and revalue his critical-historical project, see Spector, Puff, and Herzog, *After the History of Sexuality*.

14. On this historical development, see the essays in Cryle and Forth, *Sexuality at the Fin de Siècle*.

15. Doane, *Emergence of Cinematic Time*, 24.

16. See, for example, deCordova, "Emergence of the Star System in America," 17–29. For a project less directly aligned to Foucault's history but that discusses sexuality in terms that are very suggestive of an increasing nexus between new embodied forms of perception, as mobile and virtual gaze, and the constitution of modern sexual subjectivities, see Friedberg, *Window Shopping*, 32, and 222n68.

17. Miller, "The Late Jane Austen," 57.

18. See, for example, Constance Balides's study of early cinema's sexualization of women's bodies in everyday spaces: "Scenarios of Exposure,"63–80.

19. See Williams, "Film Body," 507–534. Williams revises and extends her argument in relation to early film pornography in *Hard Core*, 34–57.

20. For a brilliant summation of the "problem" of invisibility and its conceptual and historiographical impasses, see Jagose, *Inconsequence*, 1–13. On the discursive configuration of female same-sex desire in premodern England as an impossibility, see Traub, *Renaissance of Lesbianism in Early Modern England*, 1–35.

21. See Jagose, *Inconsequence*, 1–13.

22. Butler, "Imitation and Gender Insubordination," 312. In a note Butler argues, "It is this particular ruse of erasure which Foucault for the most part fails to take ac-

count of in his analysis of power. He almost always presumes that power takes place through discourse as its instrument, and that oppression is linked with subjection and subjectivation, that is, that it is installed as the formative principle of the identity of subjects" (319n11).

23. For two literary perspectives on similar modes of resistance that emerge in the late nineteenth and early twentieth centuries in Anglophone cultures, see Coviello, *Tomorrow's Parties*, and Herring, *Queering the Underworld.*

24. Lanser, "Sapphic Picaresque, Sexual Difference," 251.

25. See, generally, Halperin, Chapter 2, "The First Homosexuality?" in *How to Do the History*. While Halperin uses a literary example for the latter meaning, early films also demonstrate that it had a similar cultural currency at the turn of the twentieth century; see, for example, *A Modern Sappho* (American Mutoscope & Biograph., U.S., 1905).

26. Doan, *Fashioning Sapphism*, 29–30.

27. On the figure of the sapphist, her late-nineteenth-century transformations as proto-invert, and other models of same-sex intimacy based on friendship or other kinship relations (husband/wife; mother/daughter), see, for example, Vicinus, *Intimate Friends.*

28. On this point, see Jagose, *Inconsequence*, 13.

29. Halperin, *How to Do the History*, 32. Halperin considers the exclusionary and colonialist effects of the premodern/modern distinction at 18–20.

30. On the intransigent effects of the homo/hetero sexual binary, see, generally, Sedgwick, *Epistemology of the Closet.*

31. Halperin, *How to Do the History*, 42–43, original emphases.

32. See Cocks, "Historiographical Review," 1226–1227.

33. Judith Butler, "The Force of Fantasy," 199.

34. For example, it was Noël Burch's explicit aim to denaturalize contemporary reading practices and what he regarded as the internalization of the "Language of Cinema": Burch, *Life to Those Shadows*, 2. On the significance of the Brighton conference, see the collection of essays in Strauven, *The Cinema of Attractions Reloaded.*

35. See, especially, Villiers, *Opacity and the Closet.*

36. Eve Kosofsky Sedgwick, "Paranoid Reading and Reparative Reading, or, You're So Paranoid You Probably Think This Essay Is about You," in *Touching Feeling*, 123–151.

37. Valerie Rohy's astute reading of Sedgwick's work in "Exchanging Hours," 247–268, reminded me of these aspects of reparative reading. Rohy identifies Sedgwick's stance with that of literary scholar Barbara Johnson in their shared elaboration of an "ethics of uncertainty" (254).

38. Valerie Traub, "The Present Future of Lesbian Historiography," 82–100, in Traub, *Thinking Sex with the Early Moderns*, a revised and expanded version of the essay originally published in George E. Haggerty and Molly McGarry eds., *A Companion to Lesbian, Gay, Bisexual, Transgender, and Queer Studies* (Malden, Mass.: Blackwell Publishing, 2007).

39. Ibid., 95–97. Traub splits her list into two, the second set of additional themes

grouped together because they have had "more consequence for the history of female bodies, experiences and representations" (96).

40. Ibid., 85.

41. White, "Nazimova's Veils," 60–87.

42. Fradenburg and Freccero, "Preface," viii.

43. Valerie Traub, "Sex Ed; Or, Teach Me Tonight," in *Thinking Sex with the Early Moderns*, 320–321.

44. For a related discussion of the place of autobiography in queer methods, see Brim and Ghaziani, "Introduction," 14–27.

45. As Fradenburg and Freccero argue, the binary opposition between "trans-historicist perspectives which seek, in the past, the allure of the mirror image, and historicist perspectives that 'accept' the difference of past and present" is an ideological one: "Introduction," xix.

46. Valerie Rohy, "Ahistorical," 67.

47. Ibid.

48. As Fradenburg and Freccero write, not only does the ban on identification suggest to them that "historical knowledge is often founded on the renunciation, the *ascesis*, of 'self,'" but, as they go on to argue, "to the degree that this renunciation tries to hide its own narcissistic investments, it begs for queer scrutiny": see Fradenburg and Freccero, "Preface," viii.

49. Fradenburg and Freccero, "Introduction," xix.

50. This point is made explicitly in Halperin, *How to Do the History*, 15.

51. Traub, *Renaissance of Lesbianism*, 333.

52. Fuss, *Identification Papers*, 2–5. As Fuss argues, the place of the "other" in identification and identity-formation is one of the routine theoretical difficulties that psychoanalysis has to confront.

53. Halperin, *How to Do the History*, 15, original emphases.

54. Osborne, *Politics of Time*, 200.

55. Arondekar, "Without a Trace," 12.

56. Dinshaw, *How Soon Is Now?* 4.

57. See, respectively, Freeman, *Time Binds*; Love, *Feeling Backward*; Sedgwick, *Tendencies*, xii; Dinshaw, *How Soon Is Now?* 5; Stockton, *The Queer Child*; Edelman, *No Future*.

58. Rohy, "Exchanging Hours," 262.

59. On the first point, see Dinshaw, *How Soon Is Now?* and also Agamben's discussion of alternative, even failed, Western cultural traditions of temporality of Gnosticism (a broken linear time) and Stoicism (abrupt interrupted time) in the essay, "Time and History," 110–111.

60. Dinshaw, *How Soon Is Now?* 18. Historical teleologies are now recognized as fragmented and plural in their instantiations and discursive effects: see the recent collection of essays in Trüper, Chakrabarty, and Subrahmanyam, *Historical Teleologies in the Modern World*. They may involve, at the very least, different conceptions of the

future as finite or open-ended: see Trüper, with Chakrabarty and Subrahmanyam, "Introduction," 12, 17, in ibid.

61. Traub, "New Unhistoricism of Queer Studies," 31.

62. Ibid., 21. Queer theorists in their thinking on queer temporality have drawn on conceptual insights in other fields, including anthropology and postcolonial studies. The seminal work in anthropology is Fabian's *Time and the Other*. For a lucid and influential critique of conventional historical time from the perspective of subaltern studies and postcolonial history, including why it might be necessary both to sustain and disrupt it, see Chakrabarty, "Time of History," 35–60.

63. Rohy, "Exchanging Hours," 261.

64. Ibid., 258, 259. Dinshaw draws attention to the longer history of thinking time in this way; she writes that in "Aristotle's description of time . . . as Heidigger saw, linear sequential temporal measurement is dependent on asynchrony, and everyday life is profoundly asynchronous." See *How Soon Is Now?* 7, 10. A similar kind of claim in relation to historical rather than lived time is made by Siegfried Kracauer when he notes the difficulty, if not impossibility, of reconciling chronology with alternative periodizations and historical temporalities; see Kracauer, *History*, 154–155.

65. As Osborne notes, it is impossible to develop a materialist conception of history without also attending to "the variety of historically established social practices which make up any particular present": *Politics of Time*, xiv. Walter Benjamin's work stands as one of the most provocative and challenging articulations of historical time in the twentieth century. While an exegesis on Benjamin's influence on film historical method is beyond the scope of this note, for a brief provocation, see Russell, "New Media and Film History," 81–85.

66. White, *Uninvited*. While each chapter of *Uninvited* can be said to explore a different aspect of retrospectatorship, it is only—and fittingly—in White's final chapter that she undertakes a more explicit consideration of its elements.

67. Ibid., xxiii–xxiv.

68. Love, *Feeling Backward*, 14–17. By reworking the parameters of lesbian history and cultural criticism, Love incorporates into her historiography the mixed feelings and temporalities of queer experience, drawing on the critical insights enabled by feeling backward and linking them more explicitly to the historical project of looking backward.

69. Russell, "Parallax Historiography," 552. Russell singles out the following scholarly projects as key to this shift in feminist film studies: Bruno, *Streetwalking on a Ruined Map*; Friedberg, *Window Shopping*; Hansen, *Babel and Babylon*.

70. Russell, "Parallax Historiography," 553.

71. In the context of photographic technologies, the term *parallax* is most commonly paired with *error*, denoting the difference between the view from a viewfinder and the image formed by the lens in cameras where those two mechanisms are separated from each other.

72. Muñoz, "Ephemera as Evidence," 5–16.

73. Ibid., 10.

74. Some of the other deeper cultural and structural pressures to make evidence register as solid, stable, and weighty, beyond the scope of this Introduction, have been canvassed by a range of scholars, but they emerge with particular acuity in the writings of Berlant: see, for example, "'68, or Something," 124–155.

75. This is a slightly different point to the value of ephemera in their capacity to archive queer affects, whether those associated with nostalgia and personal memory, or the more difficult and painful experiences of trauma. On this crucial function of the ephemeral archives of lesbian and queer sexuality and intimate life, see Cvetkovich, *An Archive of Feelings*, 243–244.

Chapter 1. Troubling Sexual History

1. Like the viewers in Jackie Stacey's study of 1940s and 1950s British female spectatorship, I too employed "extra-cinematic identificatory practices" in my passing phase of Brooks fandom, to the extent that I cut my hair into an ultrashort Bubikopf and colored it jet-black: see Stacey, *Star Gazing*, 159–170.

2. Mary Ann Doane details the critical responses typical of this "compulsive fascination" in "Erotic Barter," 70–71.

3. See Elsaesser, "Lulu and the Meter Man," 259–292; and Doane, "Erotic Barter," 62–79. An earlier version of Elsaesser's essay was originally published in the journal *Screen* in 1983. Doane's essay was subsequently republished in Doane, *Femmes Fatales*, 142–162. The two essays comprise a debate between the two authors sparked by a seminar on Weimar cinema given by Doane at the University of Iowa in the spring of 1978. Doane outlines that fraught history in the first unnumbered endnote in the first publication of her essay (at 247). That Doane and Elsaesser are regarded as the preeminent *Pandora's Box* scholars is confirmed by their inclusion as paired commentators on the audio commentary track to the DVD set released in 2006 by Criterion. I have based my reading on this restored version of the film.

4. In a typical gesture, Peter Wollen writes that the "lesbian relationship" between the two characters is "vital to the film," a rhetorical move that allows him to conclude that it is Brooks herself—rather than her fictional character Lulu, Geschwitz, or even the film—who symbolizes the "polymorphous perversity" of the Weimar era: see Wollen, "Brooks and the Bob," 25.

5. Doane, "Erotic Barter," 71.

6. Ibid., 72. As Judith Halberstam points out, the presumption that masculine women "simply represent early forms of lesbianism denies them their historical specificity and covers over the multiple differences between earlier forms of same-sex desire": *Female Masculinity*, 46.

7. Gay film historian Vito Russo was perhaps the first to claim the Countess as "the first explicitly drawn lesbian character" in the history of cinema, an assertion that continues to be influential: see *Celluloid Closet*, 24. Indebted to Russo's broad assertion, popular and scholarly lesbian and gay film histories describe the character

in *Pandora's Box* as a milestone in a history of representation marred by invisibility and negative stereotypes: see, for example, Hadleigh, *Lavender Screen*, 17. The authors of a popularly oriented film encyclopedia advocate the film as must-see viewing for modern lesbians simply because the character is "well-developed": Daniel and Jackson, *Bent Lens*, 315–316. Such prescriptive advice ignores the appeal of Lulu/Brooks for lesbian spectators: see Weiss, *Vampires and Violets*, 22–24.

8. See, respectively, Dyer, *Now You See It*, 24, 54; Kuzniar, *Queer German Cinema*, 2. For a view aligned with Dyer's interpretation, see also Weiss, *Vampires and Violets*, 21–22. Already a familiar and controversial character from the early-twentieth-century German stage, gay and lesbian scholars have noted that the sexuality of the earlier literary Countess Geschwitz figure would have been intelligible in terms of late-nineteenth-century psychiatric and sexological discourses of sexual inversion and perversion. On this aspect of the Countess's cinematic genealogy, see Dyer, *Now You See It*, 24, 54; and Weiss, *Vampires and Violets*, 21–22.

9. This explains in part the continuing appeal of *Pandora's Box* to diverse popular, cult, and scholarly audiences, despite numerous attempts by film historians to suggest that it should be read primarily in terms of its construction of straight male subjectivities. Patrice Petro has argued that while the film's space of mobile and fluid identity is underwritten by a troubled and anxious assumed male spectator position, she also observes that most critics have failed to consider issues of androgyny and lesbianism in the film as they relate to the female spectator: Petro, *Joyless Streets*, 17, 80.

10. See Freeman, *Time Binds*, 59–93.

11. See, for example, Horak *Girls Will Be Boys*.

12. The film's restoration began with Henri Langlois's preservation of the film at La Cinémathèque français before James Card's first restoration at George Eastman House, Rochester, N.Y. See the brief account of this history in Elsaesser, "Lulu and the Meter Man," 259–260.

13. Elsaesser, "Film History and Visual Pleasure," 81. Patrice Petro links Elsaesser's claim to his work on *Pandora's Box* in her critique of his elision of a female spectatorial position: see *Joyless Streets*, 15–17.

14. Elsaesser, "Lulu and the Meter Man," 261–262.

15. Doane, "Erotic Barter," 62.

16. Making a subtly different historical point, Laurie Marhoefer argues that these distinct cultural phenomena were typically articulated to broader public discourses of "immorality" and "abnormality" as part of the Weimar's public refashioning of sexual and gender norms: see Marhoefer, *Sex and the Weimar Republic*, 8–10.

17. For a recent survey history, see Herzog, *Sexuality in Europe*, in particular, 56–61. Detleve J. K. Peukert notes that "attitudes towards sexuality during the Weimar Republic were marked by ambivalence towards the process of liberalization and the dropping of taboos": Peukert, *Weimar Republic*, 103–104. On the instability and ambiguities of Weimar lesbian identities—such that it seems historically inaccurate

to assemble them all under the sign "lesbian"—see, for example, Espinaco-Virseda, "I Feel that I Belong to You," 83–113. On the "fuzzy" category of "transvestite," see Marhoefer, *Sex and the Weimar Republic*, 59–61.

18. Foucault, *History of Sexuality*, 131.

19. Brooks, "Pabst and Lulu," 125. Brooks later revised this essay for two other publications: Jaccard, ed., *Louise Brooks*, 87–119; and Brooks, *Lulu in Hollywood*, 93–106. Brooks's phrase comes in an essay that comprises a significant supporting text in the efforts to restore the film's reputation, its place in the canon of silent cinema, and the place of Brooks herself in that history. For a beautifully nuanced discussion of Brooks's contributions to the film's discourses of reception, and in particular their relation to sexuality and truth, see "The Critic: Louise Brooks, Star Witness," in Hastie, *Cupboards of Curiosity*, 104–154.

20. The play is the second of a pair but the Countess character appears only briefly in the final act of the first, *Der Erdgeist* (*Earth Spirit*, 1895).

21. Finney, *Women in Modern Drama*, 80. For a more extensive discussion of the political, legal, and cultural context for the banning of Wedekind's plays, see Jelavich, *Munich and Theatrical Modernism*, 251–258.

22. Morris, "Admiring the Countess Geschwitz," 352. A contemporary anecdote mentioned by Morris on the same page, in which a writer speaks of acknowledging one's erotic interest in the same-sex as "absconding to the Geschwitzian region," suggests that the figure of Geschwitz also had a wider cultural resonance: Morris cites Margarete Schäfer, "Theatre, Theatre," in *Eldorado: Homosexuelle Frauen und Männer in Berlin 1850–1950, Geschichte, alltag und Kultur* (Berlin: Frölich und Kaufmann, 1984), 180.

23. Sutton argues that sexological theories rather than more recent psychoanalytical theories of sexuality "provided the more frequent reference point for cultural commentators of the Weimar period, and with which German audiences were assumed to be reasonably familiar": *Masculine Woman in Weimar Germany*, 19. See also her discussion of sexological discourses in popular and subcultural print media, 102–110.

24. The association of the aristocracy with perversity stretches back in time to the scandals of the French Court in the years leading up to the French Revolution, see Vicinus, *Intimate Friends*, xviii. While the eighteenth-century allegations of Marie Antoinette's purported sapphic orgies may seem a tenuous connection, discourses about dissolute upper classes continued to circulate into the early twentieth century in Germany. The Eulenburg scandal of 1905–1906 gave them fresh momentum: see Steakley, "Iconography of a Scandal," 233–263. See also Herzog, *Sexuality in Europe*, 38–41.

25. Thanks to Misha Kavka for pointing this out to me. Sarah Colvin also notes that Geschwitz's name could be translated as "sweat": Colvin, "Frank Wedekind," 475. There is another possible reading. According to Marti M. Lybeck, who cites Peter Langenmeyer, *Erläuterungen und Dokumente: Frank Wedekind: Lulu, Erdgeist, Die Büchse Der Pandora* (Stuttgart: Philipp Reclam jun., 2005), 11, Wedekind's daughter

suggested that Geschwitz's name was a condensed form of Geschlechterwitz, which translates as "gender joke": see "Gender, Sexuality and Belonging: Female Homosexuality in Germany, 1890–1933" (PhD diss., University of Michigan, 2007), 224n40.

26. Wedekind, *Five Tragedies of Sex*, 223.

27. Ibid., 256. The Countess's desires for Lulu ("the passionate assurances") and the reference to congenital abnormality ("uncompleted in your mother's womb") confirm her sexual pathology (256, 257).

28. On Wedekind's development of his Lulu material, see Finney, *Women in Modern Drama*, 80, and the works referred to in note 2. On the interrelation between the discursive field of sexuality as constituted by literary and sexological texts, see, for example, Rosario, "Inversion's Histories | History's Inversions," 89–107.

29. Oosterhuis, "Richard von Krafft-Ebing's 'Step-Children of Nature,'" 70. First published in 1886, *Psychopathia Sexualis* was reprinted as new and expanded editions between 1886 and 1924, seventeen in Germany alone, as well as translations into several languages. The circulation of new sexological knowledges in the German-speaking middle classes is attested to by the inclusion of several entries in two encyclopedias popular at the turn of the century: see Beachy, "German Invention of Homosexuality," 805.

30. Greenway, "It's What You Do with It," 27. First published in 1903, Weininger's book went through fourteen editions by 1914. The most recent English edition of *Sex and Character* appeared in 2005 through Indiana University Press and rectified the many inadequacies of the 1906 anonymous translation. Academic commentators have noted the influence of Weininger on Wedekind's work: see, for example, the commentary of Hibberd, "The Spirit of the Flesh," 336–355.

31. Wedekind, *Five Tragedies of Sex*, 213. See, for example, Doane, "Erotic Barter," 66.

32. Ibid., 214.

33. Elsaesser, "Lulu and the Meter Man," 264, and 290n24. Elsaesser cites the definitive biography on Wedekind by Artur Kutscher, *Wedekind Leben und Werk* (Munich: Paul List, 1964). See also Izenberg, *Modernism and Masculinity*, 69; and Morris, "Admiring the Countess Geschwitz," 350–351. Both Izenberg and Morris are more determined to take Wedekind's statements seriously in relation to the dramatic significance of the Countess in the plays. See also Lynda Hart's chapter-length consideration of the Countess, which takes Wedekind's preface as its starting point: Fatal Woman, 47–64.

34. See Friedberg, "An *Unheimlich* Maneuver," 41–51. On the varied reception of psychoanalysis in Germany, and its take-up by the "educated public and intellectuals" in Berlin in the 1920s, see, for example, Decker, "Reception of Pscyhoanalysis in Germany," 589–602.

35. Raitt, "Sex, Love and the Homosexual Body," 161. See Freud's description in "Psychogenesis of a Case of Homosexuality," 145–172.

36. Raitt, "Sex, Love and the Homosexual Body," 160.

37. Within Germany, the film was widely seen and discussed: see Elsaesser, "Lulu and the Meter Man," 260. Its release coincided with an intensified public discourse about an increase in lesbianism: see Marhoefer, *Sex and the Weimar Republic*, 56.

38. For example, the leading film reviewer of the *New York Times*, Mordaunt Hall, indicated his overall assessment of the film via his subheading "A Disconnected Melodrama": Hall, "The Screen," *New York Times*, December 2, 1929, 28.

39. As Giorgio Bertellini writes in relation to the restoration of *Metropolis* (dir. Fritz Lang, Germany, 1927), "there is no stable heritage to preserve. Instead, a real critique might be performed through the maintenance of the dispersion of accidents, errors, deviations of faulty calculations that have determined the film's historical reception": see "Restoration, Genealogy and Palimpsests: On Some Historiographical Questions," *Film History* 7, no. 3 (1995): 287.

40. It seems a perverse kind of enterprise to track the censored versions of *Pandora's Box*, given the intellectual, financial, institutional, and personal resources that have been devoted to its restoration and critical recuperation. The censored prints are difficult to trace. In the course of my archival research, I was unable to find a version of the censored print released in the United States. The several prints of *Pandora's Box* that I viewed at George Eastman House, Rochester, N.Y., all turned out to be later, partially restored, versions of the film.

41. This version of the film is available for viewing at the UCLA Film & Television Archive, Los Angeles. It was released in France with French inter-titles by Aubert-Franco Film. An article published in the British film journal *Close Up* notes that the versions released in New York and Maryland in the United States also included this revised "happy ending": see Weinberg, "Cinema and the Censors," 256–257.

42. Eisner, *Haunted Screen*, 306.

43. See 289n4 of Elsaesser, "Lulu and the Meter Man," which refers to the Clipping File for Pandora's Box held at the British Film Institute Library, London.

44. Herring, "For Adolescents Only," 423. Other writers for the journal seem to have had ongoing contact with Pabst: see for example H. D.'s account of her interview with the director, "An Appreciation," 139–148, originally published in vol. 4, no. 3 (March 1929). Thanks to Fiona Philip for alerting me to Herring's criticism, which she deploys to inaugurate a discussion of Bryher's role in the making of the Pool Group's silent film *Borderline* (1930): Philip, "Veiled Disclosures and Speaking Back," 146–163.

45. "Pandora's Box," *Variety*, December 11, 1929, 39.

46. J. C. M., "The Current Cinema," *New Yorker*, December 7, 1929, 96.

47. Titles were outlawed by Article 109 of the 1919 Weimar constitution: see the abridged version in Kaes, Jay, and Dimendberg, *Weimar Republic Sourcebook*, 46–49. While titles were often retained by individuals, strictly speaking they became names only: Petropoulos, *Royals and the Reich*, 18.

48. Doan, *Fashioning Sapphism*, 96.

49. See the discussion of German lesbian subcultural masculine style and the shift to popular masculine fashions by the late 1920s, in Weinstein, "(Un)Fashioning

Identities," 123. For a discussion of the public reactions to the Garçonne style, see Hake, "In the Mirror of Fashion," 195–196.

50. Patrice Petro quotes a 1925 editorial published in the magazine *BIZ* entitled "Now That's Enough! Against the Masculinization of Woman," the last sentence of which laments: "The masculinization of the female countenance takes away real attractiveness and gives women, if anything at all, an unnatural appearance: to look like a mawkish boy is disgusting for any real boy or man," see Petro, *Joyless Streets*, 105. Katie Sutton's extensive study, *Masculine Woman in Weimar Germany*, considers the contested figure of the masculine woman as she manifested across highbrow, popular, and subcultural print media. See also Frame, "Gretchen, Girl, Garçonne?" 12–40; Grossmann, "New Woman and the Rationalization," 153–171; Grossmann, "*Girlkultur* or Thoroughly Rationalized Female," in *Women in Culture and Politics*, 62–80.

51. Hake, "In the Mirror of Fashion," 194.

52. As Eric Rentschler argues in his auteur study, Pabst was interested in "dissolving spaces, collapsing borders, leading the viewer inevitably and inexorably into singular, frenzied, indeed extraterrestrial milieu": see "Problematic Pabst," 2.

Chapter 2: Traces, Specks, and Glimmers

1. Some of the scholarship that informs this list has already been cited in the Introduction. It draws from diverse fields including film studies, sexuality studies, queer theory, and the history of human sciences. A sample of key monographs and essays would include Balides, "Scenarios of Exposure"; Davidson, *Emergence of Sexuality*; Jagose, *Inconsequence*; Traub, *Thinking Sex with the Early Moderns*; White, *Uninvited*; Williams, "Film Body."

2. Catalog synopsis, reproduced in the BFI Collections Database, http://collections-search.bfi.org.uk/web/Details/ChoiceFilmWorks/150015998 (accessed April 23, 2015). My emphasis.

3. Early films emerge in an intermedial and heterogeneous context, alongside more established entertainments, including vaudeville, music hall, and fairground shows. For an account of the "cinema of attractions" and its historiographical development, see Gunning, "Attractions," 31–39.

4. As Yuri Tsivian has pointed out, variety-style programming of multifilm performances was arguably even more heterogeneous than the vaudeville tradition, typically including serious nonfiction alongside popular entertainments: see *Early Cinema in Russia*, 129–130.

5. Its historical opacities have only been enhanced by its recent remediation as a low-resolution digital video file titled *The Gavotte*, with minimal metadata, in the subscription database "Victorian Popular Culture" published by Adam Matthew. http://www.amdigital.co.uk/m-collections/collection/victorian-popular-culture (accessed July 11, 2016).

6. The remainder of the catalog entry reads: "Chalk marks on the ground to ensure

that the performers do not move out of frame can be seen. Ref: Henri Bousquet/ Riccardo Redi, Pathé Frères: Les Films de la Production Pathé (1896–1914), p 67." An earlier online version of the database entry also noted that the film was initially attributed to the Lumière film company: http://ftvdb.bfi.org.uk/sift/title/22490 (accessed March 5, 2010).

7. *Encyclopædia Britannica Online Academic Edition*, s. v. "gavotte (dance)." This entry succinctly draws on salient details of the gavotte in the more detailed historical account written by Carol G. Marsh: "Gavotte," 123–125.

8. McMahan, *Alice Guy Blaché*, 212. McMahan suggests, against the BFI catalog, that the film is possibly an early Gaumont production that may have been directed by Alice Guy or her future husband Herbert Blaché (Appendix B, 291).

9. Ibid., 212.

10. Ibid.

11. Bean, "Introduction: Toward a Feminist Historiography," 7. Lauren Rabinovitz, for example, develops close readings of the diversity of such forms of address in *For the Love of Pleasure*, 68–102. In *Babel and Babylon*, Hansen focuses on the ambivalent and paradoxical development of a normative form of spectatorship predicated on heterosexual subjectivity; see, for example, 116.

12. Respective examples are: *The Bride's First Night* (Haydon and Urry, United Kingdom, 1898); *Birth of the Pearl* (American Mutoscope & Biograph, U.S., 1901), which presents a moving image version of Sandro Botticelli's ca.1484 painting "The Birth of Venus"; and *Trapeze Disrobing Act* (Edison, U.S., 1901). Prominent exceptions to this gendered content are the films of muscleman Eugen Sandow produced by Edison, and American Mutoscope. Tom Gunning has argued that the erotic film, because it literalizes modes of exhibitionism through various scenarios of undressing and nudity, represents the fullest articulation of the cinema of attractions paradigm: see "Cinema of Attractions," 57. Eileen Bowser notes, "It could be argued that some French films portrayed actual nudity, while American films showed pretended nudity (actresses wearing flesh-colored leotards) . . . the risqué spirit was the same": Bowser, *Transformation of Cinema 1907–1915*, 23. For a broad discussion of the erotic in early cinema, see Hagan, "Erotic Tendencies in Film, 1900–1906," 231–237.

13. For Gunning, it is the direct look to camera that granted erotic films their power, a power only further privileged by the presence in the frame of an often unobserved male voyeur: Gunning, "Unseen Energy Swallows Space," 359–360.

14. The matter of determining genre—and what was regarded as an erotic genre—remains problematic since, as many leading early cinema scholars have argued, early films were "semi-finished products." See Thomas Elsaesser, "Comparative Style Analysis for European Films, 1910–1918," Deuxième Colloque International de Domitor, Lausanne, July 1, 1992, cited by Abel, *Ciné Goes to Town*, 61. See also Musser, *Before the Nickelodeon*, 103–156.

15. Miriam Hansen argues that the transposition of "familiar acts and vernacular iconography" into the new medium of film "emphasized distinctions between genres

rather than, as in later classical practice, making them variants of a relatively homogenous mode of representation known as cinema": Hansen, *Babel and Babylon*, 30.

16. See also Charles Musser's discussion of the films' cosmopolitanism in "At the Beginning," 25–26.

17. See Musser, *Emergence of Cinema*, 200.

18. Hansen, *Babel and Babylon*, 1.

19. Ibid., 2. See also 122 and 151.

20. Musser, "At the Beginning," 23.

21. Streible, "Female Spectators," 16–47.

22. See Streible's discussion of the article "Alice Rix at the Veriscope" and the accompanying illustration of two female viewers in "Female Spectators," 35–39.

23. On the emergence of a female spectator prior to cinema, in relation to consumer culture, see Friedberg, *Window Shopping*. Aspects of Miriam Hansen's epic study touch on the erotics of female spectatorship and processes of normalization in early cinema spectatorship: see, for example, *Babel and Babylon*, 114–116.

24. The critical discourse on the "deviancy" and "polymorphic perversity" of early cinema develops out of psychoanalytically inflected scholarship that understands early cinema spectatorship as "infantile": see, for example, the discussions of this strand of scholarship and its limitations by Hansen, *Babel and Babylon*, 57; and also Mayne, *Woman at the Keyhole*, 182–183.

25. See Hagan, "Erotic Tendencies," 235.

26. For example, Lauren Rabinovitz suggests the former interpretation, that the woman's look is "diegetically authorized" because she is going to buy the corset and not its model: Rabinovitz, *For the Love of Pleasure*, 95.

27. Constance Balides makes the latter argument in relation to *A Busy Day for the Corset Model* in "Scenarios of Exposure," 74–75. The former argument is developed by Friedberg in *Window Shopping*.

28. The penultimate chapter of this book further pursues the implications of this claim.

29. Russell, "Parallax Historiography," 565. Anke Gleber similarly sees the flaneuse as a figure that offers a mode of resistance by offering "an alternative to woman's status as image": Gleber, "Women on the Screens and Streets," 56–64.

30. The now well-known homoerotic photographs of Clementina, Viscountess Hawarden, taken in private and rarely exhibited publicly, suggest the cultural familiarity of the codes of female homoeroticism in mid-nineteenth-century Anglophone culture: see the book-length study by Mavor, *Becoming*. The similarity of their scenarios, poses, and gestures to other midcentury artistic and pornographic representations of love and sex between women would seem to confirm Sharon Marcus's argument that pornography and mainstream culture shared "an erotic repertoire": Marcus, *Between Women*, 114. See also Mandy Merck's discussion of another late-nineteenth-century visual archive, one that resonates more sharply with fin-de-siècle transformations in

the sexual meanings of gender similitude, the photographs of Alice Austen: Merck, "Transforming the Suit," 86–100.

31. Marcus, *Between Women*, 12.

32. Ibid., 113.

33. Ibid., 111–148.

34. Ibid., 6.

35. Keil, "Story of Uncle Josh Told," 65.

36. The film was shot in the Biograph New York City studio. The posters lend the set its authenticity since they advertise contemporary burlesquers of the period; see the Library of Congress catalog note on the film, https://lccn.loc.gov/96520173 (accessed September 12, 2018). The same set of posters was used to film *The Committee on Art* (American Mutoscope & Biograph, U.S., 1904), in which a group of women pin blouses and skirts to the burlesque images: see Hagan, "Erotic Tendencies," 236. For a discussion of the film in the context of the media history of outdoor advertising, see Corzo-Duchardt, "Paper Girls," 56–59.

37. The film also alludes to the use of projected and moving images in commercial advertising at the turn of the century: see Musser, "American Vitagraph: 1897–1901," 10.

38. *Biograph Bulletin* no. 55, quoted in the Library of Congress catalog note on the film, see note 36 above. The *Bulletin* acted as an industry newsletter, promoting the company's films to distributors and exhibitors.

39. Hennefeld, "Slapstick Comediennes in Transitional Cinema," 92.

40. As Kirby notes, "Gender seems to be irrelevant in terms of the fascination and seduction of the image": "Gender and Advertising," 4.

41. Perhaps the most widely cited example is John Sloan's 1905 etching of several young women watching and laughing at their view of several kinetoscope films, advertised with various titles such as "Girls in Their Night Gowns Spicy," "Those Naughty Chorus Girls," and "Trying on Her Stocking," in the well-known print, "Fun, One Cent" from Sloan's *New York City Life* series. This print is in the collection of the Smithsonian American Art Museum; for details, see http://americanart.si.edu/collections/search/artwork/?id=22491 (accessed September 12, 2018). Other sources mentioned by film and visual culture scholars include photographs of girls watching Mutoscope peep shows at Coney Island, and young women peering at a Mutoscope on a pier in England: see, respectively, Streible, "Female Spectators," 42, and Huhtamo, "Pleasures of the Peephole," 133. See also the example of the penny-in-the-slot machines exhibiting erotic images to "boys and girls" discussed by Sigel, "Filth in the Wrong People's Hands," 876.

42. See the three films discussed by Mayne, *The Woman at the Keyhole*, 177–178: *A Search for Evidence* (American Mutoscope & Biograph, U.S., 1903); *Die Rache der Frau Schultze* [*Mrs Schultze's Revenge*] (Germany, 1905); and *La Fille de bain indiscrete* [*The Indiscreet Bathroom Maid*] (Pathé Frères, France, 1902). The significance of the range of women's different looks to the camera is discussed by Hansen, *Babel and Babylon*, 37–39; see also Balides, "Scenarios of Exposure," 79–80, and the more

extended discussion by Rabinovitz in *For the Love of Pleasure* in Chapter 3, in particular 79–102.

43. Hansen, *Babel and Babylon*, 122.

44. As Miriam Hansen writes in relation to *Uncle Josh*, "The narrative clearly articulates a pressure for these pleasures to become integrated, subordinated to a more mature mode of reception; but it can do so only by negative example": Hansen, *Babel and Babylon*, 28. See also Keil, "Story of Uncle Josh Told," 69.

45. Elsaesser, "Archaeologies of Interactivity," 16.

46. For a review of the scholarship, see Doane, *Emergence of Cinematic Time*, 184–185. Later classical cinema, as Doane notes, disengages movement from bodies (179).

47. For a long time, this film has been known as *Ladies' Skirts Nailed to [a] Fence.* The historical origins and context of the film have been reevaluated by the BFI National Archive: see the online note for the film by Michael Brook, "Women's Rights (1899)," http://www.screenonline.org.uk/film/id/444603/index.html (accessed February 12, 2018). The film was based on a well-known magic lantern slide series produced by the same company. I am grateful to Richard Crangle, Research Officer for the United Kingdom Magic Lantern Society, for alerting me to these sources.

48. Based on the presence of its cross-dressed performers, the BFI in 2007 programmed the film as part of a lesbian- and gay-themed Mediatheque presentation called "Beautiful Things," now an ongoing collection "exploring LGBT lives on screen": see http://www.bfi.org.uk/archive-collections/introduction-bfi-collections/bfi-mediatheques/beautiful-things-2016 (accessed February 12, 2018).

49. See the two different production stills reproduced in the BFI Screenonline entry for "Come Along, Do!": http://www.screenonline.org.uk/film/id/444430 (accessed January 9, 2017).

50. Gray, "*Kiss in the Tunnel* (1899)," 54.

51. Gunning, "'Primitive' Cinema," 99. Gunning's essay recuperates the aesthetics and hidden labor of the single shot film.

52. In France, this would have included café-concert or music halls, *fêtes foraines* (fairgrounds), as well as magic theaters, wax museums, and department stores: Abel, *Ciné Goes to Town*, 15–16.

53. See Hansen, *Babel and Babylon*, 29–30.

54. Ibid., 54.

55. On the erotic identities and tastes of Parisian music hall crowds, see, for example, the mid-nineteenth-century memoir cited by Choquette, "Homosexuals in the City," 151 and 163n12.

56. Berlanstein, "Breeches and Breaches," 339–341. On the mid-nineteenth-century tradition of the female *travesti* ballet dancer, see also Garafola, "Travesty Dancer in Nineteenth-Century Ballet," 35–40.

57. Matlock, "Masquerading Women, Pathologized Men," 51–53. As Matlock argues, female cross-dressing was, until the last two decades of the nineteenth century, a common and accepted practice in certain circles. Even in those last two decades,

female celebrities or women of the *haute bourgeoisie* "could name their reasons for dressing as they pleased" (51). Horak's recent book on cross-dressing in early American cinema further supports a more nuanced interpretation of the meanings and regulation of cross-dressing: see *Girls Will Be Boys.*

58. *Travesti* continue to appear in different subgenres of dance films into the late 1900s. For an exquisite example, see the color-stencil print version of *Dans L'Hellade* (dir. Charles Decroix, France, 1909). The film adaptation of the French theater *travesti* tradition in later films, situated in certain cultural and social contexts, may have made alternative readings of same-sex desire possible. See, for example, Abel's consideration of this possibility in relation to the Pierrot-Columbine couple depicted in *Le Miracle des fleurs* (dir. René Leprince, France, 1912). Such a reading is enabled not only by the film's adoption of the French theater *travesti* tradition but also the knowledge that the actress playing the male character, Stacia Napierkowska, was part of a lesbian scene in the Parisian theater world: see Abel, *Ciné Goes to Town,* 295–296. Even here, though, I would want to distinguish between sapphic cultures and identities that may have been transformed by or absorbed into new forms of modern lesbian sexuality and the role of cinema in such historical changes.

59. This subtle transformation may have been enabled by the shift of cross-dressed performance in the 1890s away from operettas to music reviews and revivals, as noted by Berlanstein in "Breeches and Breaches," 346. Certainly by the time *Gavotte* would have been screened in a French venue, if not elsewhere, audiences were relatively mixed compared to the class hierarchies of the theater: see Abel, *Ciné Goes to Town,* 6–7.

60. This distinction draws on that discussed by Arnold Davidson in relation to the representation of the genitalia and erections of Jesus Christ in Renaissance art: Davidson, *Emergence of Sexuality*, 40–46.

61. On the significance of new performative modes for enacting, playing with, and disrupting gender norms at the end of the nineteenth century in France, see Roberts, *Disruptive Acts*, 1–17.

62. Heather Love's relation to the queer archive has influenced my thinking here, in particular in how tracing obscurity itself might allow us to "deflect questions of [sexual] identity and to acknowledge the losses of both the past and the present": *Feeling Backward*, 51.

Chapter 3. Queer Character

1. The source of the film's screenplay was a novel of the same name written by Archibald Clavering Gunter and Fergus Redmond and published in 1891. For a brief discussion of its status as popular literature, and its theatrical adaptation in 1896, see Somerville, *Queering the Color Line*, 40, 53–54. Note that a revised version of Somerville's chapter on *A Florida Enchantment* appears in the innovative anthology, *A Feminist Reader in Early Cinema*: see Somerville, "The Queer Career of Jim Crow," 251–269. I reference this later revised essay unless referring to material that appears only in the original monograph.

2. Lillian's homoerotic and cross-dressing adventures have ensured the film's place—albeit an ambivalent one—in the history of lesbian cinematic representation. Vito Russo notes the film's "higher tolerance for women who relate emotionally, or even sexually, to other women than for men who behave similarly toward other men": Russo, *Celluloid Closet*, 13. Andrea Weiss, on the other hand, refers to the film only in passing in the context of the use of cross-dressing as visual code for lesbian desire. She observes that the film's "female-to-male gender transformation serves as ironic commentary on male privilege but does not imply lesbian identity": Weiss, *Vampires and Violets*, 17.

3. Brasell, "A Seed for Change," 9, 13–14. Brasell's discussion of the concordances between sexologist Havelock Ellis's typology of the female invert and the Lillian/"Lawrence" character ends up emphasizing, perhaps inadvertently, the ridiculously expansive nature of Ellis's category, his coup de grâce being the character's sense of adventure and courage (13–14).

4. Somerville, "The Queer Career of Jim Crow," 259, 260.

5. Horak, *Girls Will Be Boys*, 93–117.

6. On the emergence in the United States of popular print discourse on psychoanalysis or "new psychology" around 1915, see Hale, *Freud and the Americans*, 397; Zaretsky, *Secrets of the Soul*, 82. One of the earliest references to "psycho-analysis" in a film magazine occurs in a 1915 review of the Thanhauser Studio production "Milestones of Life" in *Reel Life* (July 17, 18). Arclight, the data-mining tool developed by Concordia University and the University of Madison-Wisconsin that searches the Media History Digital Library collections, visualizes the appearance of the term *psychology* in the late 1900s. A relatively sharp increase in mentions across the second half of the 1910s coincides with the appearance of the terms *psychoanalysis* and its popular synonym *new psychology*. http://search.projectarclight.org, accessed and report generated September 12, 2018.

7. John Frow, "Spectacle Binding," 227. As Frow states in his more recent book, *Character and Person*, character should be approached both as "pieces of writing or imaging" and as "person-like entities" (2). For a study that develops a phenomenological approach to the parameters within which film characters are constructed, see Smith, *Engaging Characters*.

8. Doane, *Femmes Fatales*, 253, original emphasis.

9. On the "intellectual confusion and anachronism" characteristic of congenital and psychological theories of female same-sex desire in the 1910s, see Chauncey, "From Sexual Inversion to Homosexuality," 138. On the conflation of sexual inversion with homosexuality and the consequential elision of inversion's place in a history of transgender and transsexual subjectivity, see Prosser, "Transsexuals and the Transsexologists," 116–131.

10. My approach is akin to that of scholars of early cinema, such as Lauren Rabinovitz and Jonathan Auerbach. The former extends the critical archive of early films of interest to feminist film scholars through several close readings in order to develop an argument about the ambivalent positioning of female subjects and objects of

looking in early films: see Rabinovitz, *For the Love of Pleasure.* As Auerbach puts it, he selects a few early films and reads them closely in order to consider certain "conceptual problems or puzzles" concerning the representation of the body and its relation to space in early film: see Auerbach, *Body Shots*, 7.

11. The foundational, and still influential, history of the classical Hollywood style is Bordwell, Staiger, and Thompson's *Classical Hollywood Cinema.*

12. Storey's performance of masculinity has tended to overdetermine the film's generic categorization as a cross-dressing comedy, whether as the precursor of an "explosion" of such films between 1914 and 1919 or as an exemplary instance of the genre's development since the early 1910s: see, respectively, Brasell, " Seed for Change," 5; and McMahan, *Alice Guy Blaché*, 239.

13. The film's inter-titles consistently present the name of Lillian's male alter ego in quotation marks, a textual indication that her inversion is an imitation of masculinity, not the "real" thing.

14. On the film's representation of Jane, see Somerville's historical analysis that, among other things, situates her character in relation to the racial and sexual politics of blackface performance: Somerville, "The Queer Career of Jim Crow," 261–265. Somerville's larger argument is that film's playful and fluid representations of female same-sex desire (most prominently between Lillian and Bessie but never Lillian and Jane) reinforce and stabilize a historically specific "cultural architecture of racial segregation" (265).

15. Note that I am using the term *psychological character* not in any historical, disciplinary, or epistemological sense, but rather as a catchall rubric for all those internal, subjective elements typically ascribed to character as narrative agent, such as intentions, desires, motivations, feelings, thoughts, wishes, fantasies, and so forth.

16. The discussion of the film in the context of the transitional era draws on the following single monograph and anthologized histories: Bowser, *Transformation of Cinema 1907–1915*; Keil, *Early American Cinema in Transition*; Keil and Stamp, *American Cinema's Transitional Era*; Gunning, *D. W. Griffith and the Origins*. Apart from the film itself, *A Florida Enchantment*'s archive is limited to reviews, trade press articles, and fan magazine pieces. The Vitagraph studio records are missing: see Uricchio and Pearson, *Reframing Culture*, 6. There is one other, albeit unreliable, source for Vitagraph's history: the autobiography of the studio's cofounder, Smith, *Two Reels and a Crank.*

17. See the examples of trade press discourse on the need for films to develop dramatic unity in this sense in Keil, *Early American Cinema in Transition*, 104. See also, for example, the scenario guidebook and review examples discussed by Thompson, "Part Three," 175, in Bordwell, Staiger, and Thompson, *Classical Hollywood Cinema.*

18. *A Florida Enchantment* was one of Vitagraph's first longer-form narrative films or "features" of five reels or more (or just over 60 minutes of screen time). The studio changed its production set-up in mid-1913 and began to release longer features in 1914: see Slide, *Big V*, 82–85, 241–251. The year 1914 is arguably the moment when it became clear that the multireel feature would "permanently reconfigure the

[American] industry and the amusement landscape": Singer, "Feature Films, Variety Programs," 77.

19. Thompson, "Part Three," 181. This historical development aligns with theoretical understandings of the relation between character and action as defining and constraining each other's "logical development": Branigan, *Narrative Comprehension and Film*, 101.

20. See, for example, the essays in Gaines, ed., *Classical Hollywood Narrative*.

21. Charlie Keil discusses a very early example from 1907 in which the romance plot becomes intertwined with the film's other main plotline, albeit in relatively undeveloped terms: Keil, *Early American Cinema in Transition*, 49–51. As part of their joint study of the development of the Hollywood classical style, Bordwell, Staiger and Thompson, developed a statistical sample of Hollywood films from 1915 to 1960, finding that 95 percent involved romance in one line of action, while 85 percent made it the main plot: see Bordwell, "Part One," 16–17, in Bordwell, Thompson, and Staiger, *Classical Hollywood Cinema*; and "Appendix A: The Unbiased Sample," 388–396. Judith Mayne rightly criticizes Bordwell for failing to press further on the political and historical dimensions of this statistical finding: Mayne, *Woman at the Keyhole*, 118–119.

22. Historically, the chase genre marks a significant shift in spectatorship toward a mode of film viewing that required an active spectator who "knitted together the space and time of the film following the logic of the narrative": Gunning, *D. W. Griffith and the Origins*, 67. *A Florida Enchantment* inverts the gendered structure of the most popular and iconic chase films of early cinema in which the final heterosexual pairing is paradoxically reliant on the representation of an unruly female homosociality.

23. The shot/reverse-shot schema was used occasionally in films of the early 1910s, but by the end of the decade it was common in American feature films: Bordwell, "Convention, Construction and Cinematic Vision," 87. On the development of the shot/reverse-shot schema in early Vitagraph films, see Spadoni, "The Figure Seen from the Rear," and Thompson, "Narration Early in the Transition."

24. Such protoclassical techniques and their characterological outcomes consolidate the effects of earlier innovations of cinematic syntax, such as those of the chase film, and their "collusion," as Mary Ann Doane puts it, with the norms of an emergent heterosexuality: see *Emergence of Cinematic Time*, 192.

25. Keil, *Early American Cinema in Transition*, 90.

26. Trahair, "Figural Vision," 185, original emphases.

27. Branigan, *Narrative Comprehension and Film*, 18.

28. Somerville argues that the removal of the novel's dime museum scenes was consonant with Vitagraph's broader strategy to appeal to middle-class audiences, distancing its film products from earlier forms of lower-class entertainment: see Somerville, *Queering the Color Line*, 58.

29. On the American dime museum and freak show, and the bearded lady attraction, see Adams, *Sideshow U.S.A.*; Bogdan, *Freak Show*; and Dennett, *Weird and Wonderful*.

30. Sears, "Electric Brilliancy," 182.

31. Ibid., 182.

32. Burch, *Life to Those Shadows*, 154.

33. In her survey of reviews, Somerville notes that a few registered "contempt toward the transvestite performances": see Somerville, "Queer Career of Jim Crow," 260. Horak concludes that for most film critics the cross-dressing in the film was "more strongly connected to old-fashioned entertainment than to deviant identities": *Girls Will Be Boys*, 99.

34. Perhaps because of the combination of its vituperative tone and likely influence, the most cited review is the one published by the trade journal *Variety*. After describing the film's comedy as "a weary, dreary, listless collection of foolish things," the reviewer criticizes Storey's performance as "not so much a man in this instance as just mannish": Sime, "Florida Enchantment," *Variety*, August 14, 1914, 21. The terse segue from "man" to "mannish" implies that the credibility of Storey's impersonation is marred by a visually legible sex/gender dissonance—that is, she is readable as a woman who displays what are regarded as inherently masculine features—associated in this period not only with women's challenge to and transgression of highly gendered social, economic, and political boundaries but also the possibility of "sexual perversion," in particular the sexological figure of the invert. For another example, see "Feature Film Reviews" by Hex in *New York Clipper*, August 22, 1914, 13 ("a most disagreeable theme").

35. "At Alamo No. 1," *Atlanta Constitution*, November 1, 1914, B11.

36. Alongside the reviews already mentioned in note 34, the September 1914 issue of *Motion Picture Magazine* industry gossip column, "Greenroom Jottings: Little Whisperings from Everywhere in Playerdom" noted that "After seeing 'A Florida Enchantment' a popular conception of Edith Storey will be that she is a fine, manly chap and that Sydney Drew is a sweet young thing and a perfect dear" (127). The article's arch tone and ironic observation construct an address to a more sophisticated reader attuned to the subcultural requirements of sexual passing, and the misrecognitions of "normal" folk.

37. Gunning, *D. W. Griffith and the Origins*, 114.

38. deCordova, *Picture Personalities*, 98. As Patricia White points out in respect to the later role of the supporting character in Hollywood classical cinema from the 1930s, "It is impossible to grasp the ambivalence of [the character's] narrative 'support' and the function of (lesbian) typification apart from a consideration of the star text": White, *Uninvited*, 174.

39. Attuned to the sexual implications of gender, Somerville briefly considers Bessie's "unmistakable" desires for Lillian in terms of the erasure of the same-sex desires of feminine women: Somerville, "Queer Career of Jim Crow," 268n32.

40. The scene is not played for comedy but rather for melodrama. On Vitagraph's development of restrained, more psychological styles of acting, and its exploitation of this reputation in its advertising, see Keil, *Early American Cinema in Transition*, 144–145. The coexistence of these different styles reinforced certain ideological dif-

ferences including class, different forms of "white" ethnicity, and race: see Bowser, *Transformation of Cinema 1907–1915*, 88–91. Roberta E. Pearson traces the shift from the "histrionic" to "verisimilar" style of acting in the Biograph films of 1908–1913 in *Eloquent Gestures*.

Chapter 4. Mobilizing Genre

1. As Kathryn Bond Stockton notes, more than once, both terms share the same Latin root word, *movere*, to move: see *The Queer Child*, 121, 132, 157. While Stockton's focus is the queer temporal effects of legal discourse that grapples with making sense of the relation between immediate intention (or *mens rea*) and motivation, such conceptual difficulties extend to other fields that endeavor to make intention legible.

2. The quote alludes to the Ziegfeld Follies, the famous Broadway revue that ran from 1907 to 1931 in New York: see "The Wild Party," *Times*, April 1, 1929. This and subsequent reviews (unless otherwise noted) are collected in the Dorothy Arzner Scrapbook, Performing Arts Special Collections, University of California, Los Angeles.

3. Theaters in smaller towns and rural areas played the silent version of the film: see Stenn, *Clara Bow*, 162. The sound version is available to view at the UCLA Film & Television Archive. For the silent version's inter-titles, see the export script in the Paramount production file, Special Collections, Margaret Herrick Library, Los Angeles.

4. On diminishing opportunities for women and the masculinization of the Hollywood film industry by the 1920s, see Mahar, *Women Filmmakers in Early Hollywood*.

5. This understanding of Arzner's career draws on the considerable body of feminist scholarship devoted to recuperating the once-forgotten Hollywood director. Arzner's rediscovered oeuvre, shown at various forums, including women's film festivals and archive-curated programmes from the 1960s onward, provoked a sustained attention from feminist critics who discerned in her work the possibility of a feminine discourse that exposed, and disrupted, the dominant patriarchal ideologies of classical Hollywood cinema. See the essays collected in Penley, *Feminism and Film Theory*, and Wallace's astute summary of them in "Dorothy Arzner's *Wife*," 392–393.

6. R. W. Jr., "The Wild Party," *Herald-Tribune (New York)*, April 2, 1929; Joe Bigelow, "The Wild Party (Dialog)," *Variety*, April 3, 1929; Irene Thirer, "Clara Proved Just Wild Enough in Rialto's New Film Yesterday," *News (New York)*, April 1, 1929.

7. For key works on the flapper genre in film studies, see Higashi, *Virgins, Vamps and Flappers*, 110–131; Rosen, *Popcorn Venus*, 73–94; Ryan, "The Projection of a New Womanhood," 113–130.

8. Chauncey, "From Sexual Inversion to Homosexuality," 144.

9. For a compact summary of the flapper generic narrative, see Studlar, "Perils of Pleasure?" 20.

10. Ryan, "Projection of a New Womanhood," 116.

11. Landay, "Flapper Film," 234. Landay draws on dance scholar Susan Manning's historical argument that middle-class women's experience of Delsartian dance classes

and aesthetic gymnastics led them to identify more intensely with the movements of women performers on stage: see Manning, "Female Dancer and the Male Gaze," 162–163. Manning makes an important distinction between the representation of feminine types in modern dance and spectators' kinesthetic identification with the movements of dancers, a distinction that implicitly suggests the possibility of a degree of disidentification with the former.

12. Landay, "Flapper Film," 223.

13. On the evidence for women's film-going, and the Hollywood industry's assumptions about the predominance of women in film audiences, see the one-off surveys and reports discussed by Koszarski, *Evening's Entertainment*, 30.

14. Program note for a retrospective screening of *The Wild Party* by William K. Everson, cited by Weiss, *Vampires and Violets*, 14 and 167n17. Although the review is undated, it was almost certainly written for the short-lived weekly film screening series "Paris Pitt Presents," held at the Trans-Lux Cinema on 85th Street, New York, during 1966. For more information on the William K. Everson Collection held at George Amberg Memorial Film Study Center, Department of Cinema Studies, Tisch School of the Arts, New York University, see https://www.nyu.edu/projects/wke/ (accessed February 28, 2012).

15. Morgan choreographed dance and other scenes in four earlier Arzner films: a fashion show in *Fashions for Women* (1927), dance scenes in *Ten Modern Commandments* (1927) and *Manhattan Cocktail* (1928), and a waxwork tableau in *Get Your Man* (1927). On her work and longtime relationship with Arzner, see Mayne, *Directed by Dorothy Arzner*, 40–45.

16. White, *Uninvited*, xix, citing Laura Mulvey's well-known phrase from "Visual Pleasure and Narrative Cinema," reprinted in *Sexual Subject*, 22–34.

17. That the film's flappers are rendered briefly in silhouette, as dark black shapes with clothing suggestive of grass skirts, suggests how the discursive figure of the white feminine flapper masks the racial ideologies that partly enable her. One of the explicit thematics threaded through the film's story is a certain popular sense of primitivism associated with African American jazz music and new popular dances of the 1920s, which becomes linked to modern heterosexual desires. Gil's anthropological interest in certain ethnic tribes in exotic countries, for example, is a diegetic detail that allows Gil and Stella to call each other "my little savage."

18. This scene survives in the only remaining reel of the film held by the Library of Congress, Washington, D.C. For a compact summary of the flapper generic narrative, see Studlar, "Perils of Pleasure?" 20.

19. He writes that "she lives only to *consume*": Pumphrey, "Flapper, the Housewife," 186, original emphasis.

20. For a notable international project, see *The Modern Girl Around the World: Consumption, Modernity, and Globalization*, ed. The Modern Girl Around the World Research Group, Alys Eve Weinbaum, Lynn M. Thomas, Priti Ramamurthy, Uta G. Polger, Madeleine Yue Dong (Durham: Duke University Press, 2008).

21. See for example: Cynthia Felando, "Clara Bow Is *It*," in *Film Stars: Hollywood*

and Beyond, ed. Andrew Willis (Manchester: Manchester University Press, 2004), 8–24; Landay, "Flapper Film," 221–248; Ross, "Good Little Bad Girls."

22. Landay, "Flapper Film," 231.

23. Schwartz, "Torque," 85–86. As Schwartz notes, pioneer of modern dance Ruth St. Denis could write in a 1932 article for the *Journal of Health and Physical Education* that "there must be a close relation between motion and emotion; that failure or inhibition of movement, especially of movements which (so to speak) answer the call of the muscle for action, bespeaks decadence."

24. Hollander, *Seeing through Clothes*, 332.

25. Ibid., 153.

26. The most cited historical account of the emergence of these social dances in Black communities of the American South, and their popularization for white audiences via all-Black musical shows, is still that by Stearns and Stearns in *Jazz Dance*, 111–114. On the "magical purification" of the African American origins of one such dance, the Charleston, see aspects of the compelling study by Amy Koritz, *Culture Makers*, 64–85, 84.

27. This gesture became "the primary defining movement of the dance": Cohen-Stratyner, "A Thousand Raggy, Draggy Dances," 223.

28. Kendall, *Where She Danced*, 195. While Kendall is writing at a moment in dance studies before the turn toward more explicit theorizations of dance and its vernacular forms, her account remains one of the more succinct descriptions of the signature movements of 1920s social dances whose movements are often difficult to describe.

29. Cohen-Stratyner, "A Thousand Raggy, Draggy Dances," 222.

30. Stearns and Stearns, *Jazz Dance*, 112.

31. Even an account as brief as this one raises significant theoretical issues concerning the relation between choreographies of gender and sexuality, and their performance: see, for example, Foster, "Choreographies of Gender," 1–33.

32. Moral discourse registered this new mobility and its potential for both expressing and generating socially unsanctioned forms of eroticism and desire. As one commentator observed, rather hysterically, "The rhythm of the jazz age has infected our sex life. . . . The modern mad quest for stimulation is driving men and women into the arms of abnormality": S. D. Schmalhausen, "The Freudian Emphasis on Sex," in *The Sex Problem in Modern Society*, ed. John Francis McDermott (New York: Modern Library, 1931), 64, quoted in Simmons, "Companionate Marriage and the Lesbian Threat," 56. Such discourses had been developing since the early 1920s in relation to various styles of jazz dance: see Koritz, *Culture Makers*, 70–73, 75–76, 82–83.

33. For a discussion of the institutional connections between modern dance and the Hollywood film industry in the 1910s and 1920s, see Franklin, "The Terpsichorean Tramp," 58–59. On dance as a primary signifier of modern femininity (the others being smoking and "unladylike comportment"), see Landay, "Flapper Film," 233.

34. Comolli, "Machines of the Visible," 743.

35. The proposed rerelease of *The Wild Party* by Paramount in 1938 suggests that

its homoeroticism had sustained if not renewed appeal. The Production Code Administration office required further cuts to the film, however, and the request for a rerelease was eventually canceled. See the Motion Picture Producers & Distributors of America—Production Code Administration file, Special Collections, Margaret Herrick Library, Los Angeles.

36. The Tiller Girls were a well-known British precision dance troupe active from the late nineteenth century and brought to critical attention by Siegfried Kracauer's use of them as a "historico-philosophical allegory" for Fordist mass culture in his essay, "The Mass Ornament": see Hansen, "America, Paris, the Alps," 374–375; see also the translated extract from an earlier review by Kracauer of a Tiller Girls performance at 371.

37. Judith Mayne argues that the scene (particularly together with the following roadhouse scene) can be read two opposing ways, "as a repression of sexuality, or, conversely, as a refusal of stereotypical associations of women with sexual objectification": Mayne, *Directed by Dorothy Arzner*, 135. Reading the film in terms of its kinesthetic imagery suggests how its same-sex erotics might inflect both of those possible interpretations.

38. Fuss, "Fashion and the Homospectatorial Look," 737. In her later book, *Identification Papers*, Fuss continues to explore, across diverse aesthetic and institutional contexts, what she calls the "always-complicated" relation between desire and identification.

39. Glenn Chaffin, writing in *Photoplay Magazine* in 1925, describes Bow as the "ultra-flapper": see the epigraph in Addison, "Capitalizing Their Charms," 30.

40. Felando, "Clara Bow Is *It*," 13–15.

41. Landay, "Flapper Film," 237.

42. For an account that takes this story at face value, see Rosen, *Popcorn Venus*, 85. Biographer David Stenn gives a more detailed account of this incident, suggesting that the man involved had his own publicity agenda: see *Clara Bow*, 65–68. If Bow's hyper-heterosexuality was confirmed by this sexualized discourse, Bow often intervened to moderate it, whether through stories of her difficult childhood or her explicit disidentification with her on-screen characters. See, for example, Bow's famous tell-all interview with Adela Rogers St. Johns, described in Stenn, *Clara Bow*, 119–122.

43. Studlar, "Perils of Pleasure?" 20. See also Felando, "Clara Bow Is *It*," 17–19.

44. The expansiveness and cultural longevity of "it" is suggested by the censorship history of *Sex Madness* (Cinema Service Corp, 1938), an exploitation film produced more than a decade after the release of *It*. The film was rejected by several state censors in the United States, but Ohio approved the film subject to certain cuts, including a scene in which "one girl strokes another's arms in a suggestive manner" as she says "You do have plenty of IT." See the note to *Sex Madness* in *The American Film Institute Catalog of Motion Pictures Produced in the United States*, vol. F.3 (New York: R. R. Bowker, 1971), 1898.

45. The photograph appears in a clipping on p. 5 of the *Clara Bow Scrapbook*, Special Collections, Margaret Herrick Library, Los Angeles. It is dated in a pencil annotation as January 1929, though *Get Your Man*, also directed by Arzner, was first released in 1927.

46. Doan, *Fashioning Sapphism*, 109–110.

47. Mordaunt Hall, "The Screen," *New York Times*, April 2, 1929, 26.

48. For an earlier example of camera lens technology and film emulsion speed shaping acting styles, see Mayer, "Acting in Silent Film," 22–23.

49. The film's cinematography and editing suggests that it was shot with multiple cameras, a dominant studio shooting practice in the brief transitional sound era: see further Bordwell, "Introduction of Sound," 298–308, in Bordwell, Staiger, and Thompson, *Classical Hollywood Cinema*. As the authors note, studios and directors worked hard to maintain the elements of the classical style in these difficult transitional conditions.

50. The response of distributors to censorship cuts of *The Wild Party* in the United States also suggests the privileging of the image. As Donald Crafton describes it, the Ohio censors ordered substantial cuts, but "the Paramount exchange resisted by substituting black leader for the censored picture track and letting the sound on disc continue" so that "audiences and critics were aware that something was being withheld from them": see Crafton, *Talkies*, 467.

51. On the motility of the gesture, in contradistinction to the pose or "attitude," see Mayer, "Acting in Silent Film," 17–18.

52. This claim revises Laura Mulvey's argument concerning the gendered ideologies of Hollywood film spectatorship, that the visual presence of woman "tends to work against the development of story line, to freeze the flow of action in moments of erotic contemplation": "Visual Pleasure and Narrative Cinema," 27.

53. White, "Nazimova's Veils," 66–67. In her book *Uninvited*, White undertakes a more extensive examination of the ways in which femininity veils same-sex desire in her elaboration of "femme" films of the Production Code era. I have found her argument provocative for thinking through how *The Wild Party* may be part of the cinematic genealogy of those films.

54. For the paradigmatic discussion of suspicion and the connotation of homosexuality as it manifests in later Hollywood classical cinema under the regime of the Production Code, see Miller, "Anal *Rope*," 114–133.

Chapter 5. Looking Backward

1. My specific critical interest in Fuller's electric light dance performances, as a cultural site for thinking through the relations between visual pleasures in moving images and women's spectatorship, precludes an account of Fuller's considerable influence on a range of artistic movements, including the French Symbolists, Art Nouveau, and Futurism. The critical archive that I have assembled in this chapter only hints at the proliferation of Fuller's image across a variety of fin-de-siècle media and

object forms, from photographs, postcards, etchings, lithographs, and paintings, to decorative sculptures and table lamps. This more expansive archive attests to Fuller's international popularity, broad appeal, and canny career management—the latter task devolved in the early 1900s to her life partner Gabrielle Bloch—as well as her relation to a number of intersecting fields of visual culture, both "high" and "low."

2. Gaudreault, "Diversity of Cinematographic Connections," 10.

3. Gunning, "Loïe Fuller and the Art of Motion," 75–89.

4. Schwartz, "Cinema Spectatorship before the Apparatus." 316.

5. As André Gaudreault puts it, "Early cinema shares an essential characteristic with 'pre-cinema,' a characteristic that has only recently been reconceived in a sufficiently broad manner: its fundamental diversity. Cinematic history is too often the work of historians concerned with unity and homogeneity, searching in the hodgepodge that is early cinema for something that is not there": Gaudreault, "Diversity of Cinematographic Connections," 9.

6. More than 30 serpentine dance films were produced internationally: see the filmography compiled by Lista, *Loïe Fuller: Danseuse de la Belle Époque*, 638–642. Although most were produced between 1895 and 1902, the serpentine performance persists in early-twentieth-century film productions. The 1911 French film *Zigomar*, for example, includes a serpentine dance as diegetic interlude, performed by the dancer Esmée in the style of Fuller—tinted, and accompanied by a special musical score: see Abel, *Ciné Goes to Town*, 359.

7. Later in the 1920s, Fuller and her life partner and manager Gabrielle Bloch (under the stage name Gab Sorère) did make three films together: *Le Lys de la vie* (1921), *Visions des rêves* (1924), and *Les Incertitudes de Coppélius* (1927): see the discussion of these films in Garelick, *Electric Salome*, 56–62, 140.

8. The evidence is contradictory. Rhonda Garelick suggests that Fuller turned down an invitation from Thomas Edison to be filmed at his Black Maria studio in the mid-1890s: see Garelick, *Electric Salome*, 39. Elizabeth Coffman suggests that Fuller did perform for Edison's camera, but in a film attributed to another dancer, *Crissie Sheridan* (Edison, United States, 1897): see Coffman, "Women in Motion," 101n37. Giovanni Lista believes that no films featuring Loïe Fuller herself have been found: see the account of Lista's view in Brannigan, "La Loïe as Pre-cinematic Performance," n12. On the considerable back-and-forth movement of performers between the stage and screen, as both embodied and virtual performers, see Musser, "May Irwin Kiss," 111.

9. Giovanni Lista has traced several such titles, including *Loïe Fuller* (1898) and *La Danse Loïe Fuller* (1903): Lista, *Loïe Fuller*, 639, 641. Alison McMahan notes that a number of the earliest dance films in the Gaumont catalog from 1897 and 1898 are described as "danse genre Loie Fuller": McMahan, *Alice Guy Blaché*, 211, 300–301.

10. Guido, "Between Paradoxical Spectacles and Technical Dispositives," 263–265.

11. American dancer Jody Sperling and German choreographer Brygida Ochaim are notable for their recent recreations of Fuller's dances: see Garelick, *Electric Salome*, 224–227, and the Fuller biopic *La danseuse* (dir. Stéphanie Di Giusto, France, 2016). Although rendered in black and white, the most convincing imitation of Fuller

that I have viewed is *Serpentine Dance* aka *Danse Serpentine* (dir. Alice Guy Blaché, Gaumont, France, 1900), held at the BFI National Archive in London. The lightweight, silklike quality of the costume, the extended length and bamboolike flex of the concealed rods that support it, together with the dancer's physical resemblance to Fuller, blend into a superb serpentine performance.

12. This short film is digitally archived on the DVD, *The Lumière Brothers' First Films* (New York: Kino on Video, 1998). There are two versions of this film, one of which "remakes" the first by juxtaposing end to end two copies of the same performance: see Gaudreault, Lamotte, and Barnard, "Fragmentation and Segmentation," 129n4.

13. See the excellent discussion of the history of color in early cinema, in particular its association with femininity and eroticism, and color's amplification of the "gendered and generic erotics of early dance films," in Joshua Yumibe, *Moving Color*, 49–58.

14. Mayne, *Woman at the Keyhole*, 161–163.

15. See McMahan, *Alice Guy Blaché*, 211–212. In Austria in 1898, an erotic film program promoted by Josef Stiller included the film *Loïe Fuller Serpentintänzerin*: see Achenbach and Canappele, "Born under the Sign of Saturn," 129.

16. See the various advertisements and articles in provincial and city newspapers such as *Thames Star*, *Hawke's Bay Herald*, *Evening Post*, and *Otago Daily Times*, from 1897. Unless otherwise noted, newspaper articles and advertisements are accessible through the ProQuest Historical Newspapers full-image digital archive.

17. See Albright, *Traces of Light*, 117, and Current and Current, *Loie Fuller*, 72–74.

18. The following reviews indicate the range and difference of this discourse: "[Untitled]," *Taranaki Herald*, November 21, 1898, 2 ("more a matter of posing than of dancing properly so-called"); "Foreign," *Star*, October 28, 1893, 2 ("not a dancer in the strict meaning of the word"); D. F., "Some Gossip from Paris," *New York Times*, January 22, 1893, 2 ("the exquisite posing is something more original"). While I call these "reviews," and use this term throughout the chapter, the writing on Fuller in the late nineteenth and early twentieth centuries comprises a diverse body of descriptive and critical writing from which the genre of the dance review emerged: see Doran, "Figuring Modern Dance," 25–26.

19. Elizabeth Coffman discusses in detail the links between new forms of physical culture for women and Fuller's dance forms: Coffman, "Women in Motion," 79–84.

20. See, for example, J. O., "Loie and Her Dance," *Atlanta Constitution*, February 28, 1892, 5; "Theatrical and Musical Notes," *Otago Witness*, November 17, 1892, 35.

21. See Fellom, "Skirt Dance," 605; and Hindson, *Female Performance Practice*, 71–73. There is also evidence that Fuller's dance assemblage drew on the conventions of *Nautch dancing*, a term that referred both to dances performed by touring Indian troupes, and those dance styles as they were adapted to Orientalist stage shows: see Kraut, "White Womanhood, Property Rights," 11–12.

22. Carl Van Vechten, "Terpsichorean Souvenirs," *Dance Magazine*, January 1957, 16, quoted by Garelick, *Electric Salome*, 28.

23. Review of Fuller's performance in Boston, United States, in 1896, quoted in Albright, *Traces of Light*, 23.

24. On the techniques of 1870s stagecraft that likely influenced Fuller's dance innovations, see Sommer, "Loie Fuller," 90–91.

25. On Fuller's screened images and projections, see Garelick, *Electric Salome*, 52–54.

26. The latter connects Fuller's innovations to a broader history of the virtual gaze and nineteenth-century forms of visual spectacle, such as the panorama and photography: see Friedberg, *Window Shopping*.

27. See Tom Gunning's discussion of this element of Fuller's shows and his references to a contemporary review and a cartoon that depict latecomers having to light matches in order to find their seats: Gunning, "Loïe Fuller and the Art of Motion," 85–86, 89n39.

28. Schivelbusch, *Disenchanted Night*, 217.

29. McCarren, *Dance Pathologies*, 157.

30. Mallarmé's short essay on Fuller, "Autre études de danse: les fonds dans le ballet," *Oeuvres complètes de Stéphane Mallarmé* (Paris: Editions Gallimard, 1951), 307–309, has exercised considerable influence on her critical reception.

31. *New York Spirit of the Times*, January 12, 1892, quoted in Current and Current, *Loie Fuller*, 35, 356n13.

32. These associations were only reinforced by Fuller's use of electricity, a form of energy regarded as both a modern and life-sustaining force. On the utopian and salvational meanings of electricity at the fin de siècle, see, for example, Schivelbusch, "The Force," 57–61. Fuller became widely known as "the electric fairy": see Albright, *Traces of Light*, 92.

33. Gunning, "Attraction of Motion," 166. See also Gunning, "Loïe Fuller and the Art of Motion," 86–87.

34. Gunning, "Loïe Fuller and the Art of Motion," 84. Gunning's argument is part of a larger, and well-established, critical perspective on the gendered dimensions of modernity. Mary Ann Doane traces the implications of this gendered discourse in relation to the representation of the body and spectatorship in "Technology's Body," 530–551.

35. Gunning, "Loïe Fuller and the Art of Motion," 84.

36. Latimer, "Loïe Fuller," 86. Latimer's point about the enumerability of Fuller's body alludes to her mirror dance in which audience members viewed several mirror reflections of Fuller's dance on stage.

37. Ibid.

38. Quoted by Townsend, "Alchemic Visions and Technological Advances," 75.

39. Garelick, "Setting the Air on Fire," 200. Julie Townsend's interpretation of Fuller's performances in terms of their visualization of female genitalia, which for Townsend suggests "a kind of searching for, or researching of, an artistic identity that had implications for sexual identity," arguably takes the impulse to absent the

lesbian body to its other extreme: see Townsend, "Alchemic Visions and Technological Advances," 84, 94.

40. Albright, *Traces of Light*, 141. She notes later, again, that she "never self-identified as a lesbian" (142). Sally Banes also glosses the public/private nature of Fuller's sexuality by describing her as "an openly identified lesbian": Banes, *Dancing Women*, 74. The grammatically passive construction renders the terms of this identificatory process quite ambiguous.

41. Garelick, *Electric Salome*, 4.

42. Albright, *Traces of Light*, 118.

43. These processes occurred during Fuller's lifetime. The historical constitution of female homosexuality by the 1920s as a connotative textual effect is exemplified by Isadora Duncan's account of a tour early in her career with Fuller and her troupe, and Fuller's response on hearing of the content of the manuscript through some friends and journalists. In her memoir, Duncan alludes to the lack of scandal associated with Fuller, before describing a group of young women "stroking [Fuller's] hands and kissing her," and noting how she was "taken aback by coming upon this extreme attitude of expressed affection"; a couple of pages later she describes Gabrielle Bloch as "a strange figure in a black tailor-made" whose "enthusiasm for Loie Fuller possessed her entire emotional force": see Duncan, *My Life*, 94–95, 96. According to her autobiographers, Fuller engaged a lawyer to try and prevent the publication of Duncan's memoir: see Current and Current, *Loie Fuller*, 328–329. There is no evidence that publication of *My Life* caused a scandal, unlike the publication in the same year of Radclyffe Hall's *The Well of Loneliness*, perhaps because the register in which Duncan writes is one of female intimacy and friendship, rather than female masculinity or sexual inversion. Though Fuller's reaction needs to be read in the context of her competitive relation with Duncan, her concern suggests how, by the 1920s, such passages could be read in quite phobic terms, in a way that could be potentially damaging to Fuller's reputation.

44. See Garelick, *Electric Salome*, 4. See also Coleman, "Electric Fairy," 325–326.

45. In Fuller's 1913 memoir she describes how she came to create her performance as a result of being asked to improvise a hypnosis scene for *Quack M.D.*, a play in which she took the lead role: see Fuller, *Fifteen Years of a Dancer's Life*, 25–32.

46. While some critics fault Fuller as a notoriously unreliable narrator, Catherine Hindson argues that Fuller was not only adept at playing the media, but made strategic use of the conventions associated with contemporary constructions of female celebrity: Hindson, *Female Performance Practice*, 129–132.

47. On the immense popularity of hypnosis in literature at the end of the nineteenth century, see Thurschwell, *Literature, Technology and Magical Thinking*, 37.

48. Debora Silverman argues that one of the key meanings of Fuller's dance in French culture was its articulation in physical motion of the experience of ideodynamism, that is, the notion that ideas can be implanted in a person's mind and materialized in their unconscious acts: Silverman, *Art Nouveau in Fin-de-Siècle France*, 300.

49. While ostensibly a cure for mental illness, hypnosis was employed—most notoriously and publicly by Jean-Martin Charcot at the Saltpêtrière Hospital in Paris—to demonstrate and dramatize the symptoms of hysteria. George Didi-Huberman argues that for Charcot hypnosis became not only a conceptual paradigm but a model for hysteria: Didi-Huberman, *Invention of Hysteria*, 184–185. Yet, hypnosis and its associations with hysteria were contingent and contested. Experiments by another French doctor, Hippolyte Berheim, suggested that the ability to be hypnotized was not a sign of pathology or abnormality but rather characteristic of all human subjects: see the extended discussion of the French "psychologie nouvelle" in Silverman, *Art Nouveau in Fin-de-Siècle France*, 83–91.

50. Foucault, *History of Sexuality*, 55.

51. Ibid., 56.

52. "London Chat," *Wanganui Chronicle*, January 17, 1894, 2. The article purports to be from a special correspondent though it seems the story has been syndicated, since it also appears in other publications, including "Chit-Chat," *Taranaki Herald*, January 19, 1894, 2; and "London Chat," *Otago Daily Times*, January 20, 1894, 5. Accounts of Fuller's connection to her "husband," William Hayes, differ as to whether it was in fact a legal marriage or only a financial arrangement: see, for example, Current and Current, *Loie Fuller*, 24–26, 36–40; and Garelick, *Electric Salome*, 27.

53. See Gunning, "Loïe Fuller and the Art of Motion," 84. Gunning also cites the study of Fuller by Lista who draws attention to her family's spiritualist background and their interest in mesmerism: *Danseuse de la Belle Époque*, 89n30.

54. On Fuller as magician or wizard, see Catherine Hindson, "Female Illusionist—Loïe Fuller," 161–174.

55. As Diana Fuss notes, mesmerism is one of the central Romantic tropes in the nineteenth and twentieth centuries for figuring lesbian desire: Fuss, *Identification Papers*, 127–128. See also Felicia McCarren's reading of Fuller's use of hypnosis and electricity as culturally familiar practices and technologies that enable the dancer to enact multiple artistic and performative identities: McCarren, *Dance Pathologies*, 154–159.

56. See Plates 187–189, "Dancing (fancy)" in Eadweard Muybridge, *Muybridge's Complete Human and Animal Locomotion*.

57. Nancy Mowll Mathews, "The Body in Motion," in *Moving Pictures: American Art and Early Film 1880–1910*, ed. Nancy Mowll Mathews (Manchester, Vt.: Hudson Hills Press, 2005), 79, 82. Mathews refers to "the premiere danseuse of a Philadelphia theatre," citing Robert Bartlett Haas, *Muybridge: Man in Motion* (Berkeley: University of California Press, 1976), 149.

58. A similar approach can be seen in Muybridge's photographic studies of two naked women together, always scenarios in which care has been taken to establish some external motivation for their movements in the scene, whether everyday narratives (Plate 444 "Two women shaking hands and kissing each other") or scenes that draw on the iconographies of classical painting (Plate 453 "Woman kneels and drinks from the water jar of another woman and both walk off").

59. Williams, "Film Body," 508, original emphasis.

60. Williams, *Hard Core*, 35–36. Chapter 2 of *Hard Core*, "Prehistory: The 'Frenzy of the Visible,'" is a revision and extension of Williams's argument in "Film Body" in relation to early film pornography.

61. The photograph is part of a group of thirteen photographs in a collection housed in the Metropolitan Museum of Art, New York.

62. Hansen, *Babel and Babylon*, 36.

63. See Apter, "Acting Out Orientalism," 15–34.

64. J. O., "Loie and Her Dance," *Atlanta Constitution*, February 28, 1892, 5.

65. Many female spectators would have been already familiar with some of the conventions of the skirt dance reworked by Fuller, and with the physical vocabulary of her dance moves borrowed from physical culture. On the 1890s skirt dance craze, one that brought the form "into the classroom and the domestic space," see Hindson, "Interruptions by Inevitable Petticoats," 48–64.

66. As Amy Koritz notes, transformations in the class status of dancers and their performances were a precondition for establishing certain forms of dance as art forms rather than popular entertainments: see Koritz, *Gendering Bodies / Performing Art*, 6–7.

67. For a biographical account of this season, and Fuller's popular and critical reception, see Current and Current, *Loie Fuller*, 46–58.

68. See, for example, the reviews quoted in ibid.

69. Reviewer quoted by Garelick, *Electric Salome*, 33.

70. A February 1893 review quoted in Current and Current, *Loie Fuller*, 53, 357n12. This review, slightly misquoted by Current and Current but in a way that does not affect its meaning, was syndicated across several other national English-language newspapers in 1893.

71. Fuller, *Fifteen Years of a Dancer's Life*, 169–170.

72. Albright draws attention to the anecdote for how "it reveals Fuller's awareness of and responses to a markedly voyeuristic gaze," though she cautions that she explicitly refrains from "projecting too much into the situation": Albright, *Traces of Light*, 119. Felicia McCarren highlights this same anecdote in relation to an argument about Fuller's use of electricity and its relation to her identity as a performer: McCarren, *Dance Pathologies*, 158–159.

73. Fuller was no doubt aware of the potentially dangerous consequences of such scrutiny as they manifested in the trials of Oscar Wilde. For further context on the timing of the performance of a Fuller dance inspired by Wilde's *Salomé*, see Farfan, *Performing Queer Modernism*, 29–30.

74. A significant contemporary discourse emphasized the difference between Fuller's ordinary body—various critics and friends described her as "plump," "badly dressed," and "myopic"—and her extraordinary performances, underscoring the scale of her technical ability and artistic accomplishments. For a representative sample of such descriptions, see Garelick, *Rising Star*, 100–101.

75. Such co-present modes of viewing are remarkably similar to two styles of visuality first theorized by the art historian Alöis Riegl at the turn of the twentieth

century, the haptical and the optical. Simply put, the haptical describes a visual style invested in surface, flatness, and the textural or decorative. The optical, in contrast, articulates a ground and figures distinct from it in order to establish the illusion of spatial depth and individuated subjects. In her theoretical extension of the former concept in relation to alternative video and avant-garde films, Laura U. Marks argues that "haptic images . . . make viewers unsure of their relationship to the image and the knowledge it implies": see Marks, *Skin of the Film*, 177. The epistemological uncertainty sustained by haptical modes of visuality is particularly suggestive in relation to the abstract elements of Fuller's performances, given their historical coincidence with new visual epistemologies of sexuality.

76. Here I am deliberately alluding to Patricia White's notion of retrospectatorship: see *Uninvited*, 197.

77. Phelan, "'I Never See You as You Are,'" 418. Fuller writes about her relationship with Gabrielle Bloch in Chapter 22 of her memoir: Fuller, *Fifteen Years of a Dancer's Life*, 250–266.

78. Fuller, *Fifteen Years of a Dancer's Life*, 263–265.

79. Ibid., 266.

80. Phelan, "'I Never See You as You Are,'" 418. Patrizia Veroli also discusses Phelan's suggestive reading of Fuller's memoir in the context of the fragmentary archival texts that attest to Bloch and Fuller's relationship, considering, more specifically, Bloch's place in how Fuller perceived herself and her performances: see Veroli, *Loie Fuller*, 256–258. My thanks to Laurence Simmons for assisting me with the Italian translation of this passage.

Chapter 6. Valentino's Lesbianism

1. See, in particular, the work of Hansen, *Babel and Babylon*, 245–294. Hansen's work is based on her earlier essay, "Pleasure, Ambivalence, Identification," 6–32. Gaylyn Studlar has also developed a significant body of work on Valentino's stardom, though her approach and claims differ in some significant respects from Hansen's: see Studlar, "Dialogue," 51–53; Studlar, "Discourses of Gender and Ethnicity," 18–35; Studlar, "Valentino, 'Optic Intoxication,' and Dance Madness," 23–45. The latter essay appears in revised form in Studlar, *This Mad Masquerade*, 150–198. For a recent recuperation of another significant sexual element of Valentino's star persona—his association with Elinor Glyn's female- and pleasure-centered sexual philosophy—see Horak, "'Would You Like to Sin?'" 85–90.

2. Hansen, *Babel and Babylon*, 254. For an example of a newspaper report that manages to mock in a lighthearted tone both Valentino's fans and his masculinity, while functioning as publicity for a Valentino dance show, see "Rudolph Runs as Women Fans Surge in Lobby," *Los Angeles Times*, February 23, 1923, II10.

3. See the chapter entitled "Rudy's Rep" (106–115) in the 1975 English edition of *Hollywood Babylon* published by Straight Arrow Books in San Francisco. The "labyrinthine" history of the publication and revision of *Hollywood Babylon*—a multivolume text and work in progress—is recounted by Tinkcom in *Working like a Homosexual*, 211n37. Framing Anger's *Hollywood Babylon* volumes or "Holy Babies" as insightful

"camp and queer male fan textual production[s] of Hollywood history," Tinkcom argues that Anger's work should not be read literally but rather in light of practices of sharing and reading gossip: *Working like a Homosexual*, 140–153.

4. Anderson, *Twilight of the Idols*, 70–126. As part of his argument for revaluing Valentino's queer stardom, Anderson undertakes an important rereading of the famous "Pink Powder Puffs" editorial published in the *Chicago Sunday Tribune*, July 18, 1926, arguing that its bitchy tone and sensationalist rhetoric should be read as the means by which Valentino could be acknowledged "as an important mass cultural figure for fairies and other queers" (95). For a more obscure article early in Valentino's career that adopts similar strategies, detailing Valentino's new freedom after his first divorce to peruse his "'lady-fan' mail," and presumably take up some of the offers therein, see "Plays and Players—East and West," *Photoplay*, April 1922, 80. Richard Dyer has suggested that Valentino's gay iconicity extended beyond American borders and was a model for trends in other gay subcultures, such as the fashions of West End Berlin men for powder, lipstick, perfume, and heavily kohled eyes: see Dyer, "Less and More than Women and Men," 22.

5. White, *Uninvited*, 41.

6. Traub, *The Renaissance of Lesbianism*, 27. The influence of psychoanalytic fantasy theory in film studies, in particular the revisions of Freud's theories by Jean Laplanche and Jean-Bertrand Pontalis, can be traced to an article by Elizabeth Cowie, first published in the journal *m/f* in 1984 and reprinted as Cowie, "Fantasia," 149–196. See also the collection edited by James Donald, *Fantasy and the Cinema* (London: BFI Publishing, 1989).

7. For subsequent developments and critiques of fantasy theory, in particular the tendency to theorize an ahistorical mobile spectator, unanchored by any social identity or relations, see, for example, De Lauretis, *Practice of Love*, 123–130; Stacey, *Star Gazing*, 30–33. See also the account of the turn to fantasy theory in Robert Lapsley and Michael Westlake, *Film Theory: An Introduction* (Manchester: Manchester University Press, 1988), 90–95.

8. Farmer, *Spectacular Passions*, 64.

9. Jean Laplanche, and Jean-Bertrand Pontalis, "Fantasy and the Origins of Sexuality," in *Formations of Fantasy*, edited by Victor Burgin, James Donald, and Cora Kaplan (London: Methuen, 1986), 5–34.

10. Ibid., 26.

11. This insight arises in terms of the so-called primal fantasies that preexist the emergent sexual subject. For a brief but lucid account, see De Lauretis, *Practice of Love*, 82–83.

12. Laplanche and Pontalis, *Language of Psycho-Analysis*, 317. Farmer develops Laplanche and Pontalis's term as the critical theoretical foundation for his study of gay spectatorship: see, in particular, *Spectacular Passions*, 63–67.

13. Farmer, *Spectacular Passions*, 66.

14. White, *Uninvited*, 197.

15. This aspect of my argument owes its inspiration to a small body of scholarship concerned with the identifications of nineteenth-century male artists and authors

with female same-sex desire: see Morgan, "Male Lesbian Bodies," 37–57; Ladenson, *Proust's Lesbianism*; Schor, "Male Lesbianism," 391–399.

16. Anderson, *Twilight of the Idols*, 90.

17. Hansen, *Babel and Babylon*, 292.

18. Ibid., 264.

19. Ibid., 261.

20. Ibid., 285.

21. Ibid., 293.

22. For a cogent outline of the novel elements of homosexuality compared to earlier erotic formations, in particular the diminished significance of gender differences and identities, and homosexuality's registration of "sameness and mutuality," see Halperin, *How to Do the History*, 131–134.

23. Kay and Peary, "Interview with Dorothy Arzner," 155–156. See also Mayne, *Directed by Dorothy Arzner*, 25.

24. Gaines, "Of Cabbages and Authors," 99.

25. See Alexander Doty's discussion of Arzner's cross-gendered identification with the eponymous protagonist of *Christopher Strong* (1933) in *Making Things Perfectly Queer*, 22–23. Doty's specific point is that such identifications in erotic narratives can establish a "lesbian mode of expression within traditional film forms" (22).

26. DeCordova, "Emergence of the Star System in America," 26. See the more extensive history of this development in deCordova, *Picture Personalities*, 98–116.

27. For one of the more complete lists of Valentino biographies and memoirs published since 1926—over forty—see Ellenberger, *Valentino Mystique*, 216–218. The issue of Valentino's personal sexual identity has been raised again in recent years with the publication of an account of a sexual encounter with Valentino, apparently documented by Samuel M. Steward as part of his card catalog "Stud File," described in Spring, *Secret Historian*, 15–16. Thanks to Rostom Mesli who gave me the citation for Steward's brief but significant archive. Valentino scholars have disputed the accuracy of Steward's claim, based on the documented whereabouts of Valentino on the date in question: see Thomas Gladysz, "The Secret Historian and the Silent Film Star: One Was Gay," *Huffington Post*, posted August 31, 2010, http://www.huffingtonpost.com/thomas-gladysz/the-secret-historian-and-_b_700927.html (accessed February 14, 2018). Though the Valentino scholars mentioned in the Gladysz article base their arguments on the issue of reliable evidence—newspaper reports are pitted against an eclectic sexual archive—there is a sense that, in seeking to prove once and for all Valentino's heterosexual identity, such scholars disavow the fantasmatic elements of all sexual identities, affirming heterosexuality as a coherent and real sexual truth while sustaining the association of gay sexuality with a seemingly more desperate relation to the fantastic or fictional.

28. DeCordova, *Picture Personalities*, 141.

29. See Studlar, "Perils of Pleasure?" 7.

30. On the brief lesbian cameo in *The Four Horsemen of the Apocalypse*, see Horak, *Girls Will Be Boys*, 127–130. An early instance in which Valentino is visually aligned

to a queer female couple, the sequence might also be understood as deploying a visual representation of same-sex coupledom in order to guarantee the promise of heterosexual mutuality.

31. Hansen, *Babel and Babylon*, 259.

32. Ibid., 256.

33. The two main periods of Valentino's career as a film star—from 1921 to late 1922, and then from early 1924 to late 1926—are bifurcated by a significant period during which Valentino was engaged in a protracted dispute with his studio, Famous Players-Lasky (the production arm of Paramount). During this period, Valentino and his second wife Natacha Rambova embarked on a number of dance appearances, including a dance tour sponsored by the cosmetics company Mineralava, before Valentino resumed acting on the production *Monsieur Beaucaire* (dir. Sidney Olcott, Famous Players-Lasky, 1924). Even during this disruption, however, Valentino's stardom and Famous Players-Lasky's box office earnings continued to be sustained by the screenings of his earlier film productions.

34. White, "Nazimova's Veils," 78.

35. Apart from Rambova's aesthetic, the most remarkable aspect of the set design is the large arched window and door between Gautier's bedroom and the lounge of her apartment, so that the two spaces are transparent to each other.

36. See, for example, a brief notice about an upcoming screening of *Camille*: "Rudolph Valentino at the Alamo 2 Monday," *Atlanta Constitution*, February 19, 1922, C6.

37. DeCordova, *Picture Personalities*, 140.

38. In covering the trial, newspapers reported Acker's relationship to her "friend," Grace Darmond, with whom Acker had spent her wedding night. One newspaper report, featuring a large photographic portrait of Darmond, is careful to include Acker's testimony that another hotel room in which Acker and Darmond met had two beds: see "Wedded, Found Spouse Broke?" *Los Angeles Times*, November 24, 1921, II1. Thus, the contagious force of suspicion is enlisted by newspaper reports to suggest, without ever having to name, Acker and Darmond's lesbianism. Acker was also reputed to have been one of Nazimova's protégés and lovers.

39. See, for example, the newspaper headlines and reports discussed by Leider, *Dark Lover*, 213, 465.

40. Review of *Cobra* in *Graphic*, December 8, 1925, cited in Hansen, *Babel and Babylon*, 262; caption to photograph of Valentino in *Photoplay*'s regular "Rotogravure" portrait series, September 1922, 15; "Vogue of Valentino," *Motion Picture Magazine*, February 1923, 28.

41. See also Adele Rogers St. John's contemporary analysis and polemic concerning anti-Valentino discourse: "The men of America have resented Rudolph's popularity. . . . They resent it because they believe he appeals to the worst side of women, because they claim his is the same attraction for women that a vampire has for men": "What Kind of Men Attract Women Most?" *Photoplay*, March 1924, 17; quoted in Studlar, "Discourses of Gender and Ethnicity," 25. While St. John draws a direct parallel

between the erotic power of Valentino and the screen vamp, the final clause of her second sentence harbors some significant ambiguity. It can also be read as suggesting that Valentino/the ungendered vampire is attracted to men, leaving it open as to whether St. John's point is situated within a heterosexual or homosexual erotic discourse.

42. "Are Wives of Screen Lovers Jealous? " *Moving Picture Stories*, January 6, 1925, 3.

43. Studlar, "Perils of Pleasure?" 16.

44. Fan magazines tended not to cover Hollywood scandals directly but, nevertheless, as Studlar argues, they "often crucially depended upon their readership being well versed in the sensational details of the film colony's behavioral excesses": Studlar, "Perils of Pleasure?" 12.

45. See, for example, Edwin Schallert, "Actors' Benefit Dazzles," *Los Angeles Times*, October 30, 1923, II1–2; "Frisco's Film Folks' Ball Drew Heavily and Pleased," *Variety*, January 31, 1924, 18.

46. The fan magazine photographs appear with the following captions or article titles: "Natacha and Rudie!" *Photoplay*, January 1924, 67; "No—Guess Again!" *Motion Picture*, February 1924, 58; "Our Own News Reel," *Screenland*, February 1924, 62; Edwin and Elza Schallert, "Hollywood High Lights," *Picture-Play Magazine*, February 1924, 71. The imitation is subsequently referred to in Cal York, "Gossip East and West," *Photoplay*, April 1924, 74; and Myrtle Gebhart, "Hollywood's Biggest Party," *Picture-Play Magazine*, May 1924, 24.

47. Schallert, "Actors' Benefit Dazzles," II2; "Wampas will make fun over Sheik 'Roodie,'" *San Francisco Chronicle*, December 24, 1923, 3. One trade paper published a photograph of Dana as Valentino with a brief caption linking her impersonation to her latest film role: "Pictorial Section of Exhibitors' Herald," *Exhibitors' Herald*, December 22, 1923, 27.

48. The film borrowed its sexual scenario from an Ernst Lubitsch film of 1924, *Forbidden Paradise*, cowritten by *The Eagle*'s screenwriter Hans Kräly, with Agnes Christine Johnson: see Jacobs, *Decline of Sentiment*, 233–234. Jacobs argues that in its critical reception the film "managed to avoid the charges of over-seriousness and sexual timidity that had been leveled against Valentino's previous films."

49. As Lea Jacobs notes, reviewers praised the film's central comedic conceit "a Russian czarina aggressively pursuing the men in her own guard, exchanging sex for military favours": see *Decline of Sentiment*, 233.

50. The *Variety* trade review of November 11, 1925, 38–39, observed that "there is enough suggestion in the scenes with the Czarina to make money come to the box office," while noting, "Whether they will be able to get away with these scenes and what they imply in certain censor spots remains to be seen" (39).

51. One review of the film by Jimmy Starr of the Los Angeles *Record* alludes to the action in this scene while suggesting that its flavor, left tantalizingly undefined, pervades the film's other scenes: "[The *Eagle*] leaves a never-to-be-forgotten taste in

your mouth." See the snippet published in *Film Daily*, December 1, 1925, 8. Another excerpt from this review—"a rare and spicy picture"—is quoted in some of the film's publicity. See, for example, the advertisement published in the *San Bernadino Daily Sun*, November 18, 1925, 4.

52. Studlar, *This Mad Masquerade*, 176.

53. Anderson, *Twilight of the Idols*, 110, 118–124.

54. Ibid., 124.

55. "Fate" by Susan Marr Spalding (1841–1908).

56. Anderson, *Twilight of the Idols*, 121.

57. The inter-titles that I refer to are based on those in the restored version of *Moran of the Lady Letty* on the DVD set *Valentino: Rediscovering an Icon of Silent Film* (Los Angeles: Flicker Alley, 2007). The DVD back cover and the accompanying booklet both note that this version of the film restores the inter-titles from the original Paramount cutting copy.

58. In another version of *Moran of the Lady Letty*, the George Eastman House viewing copy (Rochester, N.Y.), this final line instead has Moran stating "No, nor for women either. At all events, mate, I'm not a girl. I'm just Moran of *Lady Letty*": see Anderson, *Twilight of the Idols*, 122, 195n94. Commenting on this version, Anderson notes that the inter-title seems to have been included to disclaim the lesbianism implied by Moran's previous statement, and he argues that it "does absolutely nothing to normalize her sexuality or her gender identity" (122). Moran, in this version of the film's dialogue, demonstrates David M. Halperin's point that sexual inversion was defined as a "psychological orientation without a sexuality"; in other words, the category of inversion did not depend on any sexual act or behavior: Halperin, *How to Do the History*, 129.

59. There remains, nevertheless, a normalizing tension or undercurrent in this scene, since it is intercut with the scene of Kitchell meeting the other smuggler that includes a bit of business in which the Chinese cook, "Chopstick Charlie," imagines Moran wearing a dress and then proceeds to buy a dress from a young woman enslaved to the Mexican smuggler Poncho.

60. Though he does not attend to Valentino's lesbianism, Anderson makes a similar claim, drawing on Alexander Doty's work in *Making Things Perfectly Queer*, that "the star's involvement in the production of queer meaning does not entail that there must be an assignment of a recognizable queer identity to any particular person, including Valentino himself, though this might and undoubtedly did happen quite often": Anderson, *Twilight of the Idols*, 82.

61. Williams, *Marxism and Literature*, 128–135.

62. Studlar, "Perils of Pleasure?" 7.

63. Ibid., 10.

64. Valentino memorabilia is highly collectable and I have been unable to locate the *Screenland* cover in a United States public library or archive. The March issue is not part of the online collection available through the Media History Digital

Library. This scanned cover from a magazine held in a private collection is reproduced from an online amateur database: see http://www.moviemags.com/main.php?title=SCREENLAND&year=1923 (accessed February 14, 2018).

65. *Motion Picture*'s main competitor was *Photoplay*: Slide, *Inside the Hollywood Fan Magazine*, 27.

66. The composition of "The Valentinos"—their mapping onto one another—echoes the iconography of a photographic portrait of the couple taken by James Abbe in 1922 but not widely published until 1923: see Pepper, *Limelight*, 21, 65. The portrait is reproduced in many Valentino-focused books and biographies: see, for example, Anger, *Hollywood Babylon*, 110–111; and Leider, *Dark Lover*, in the plates between 210–211. Hansen reads the Abbe portrait as emblematic of Valentino's "incestuous-narcissistic aura": Hansen, *Babel and Babylon*, 364n32.

67. The image draws on the same costuming, but alters the composition to bring their faces closer together, of a double profile portrait of Valentino and Rambova taken by Russell Ball, circa 1922: see the plate reproduction in Rambova, *Rudy*, facing page 92.

68. Comparing the double portraits of the Valentinos to another series of images featuring the couple underlines the different queer sensibilities within which their erotic identities could be made intelligible. The most well-known of this photographic series depicts a bare-chested Valentino in profile playing a flute, wearing only a discreet black jockstrap with his legs painted in large swaths of black and white, an homage to the Russian dancer Vaslav Nijinsky, the lead male dancer and choreographer of the Diaghilev-Ballets Russes, and his role in the 1913 production of *L'après midi d'un faune*. While the photographic series was never published in its entirety, the faun photograph was published in the August 1923 issue of *Shadowland: Expressing the Arts*, a short-lived arts and culture magazine, suggesting an attempt to capitalize on the photograph's notoriety (it had been produced as evidence in Valentino's divorce trial) as well as to enlist its direct citation of Nijinsky, and his European aesthetic, in shaping Valentino's gay image (the pages are missing from the most accessible online copy in the Media History Digital Library). The knowledge that Rambova appeared in the other unpublished photographs in the series suggests the possibility that her participation was designed to act as a visual citation of Nijinsky's stage partner, Ida Rubenstein, not only in reference to her relation to Nijinsky as coperformer but as his female equivalent in a homosexual visual and performance aesthetic: see the critical recuperation of both Ida Rubenstein's and Nijinsky's public personas and their lesbian and gay dimensions in Moon, "Flaming Closets," 19–30.

69. Castle, *Noël Coward & Radclyffe Hall*, 27. My thanks to Heather Love for drawing my attention to Castle's small but perfectly formed book. The style of this image also has significant parallels with the queer visual style that Christopher Reed identifies in the pages of 1920s British *Vogue*, one that "delights in destabilizing institutionally sanctioned hierarchies": see Reed, "Design for (Queer) Living," 377–403.

70. Sedgwick, *Epistemology of the Closet*, 159. Sedgwick tucks away in a footnote her equally audacious claim that homosexual discourse "posed a radical question

to cross-gender relations and, in turn, to gender definition itself. For the first time since at least the Renaissance, there existed the potential for a discourse in which a man's desire for a woman could not guarantee his difference from her—in which it might even, rather, suggest his likeness to her": 159n34.

71. While a number of trade and fan magazines are increasingly being made available online, through well-resourced initiatives such as the Media History Digital Library (mediahistoryproject.org), this particular cover image is sourced from a fan website: http://thesilentmovieblog.files.wordpress.com/2010/12/12–23-mw-08–11–23-cover.jpg (accessed July 23, 2014). The photograph is by James Abbe. It appears in an earlier fan magazine issue, on page 20 of the June 1923 issue of *Motion Picture*, illustrating the article "We Discover Who Discovered Valentino," by Gladys Hall and Adele Whitely Fletcher.

Coda

1. Any Internet search should reveal that the clip has been made available as a streaming video file by a number of YouTube users. Several online news articles and blogs include embedded clips, and someone has even converted it to a gif. I do not include URLs or dates of access since, across the lifetime of this book, they will no doubt disappear and reappear in forms that I cannot quite yet imagine.

2. When taken out of context, viewers may not realize that he is the film's central character, Jack Powell (played by Charles Rogers). In terms of the history of cinema and its representations of same-sex desire, the film is more notable for the passionate kiss toward the end of the film, when Jack farewells his dying friend David Armstrong (Richard Arlen).

3. Horak, *Girls Will Be Boys*, 154. As Horak later notes, the women's apparel connotes an exotic Parisian sexual identity (156).

4. Traub, "Sex Ed; Or, Teach Me Tonight," in *Thinking Sex with the Early Moderns, 320.*

Bibliography

Abel, Richard. *The Ciné Goes to Town: French Cinema, 1896–1914*. Berkeley: University of California Press, 1994.

———. "The Cinema of Attractions in France, 1896–1904." In *The Silent Cinema Reader*, edited by Lee Grieveson and Peter Krämer, 63–75. London: Routledge, 2004.

Abelove, Henry, Michèle Aina Barale, and David M. Halperin, eds. *The Lesbian and Gay Studies Reader*. New York: Routledge, 1993.

Achenbach, Michael, and Paola Canappele. "Born under the Sign of Saturn: The Erotic Origins of Cinema in the Austra-Hungarian Empire." *Griffithiana* 65 (1999): 127–139.

Adams, Rachel. *Sideshow U.S.A.: Freaks and the American Cultural Imagination*. Chicago: University of Chicago Press, 2001.

Addison, Heather. "Capitalizing Their Charms: Cinema Stars and Physical Culture in the 1920s." *Velvet Light Trap* 50 (2002): 15–35.

Agamben, Giorgio. *Infancy and History: The Destruction of Experience*, translated by Liz Heron. London: Verso, 1993.

Ahmed, Sara. *The Cultural Politics of Emotion*. Edinburgh: Edinburgh University Press, 2004.

Albright, Ann Cooper. *Traces of Light: Absence and Presence in the Work of Loïe Fuller*. Middletown, Conn.: Wesleyan University Press, 2007.

Anderson, Mark Lynn. *Twilight of the Idols: Hollywood and the Human Sciences in 1920s America*. Berkeley: University of California Press, 2011.

Anger, Kenneth. *Hollywood Babylon*. San Francisco: Straight Arrow Books, 1975.

Ankum, Katharina von, ed. *Women in the Metropolis: Gender and Modernity in Weimar Culture*. Berkeley: University of California Press, 1997.

Apter, Emily. "Acting Out Orientalism: Sapphic Theatricality in Turn-of-the-Century

Paris." In *Performance and Cultural Politics*, edited by Elin Diamond, 15–34. London: Routledge, 1996.

Arondekar, Anjali. "Without a Trace: Sexuality and the Colonial Archive." *Journal of the History of Sexuality* 14, no. 1/2 (2005): 10–27.

Auerbach, Jonathan. *Body Shots: Early Cinema's Incarnations*. Berkeley: University of California Press, 2007.

Balides, Constance. "Scenarios of Exposure in the Practice of Everyday Life: Women in the Cinema of Attractions." In *Screen Histories: A* Screen *Reader*, edited by Annette Kuhn and Jackie Stacey, 63–80. Oxford: Clarendon Press, 1998.

Banes, Sally. *Dancing Women: Female Bodies on Stage*. London: Routledge, 1998.

Bauer, Heike. "Theorizing Female Inversion: Sexology, Discipline, and Gender at the Fin de Siècle." *Journal of the History of Sexuality* 18, no. 1 (2009): 84–102.

Beachy, Robert. "The German Invention of Homosexuality." *Journal of Modern History* 82, no. 4 (2010): 801–838.

Bean, Jennifer M. "Introduction: Toward a Feminist Historiography of Early Cinema." In *A Feminist Reader in Early Cinema*, edited by Jennifer M. Bean and Diane Negra, 1–26. Durham: Duke University Press, 2002.

Bergstrom, Janet. "Sexuality at a Loss: The Films of F. W. Murnau." *Poetics Today* 6, no. 1/2 (1985): 185–203.

Berlanstein, Lenard R. "Breeches and Breaches: Cross-Dress Theatre and the Culture of Gender Ambiguity in Modern France." *Comparative Studies in Society and History* 38, no. 2 (1996): 338–369.

Berlant, Lauren. "'68, or Something." *Critical Inquiry* 21, no. 1 (1994): 124–155.

Berlant, Lauren, and Michael Warner. "Sex in Public" *Critical Inquiry* 24, no. 2 (1998): 547–566.

Blackbourn, David. "'The Horologe of Time': Periodization in History." *PMLA* 127, no. 2 (2012): 301–307.

Bogdan, Robert. *Freak Show: Presenting Human Oddities for Amusement and Profit*. Chicago: University of Chicago Press, 1988.

Bordwell, David. "Convention, Construction and Cinematic Vision." In *Post-Theory: Reconstructing Film Studies*, edited by David Bordwell and Noël Carroll, 87–107. Madison: University of Wisconsin Press, 1996.

———. *On the History of Film Style*. Cambridge: Harvard University Press, 1997.

Bordwell, David, Janet Staiger, and Kristin Thompson. *The Classical Hollywood Cinema: Film Style and Mode of Production to 1960*. New York: Columbia University Press, 1985.

Bottomore, Stephen. "Shots in the Dark: The Real Origins of Film Editing." In *Early Cinema: Space, Frame, Narrative*, edited by Thomas Elsaesser and Adam Barker, 104–113. London: British Film Institute, 1990.

Bowser, Eileen. *The Transformation of Cinema 1907–1915*, edited by Charles Harpole. Vol. 2 of *History of the American Cinema*. New York: Charles Scribner's Sons, 1990.

Branigan, Edward. *Narrative Comprehension and Film*. London: Routledge, 1992.

Brannigan, Erin. "La Loïe as Pre-cinematic Performance—Descriptive Continuity of Movement." *Senses of Cinema* 28 (2003). Accessed September 9, 2018. http://sensesofcinema.com/2003/feature-articles/la_loie/.

Brasell, R. Bruce. "A Seed for Change: The Engenderment of *A Florida Enchantment*." *Cinema Journal* 36, no. 4 (1997): 3–21.

Brewster, Ben, and Lea Jacobs. *Theatre to Cinema: Stage Pictorialism and the Early Feature Film*. Oxford: Oxford University Press, 1997.

Brim, Matt, and Amin Ghaziani, "Introduction: Queer Methods," *WSQ: Women's Studies Quarterly* 44, no. 3, 4 (2016): 14–27.

Brooks, Louise. *Lulu in Hollywood*. New York: Limelight Editions, 1989.

———. "Pabst and Lulu." *Sight and Sound* 34, no. 3 (1965): 123–127.

Brooks, Peter. *Reading for the Plot: Design and Intention in Narrative*. New York: A. A. Knopf, 1984.

Bruno, Giuliana. *Streetwalking on a Ruined Map: Cultural Theory and the City Films of Elvira Notari*. Princeton, N.J.: Princeton University Press, 1993.

Burch, Noël. *Life to Those Shadows*, translated by Ben Brewster. Berkeley: University of California Press, 1990.

Burnham, John. "From Avant-Garde to Specialism: Psychoanalysis in America." *Journal of the History of Behavioral Sciences* 15 (1979): 128–134.

———. "The Reception of Psychoanalysis in Western Cultures: An Afterword on Its Comparative History." *Comparative Studies in Society and History* 24, no. 4 (1982): 603–610.

Butler, Judith. "The Force of Fantasy." In *The Judith Butler Reader*, edited by Sara Salih, 183–203. Malden, Mass.: Blackwell Publishing, 2004.

———. *Gender Trouble: Feminism and the Subversion of Identity*. 1990. Reprint. New York: Routledge, 1999.

———. "Imitation and Gender Insubordination." In *The Lesbian and Gay Studies Reader*, edited by Henry Abelove, Michèle Aina Barale, and David M. Halperin, 307–320. New York: Routledge, 1993.

Callahan, Vicki. "Call to Action: Who Will Write History and How in the Digital Age?" Paper presented at Women and Silent Screen V, Stockholm, June 13, 2008.

Carroll, Noël. "Notes on the Sight Gag." In *Cinema/Comedy/Theory*, edited by Andrew Horton, 25–42. Berkeley: University of California Press, 1991.

Castle, Terry. *The Apparitional Lesbian: Female Homosexuality and Modern Culture*. New York: Columbia University Press, 1993.

———. *Noël Coward & Radclyffe Hall: Kindred Spirits*. New York: Columbia University Press, 1996.

Chakrabarty, Dipesh. "The Time of History and the Times of Gods." In *The Politics of Culture in the Shadow of Capital*, edited by Lisa Lowe and David Lloyd, 35–60. Durham: Duke University Press, 1997.

Charney, Leo, and Vanessa R. Schwartz, eds. *Cinema and the Invention of Modern Life*. Berkeley: University of California Press, 1995.

Chauncey, George. "From Sexual Inversion to Homosexuality: Medicine and the

Changing Conceptualization of Female Deviance." *Salmagundi* 58–59 (1983): 114–146.

———. *Gay New York: Gender, Urban Culture, and the Making of the Gay Male World 1890–1940*. New York: Basic Books, 1994.

Choquette, Leslie. "Homosexuals in the City: Representations of Lesbian and Gay Space in Nineteenth-Century Paris." *Journal of Homosexuality* 41, no. 3/4 (2002): 149–167.

Cocks, H. G. "Historiographical Review: Modernity and the Self in the History of Sexuality." *Historical Journal* 49, no. 4 (2006): 1211–1227.

Coffman, Elizabeth. "Women in Motion: Loie Fuller and the 'Interpenetration' of Art and Science." *Camera Obscura: Feminism, Culture and Media Studies* 17, no. 1 (2002): 73–104.

Cohen-Stratyner, Barbara. "'A Thousand Raggy, Draggy Dances': Social Dance in Broadway Musical Comedy in the 1920s." In *Ballroom, Boogie, Shimmy Sham, Shake: A Social and Popular Dance Reader*, edited by Julie Malnig, 217–233. Urbana: University of Illinois Press, 2009.

Coleman, Bud. "The Electric Fairy: The Woman behind the Apparition of Loie Fuller." In *Staging Desire: Queer Readings of American Theater History*, edited by Kim Marra and Robert A. Schanke, 311–337. Ann Arbor: University of Michigan Press, 2002.

Colvin, Sarah. "Frank Wedekind." In *Who's Who in Gay and Lesbian History*, edited by Robert Aldrich and Garry Wotherspoon. London: Routledge, 2001.

Comolli, Jean-Louis. "Machines of the Visible." In *Film Theory and Criticism*, edited by Gerald Mast and Marshall Cohen, 741–760. New York: Oxford University Press, 1985.

Cook, Pam. "Approaching the Work of Dorothy Arzner." In *Feminism and Film Theory*, edited by Constance Penley, 36–45. New York: Routledge, 1988.

Corzo-Duchardt, Beth. "Paper Girls: Gender and Materiality in Turn-of-the-Century Outdoor Advertising." *Feminist Media Histories* 1, no. 3 (2015): 38–65.

Coviello, Peter M. *Tomorrow's Parties: Sex and the Untimely in Nineteenth-Century America*. New York: NYU Press, 2013.

Cowie, Elizabeth. "Fantasia." In *The Woman in Question*, edited by Parveen Adams and Elizabeth Cowie, 149–196. Cambridge: MIT Press, 1990.

Crafton, Donald. *The Talkies: American Cinema's Transition to Sound, 1926–1931*, edited by Charles Harpole. Vol. 4 of History of American Cinema. Berkeley: University of California Press, 1999.

Cryle, Peter, and Christopher E. Forth, eds. *Sexuality at the Fin de Siècle: The Makings of a "Central Problem."* Newark: University of Delaware Press, 2008.

Current, Richard Nelson, and Marcia Ewing Current. *Loie Fuller: Goddess of Light*. Boston: Northeastern University Press, 1997.

Cvetkovich, Ann. *An Archive of Feelings: Trauma, Sexuality, and Lesbian Public Cultures*. Durham: Duke University Press, 2003.

Daniel, Lisa, and Claire Jackson. *The Bent Lens: A World Guide to Gay and Lesbian Film*. 2nd ed. Los Angeles: Alyson Books, 2003.

Davidson, Arnold I. "Archaeology, Genealogy, Ethics." In *Foucault: A Critical Reader*, edited by David Couzens Hoy, 221–233. Oxford: Basil Blackwell, 1986.

———. *The Emergence of Sexuality: Historical Epistemology and the Formation of Concepts*. Cambridge: Harvard University Press, 2001.

Decker, Hannah S. "The Reception of Pscyhoanalysis in Germany." *Comparative Studies in Society and History* 24, no. 4 (1982): 589–602.

deCordova, Richard. "The Emergence of the Star System in America." In *Stardom: Industry of Desire*, edited by Christine Gledhill, 17–29. London: Routledge, 1991.

———. *Picture Personalities: The Emergence of the Star System in America*. Urbana: University of Illinois Press, 2001.

De Lauretis, Teresa. *The Practice of Love: Lesbian Sexuality and Perverse Desire*. Bloomington: Indiana University Press, 1994.

D'Emilio, John, and Estelle B. Freedman. *Intimate Matters: A History of Sexuality in America*. 2nd ed. Chicago: University of Chicago Press, 1997.

Dennett, Andrea Stulman. *Weird and Wonderful: The Dime Museum in America*. New York: New York University Press, 1997.

Didi-Huberman, Georges. *The Invention of Hysteria: Charcot and the Photographic Iconography of the Salpêtrière*. Cambridge: MIT Press, 2003.

Dinshaw, Carolyn. *Getting Medieval: Sexualities and Communities, Pre- and Postmodern*. Durham: Duke University Press, 1999.

———. *How Soon Is Now? Medieval Texts, Amateur Readers, and the Queerness of Time*. Durham: Duke University Press, 2012.

Dinshaw, Carolyn, Lee Edelman, Roderick A. Ferguson, Carla Freccero, Elizabeth Freeman, Judith Halberstam, Annamarie Jagose, Christopher S. Nealon, and Tan Hoang Nguyen. "Theorizing Queer Temporalities: A Roundtable Discussion." *GLQ: A Journal of Lesbian and Gay Studies* 13, no. 2 (2007): 177–195.

Doan, Laura. *Disturbing Practices: History, Sexuality, and Women's Experience of Modern War*. Chicago: University of Chicago Press, 2013.

———. *Fashioning Sapphism: The Origins of a Modern English Lesbian Culture*. New York: Columbia University Press, 2001.

———. "Forgetting Sedgwick." *PMLA* 125, no. 2 (2010): 370–373.

———. "Topsy-turvydom: Gender Inversion, Sapphism, and the Great War." *GLQ: A Journal of Lesbian and Gay Studies* 12, no. 4 (2006): 517–542.

Doan, Laura, and Jane Garrity, eds. *Sapphic Modernities: Sexuality, Women, and National Culture*. New York: Palgrave Macmillan, 2006.

Doane, Mary Ann. *The Emergence of Cinematic Time: Modernity, Contingency, The Archive*. Cambridge: Harvard University Press, 2002.

———. "The Erotic Barter: *Pandora's Box* (1929)." In *The Films of G. W. Pabst: An Extraterritorial Cinema*, edited by Eric Rentschler, 62–79. New Brunswick, N.J.: Rutgers University Press, 1990.

———. *Femmes Fatales: Feminism, Film Theory, Psychoanalysis*. New York: Routledge, 1991.

———. "Technology and Sexual Difference: Apocalyptic Scenarios at Two 'Fins de Siècles.'" *differences: A Journal of Feminist and Cultural Studies* 9, no. 2 (1997): 1–24.

———. "Technology's Body: Cinematic Vision in Modernity." In *A Feminist Reader in Early Cinema*, edited by Jennifer M. Bean and Diane Negra, 530–551. Durham: Duke University Press, 2002.

Doran, Emma. "Figuring Modern Dance within Fin-De-Siècle Visual Culture and Print: The Case of Loïe Fuller." *Early Popular Visual Culture* 13, no. 1 (2015): 21–40.

Doty, Alexander. *Making Things Perfectly Queer: Interpreting Mass Culture*. Minneapolis: University of Minnesota Press, 1993.

Duncan, Isadora. *My Life*. 1927. New York: Liveright, 1955.

Dyer, Richard. "Don't Look Now: The Male Pin-Up." In *The Sexual Subject: A Screen Reader in Sexuality*, edited by Screen, 265–276. London: Routledge, 1992.

———. "Less and More than Women and Men: Lesbian and Gay Cinema in Weimar Germany." *New German Critique* 51 (Autumn 1990): 5–60.

———. *Now You See It: Studies in Lesbian and Gay Film*. 2nd ed. (1st ed. 1990) London: Routledge, 2003.

———. *Stars*. New ed. London: BFI Publishing, 1998.

Edelman, Lee. *No Future: Queer Theory and the Death Drive*. Durham: Duke University Press, 2004.

Eisner, Lotte H. *The Haunted Screen: Expressionism in the German Cinema and the Influence of Max Reinhardt*. Berkeley: University of California Press, 1973.

Ellenberger, Allan R. *The Valentino Mystique: The Death and Afterlife of the Silent Film Idol*. Jefferson, N.C.: McFarland and Company, 2005.

Elsaesser, Thomas. "Archaeologies of Interactivity: Early Cinema, Narrative and Spectatorship." In *Film 1900: Technology, Perception, Culture*, edited by Klaus Kreimeier and Annemone Ligensa, 9–21. New Barnet, U.K.: John Libbey Publishing, 2009.

———. "Early Cinema: From Linear History to Mass Media Archaeology." In *Early Cinema: Space, Frame, Narrative*, edited by Thomas Elsaesser and Adam Barker, 1–8. London: British Film Institute, 1990.

———. "Film History and Visual Pleasure." In *Cinema Histories, Cinema Practices*, edited by Patricia Mellencamp and Philip Rosen. Los Angeles: American Film Institute, 1984.

———. "Lulu and the Meter Man: Louise Brooks, G. W. Pabst and *Pandora's Box*." In *Weimar Cinema and After: Germany's Historical Imaginary*, 259–292. London: Routledge, 2000.

Espinaco-Virseda, Angeles. "'I Feel that I Belong to You': Subculture, *Die Freundin* and Lesbian Identities in Weimar Germany." *Spaces of Identity: Tradition, Cultural Boundaries, and Identity Formation in Central Europe and Beyond* 4, no. 1 (2004): 83–113.

Fabian, Johannes. *Time and the Other: How Anthropology Makes Its Object*. 1983. New York: Columbia University Press, 2014.

Farfan, Penny. *Performing Queer Modernism*. Oxford: Oxford University Press, 2017.

Farmer, Brett. *Spectacular Passions: Cinema, Fantasy, Gay Male Spectatorships*. Durham: Duke University Press, 2000.

Felando, Cynthia. "Clara Bow Is *It*." In *Film Stars: Hollywood and Beyond*, edited by Andrew Willis, 8–24. Manchester, U.K.: Manchester University Press, 2004.

Fellom, Martie. "Skirt Dance." In *International Encyclopedia of Dance*, edited by Selma Jeanne Cohen and the Dance Perspectives Foundation, 5: 605. New York: Oxford University Press, 1998.

Finney, Gail. *Women in Modern Drama: Freud, Feminism, and European Theater at the Turn of the Century*. Ithaca, N.Y.: Cornell University Press, 1989.

Fischer, Lucy. "The Lady Vanishes: Women, Magic, and the Movies." *Film Quarterly* 33, no. 1 (1979): 30–40.

Foster, Susan Leigh. "Choreographies of Gender." *Signs: Journal of Women in Culture and Society* 24, no. 1 (1998): 1–33.

Foucault, Michel. *The History of Sexuality: The Will to Knowledge, Volume 1*, translated by Robert Hurley. New York: Random House, 1978. Reprint. Camberwell, Vic., Australia: Penguin, 2008.

———. "Nietzsche, Genealogy, History." In *Language, Counter-memory, Practice: Selected Essays and Interviews*, edited by Michel Foucault and Donald F. Bouchard, 139–164. Ithaca, N.Y.: Cornell University Press, 1977.

———. *"Society Must Be Defended": Lectures at the Collège de France, 1975–76*. Edited by Mauro Bertani and Alessandro Fontana, translated by David Macey. New York: Picador, 2003.

Fradenburg, Louise, and Carla Freccero. "Introduction: Caxton, Foucault, and the Pleasures of History." In *Premodern Sexualities*, edited by Louise Fradenburg and Carla Freccero, xiii–xxiv. New York: Routledge, 1996.

———. "Preface." In *Premodern Sexualities*, edited by Louise Fradenburg and Carla Freccero, vii–xii. New York: Routledge, 1996.

Frame, Lynne. "Gretchen, Girl, Garçonne? Weimar Science and Popular Culture in Search of the Ideal New Woman." In *Women in the Metropolis: Gender and Modernity in Weimar Culture*, edited by Katharina von Ankum, 12–40. Berkeley: University of California Press, 1997.

Franklin, Paul B. "The Terpsichorean Tramp: Unmanly Movement in the Early Films of Charlie Chaplin." In *Dancing Desires: Choreographing Sexualities On and Off the Stage*, edited by Jane Desmond, 35–72. Madison: University of Wisconsin Press, 2001.

Freeman, Elizabeth. "Introduction [to Queer Temporalities Special Issue]." *GLQ: A Journal of Lesbian and Gay Studies* 13, no. 2–3 (2007): 159–176.

———. "Time Binds, or, Erotohistoriography." *Social Text* 84–85, no. 3–4 (2005): 57–68.

———. *Time Binds: Queer Temporalities, Queer Histories*. Durham: Duke University Press, 2010.

Freud, Sigmund. "The Psychogenesis of a Case of Homosexuality in a Woman" (1920).

In *The Standard Edition of the Complete Psychological Works of Sigmund Freud*, translated and edited by James Strachey, 145–172. Vol. 18. London: Hogarth Press, 1955.

Friedberg, Anne. "An *Unheimlich* Maneuver between Psychoanalysis and the Cinema: *Secrets of a Soul* (1926)." In *The Films of G. W. Pabst: An Extraterritorial Cinema*, edited by Eric Rentschler, 41–51. New Brunswick, N.J.: Rutgers University Press, 1990.

———. *Window Shopping: Cinema and the Postmodern*. Berkeley: University of California Press, 1993.

Frow, John. *Character and Person*. Oxford: Oxford University Press, 2014.

———. "Spectacle Binding: On Character." *Poetics Today* 7, no. 2 (1986): 227–250.

Fuhrich, Angelika. "Woman and Typewriter: Gender, Technology, and Work in Late Weimar Film." *Women in German Yearbook* 16 (2000): 151–166.

Fuller, Loie. *Fifteen Years of a Dancer's Life; with Some Account of Her Distinguished Friends*. Boston: Small, Maynard and Company, 1913. Reprint. Brooklyn, N.Y.: Dance Horizons, 1977.

Fuss, Diana. "Fashion and the Homospectatorial Look." *Critical Inquiry* 18, no. 4 (1992): 713–737.

———. *Identification Papers*. New York: Routledge, 1995.

Gaines, Jane M. "Of Cabbages and Authors." In *A Feminist Reader in Early Cinema*, edited by Jennifer M. Bean and Diane Negra, 88–118. Durham: Duke University Press, 2002.

———, ed. *Classical Hollywood Narrative: The Paradigm Wars*. Durham: Duke University Press, 1992.

Garafola, Lynn. "The Travesty Dancer in Nineteenth-Century Ballet." *Dance Research Journal* 17/18, no. 2/1 (1985–86): 35–40.

Garelick, Rhonda K. *Electric Salome: Loie Fuller's Performance of Modernism*. Princeton, N.J.: Princeton University Press, 2007.

———. *Rising Star: Dandyism, Gender, and Performance in the Fin de Siècle*. Princeton, N.J.: Princeton University Press, 1998.

———. "Setting the Air on Fire: Loie Fuller and the Task of 'New Biography.'" In *Looking Back/Moving Forward: International Symposium on Dance Research*, 198–202. Saratoga Springs, N.Y.: Skidmore College, 2008.

Gaudreault, André. "The Diversity of Cinematographic Connections in the Intermedial Context of the Turn of the 20th Century." In *Visual Delights: Essays on the Popular and Projected Image in the 19th Century*, edited by Simon Popple and Vanessa Toulmin, 8–15. Trowbridge, Wiltshire, England: Flicks Books, 2000.

———. "From 'Primitive Cinema' to 'Kine-attractography.'" In *The Cinema of Attractions Reloaded*, edited by Wanda Strauven, 85–104. Amsterdam: Amsterdam University Press, 2006.

Gaudreault, André, and Tom Gunning. "Introduction: American Cinema Emerges (1890–1909)." In *American Cinema, 1890–1909: Themes and Variations*, edited by André Gaudreault, 1–21. New Brunswick, N.J.: Rutgers University Press, 2009.

Gaudreault, André, Jean-Marc Lamotte, and Tim Barnard. "Fragmentation and Segmentation in the Lumière 'Animated Views.'" *The Moving Image* 3, no. 1 (2003): 110–131.

Gleber, Anke. "Women on the Screens and Streets of Modernity: In Search of the Female Flâneur." In *The Image in Dispute: Art and Cinema in the Age of Photography*, edited by Dudley Andrew, 55–85. Austin: University of Texas Press, 1997.

Gomery, Douglas. "Writing the History of the American Film Industry: Warner Bros and Sound." In *Screen Histories: A* Screen *Reader*, edited by Annette Kuhn and Jackie Stacey, 139–147. Oxford: Clarendon Press, 1998.

Gray, Frank. "*The Kiss in the Tunnel* (1899), G. A. Smith and the Emergence of the Edited Film in England." In *The Silent Cinema Reader*, edited by Lee Grieveson and Peter Krämer, 51–62. London: Routledge, 2004.

Greenway, Judy. "It's What You Do with It That Counts: Interpretations of Otto Weininger." In *Sexology in Culture: Labelling Bodies and Desires*, edited by Lucy Bland and Laura Doan, 27–43. Cambridge, U.K.: Polity Press, 1998.

Grossmann, Atina. "*Girlkultur* or Throughly Rationalized Female: A New Woman in Weimar Germany." In *Women in Culture and Politics: A Century of Change*, edited by Judith Friedlander, and New Family and New Woman Research Planning Group, 62–80. Bloomington: Indiana University Press, 1986.

———. "The New Woman and the Rationalization of Sexuality in Weimar Germany." In *Powers of Desire: The Politics of Sexuality*, edited by Christine Stansell, Sharon Thompson, and Ann Barr Snitow, 153–171. New York: Monthly Review Press, 1983.

Guido, Laurent. "Between Paradoxical Spectacles and Technical Dispositives: Looking Again at the (Serpentine) Dances of Early Cinema." In *Cine-Dispositives: Essays in Epistemology Across Media*, edited by François Albera and Maria Tortajada, 249–273. Amsterdam: Amsterdam University Press, 2015.

Gunning, Tom. "An Aesthetic of Astonishment: Early Film and the (In)Credulous Spectator." In *Viewing Positions: Ways of Seeing Film*, edited by Linda Williams, 114–133. New Brunswick, N.J.: Rutgers University Press, 1995.

———. "The Attraction of Motion: Modern Representation and the Image of Movement." In *Film 1900: Technology, Perception, Culture*, edited by Klaus Kreimeier and Annemone Ligensa, 165–173. New Barnet, U.K.: John Libbey Publishing, 2009.

———. "Attractions: How They Came into the World." In *The Cinema of Attractions Reloaded*, edited by Wanda Strauven, 31–39. Amsterdam: Amsterdam University Press, 2006.

———. "The Cinema of Attractions: Early Film, Its Spectator and the Avant-garde." In *Early Cinema: Space, Frame, Narrative*, edited by Thomas Elsaesser and Adam Barker, 56–62. London: BFI Publishing, 1990.

———. "Dance Films." In *Encyclopedia of Early Cinema*, edited by Richard Abel, 233–234. London: Routledge, 2005.

———. *D. W. Griffith and the Origins of American Narrative Film: The Early Years at Biograph*. Urbana: University of Illinois Press, 1994.

———. "Loïe Fuller and the Art of Motion." In *Camera Obscura, Camera Lucida: Essays in Honor of Annette Michelson*, edited by Richard Allen and Malcolm Turvey, 75–89. Amsterdam: Amsterdam University Press, 2003.

———. "'Now You See It, Now You Don't: The Temporality of the Cinema of Attractions." In *The Silent Cinema Reader*, edited by Lee Grieveson and Peter Krämer, 41–50. London: Routledge, 2004.

———. "'Primitive' Cinema: A Frame-up? Or the Trick's on Us." In *Early Cinema: Space, Frame, Narrative*, edited by Thomas Elsaesser and Adam Barker, 95–103. London: BFI Publishing, 1990.

———. "An Unseen Energy Swallows Space: The Space in Early Film and Its Relation to American Avant-Garde Film." In *Film before Griffith*, edited by John L. Fell, 355–366. Berkeley: University of California Press, 1983.

H. D. "An Appreciation." In *Close Up, 1927–1933: Cinema and Modernism*, edited by James Donald, Anne Friedberg, and Laura Marcus, 139–148. London: Cassell, 1929. Originally published in vol. 4, no. 3 (March 1929).

Hadleigh, Boze. *The Lavender Screen: The Gay and Lesbian Films; Their Stars, Makers, Characters, and Critics*. New York: Citadel Press, 2001.

Hagan, John. "Erotic Tendencies in Film, 1900–1906." In *Cinema 1900–1906: An Analytical Study by the National Film Archive (London) and the International Federation of Film Archives*, edited by Roger Holman, 231–238. Brussels: Federation Internationales de Archives du Film, 1982.

Hake, Sabine. "In the Mirror of Fashion." In *Women in the Metropolis: Gender and Modernity in Weimar Culture*, edited by Katharina von Ankum, 185–201. Berkeley: University of California Press, 1997.

Halberstam, Judith. *Female Masculinity*. Durham: Duke University Press, 1998.

———. *In a Queer Time and Place: Transgender Bodies, Subcultural Lives. Sexual Cultures*. New York: New York University Press, 2005.

Hale, Nathan G. *Freud and the Americans: The Beginnings of Psychoanalysis in the United States, 1876–1917*. New York: Oxford University Press, 1971.

Halperin, David M. *How to Do the History of Homosexuality*. Chicago: University of Chicago Press, 2002.

Hansen, Miriam. "America, Paris, the Alps: Kracauer (and Benjamin) on Cinema and Modernity." In *Cinema and the Invention of Modern Life*, edited by Leo Charney and Vanessa R. Schwartz, 362–402. Berkeley: University of California Press, 1995.

———. *Babel and Babylon: Spectatorship in American Silent Film*. Cambridge: Harvard University Press, 1991.

———. "Early Cinema: Whose Public Sphere?" *New German Critique* 29 (1983): 147–184.

———. "Early Cinema, Late Cinema: Transformations in the Public Sphere." In *Viewing Positions: Ways of Seeing Film*, edited by Linda Williams, 134–152. New Brunswick, N.J.: Rutgers University Press, 1995.

———. "Pleasure, Ambivalence, Identification: Valentino and Female Spectatorship." *Cinema Journal* 25, no. 4 (1986): 6–32.

Hart, Lynda. *Fatal Women: Lesbian Sexuality and the Mark of Aggression*. Princeton, N.J.: Princeton University Press, 1994.

Hastie, Amelie. *Cupboards of Curiosity: Women, Recollection, and Film History*. Durham: Duke University Press, 2007.

Heath, Stephen. *Questions of Cinema*. Bloomington: Indiana University Press, 1981.

Hennefeld, Maggie. "Slapstick Comediennes in Transitional Cinema: Between Body and Medium." *Camera Obscura: Feminism, Culture and Media Studies* 29, no. 2 (2014): 85–116.

Herring, Robert [R. H.]. "For Adolescents Only." *Close Up* 6, no. 5 (1930): 423–424.

Herring, Scott. *Queering the Underworld: Slumming, Literature, and the Undoing of Lesbian and Gay History*. Chicago: University of Chicago Press, 2009.

Herzog, Dagmar. *Sexuality in Europe: A Twentieth-Century History*. Cambridge: Cambridge University Press, 2011.

Hibberd, J. T. "The Spirit of the Flesh: Wedekind's Lulu." *The Modern Language Review* 79, no. 2 (1984): 336–355.

Higashi, Sumiko. *Virgins, Vamps and Flappers: The American Silent Movie Heroine*. Montreal: Eden Press Women's Publications, 1978.

Hindson, Catherine. "The Female Illusionist—Loïe Fuller: Fairy or Wizardess?" *Early Popular Visual Culture* 4, no. 2 (2006): 161–174.

———. *Female Performance Practice on the Fin-de-Siècle Popular Stages of London and Paris: Experiment and Advertisement*. Manchester. U.K.: Manchester University Press, 2007.

———. "Interruptions by Inevitable Petticoats: Skirt Dancing and the Historiographical Problem of Late Nineteenth-Century Dance." *Nineteenth Century Theatre & Film* 35, no. 2 (2009): 48–64.

Hollander, Anne. *Seeing through Clothes*. New York: Viking Press, 1978.

Horak, Laura. *Girls Will Be Boys: Cross-Dressed Women, Lesbians, and American Cinema*. New Brunswick, N.J.: Rutgers University Press, 2016.

———. "'Would You Like to Sin with Elinor Glyn?': Film as a Vehicle of Sensual Education." *Camera Obscura: Feminism, Culture and Media Studies* 25, no. 2 (2010): 75–117.

Huhtamo, Erkki. "The Pleasures of the Peephole: An Archaeological Exploration of Peep Media." In *The Book of Imaginary Media: Excavating the Dream of the Ultimate Communication Medium*, edited by Eric Kluitenberg, 74–155. Rotterdam: NAI, 2006.

Izenberg, Gerald N. *Modernism and Masculinity: Mann, Wedekind, Kandinsky through World War I*. Chicago: University of Chicago Press, 2000.

Jaccard, Roland, ed. *Louise Brooks: Portrait of an Anti-star*. London: Columbus Books, 1988.

Jacobs, Lea. *The Decline of Sentiment: American Film in the 1920s*. Berkeley: University of California Press, 2008.

Jagose, Annamarie. *Inconsequence: Lesbian Representation and the Logic of Sexual Sequence*. Ithaca, N.Y.: Cornell University Press, 2002.

Jelavich, Peter. *Munich and Theatrical Modernism: Politics, Playwriting, and Performance, 1890–1914*. Cambridge: Harvard University Press, 1996.

Jewell, Richard B. *The Golden Age of Cinema: Hollywood, 1929–1945*. Malden, Mass.: Blackwell Publishing, 2007.

Johnston, Claire. "Dorothy Arzner: Critical Strategies." In *Feminism and Film Theory*, edited by Constance Penley, 46–56. New York: Routledge, 1988.

———, ed. *The Works of Dorothy Arzner: Towards a Feminist Cinema*. London: British Film Institute, 1975.

Kaes, Anton, Martin Jay, and Edward Dimendberg, eds. *The Weimar Republic Sourcebook*. Berkeley: University of California Press, 1994.

Kaplan, E. Ann. "Unfixings: Archiving the Future." *Camera Obscura: Feminism, Culture, and Media Studies* 22, no. 3 (2007): 185–190.

Kay, Karyn, and Gerald Peary. "Interview with Dorothy Arzner." In *Women and the Cinema: A Critical Anthology*, edited by Karyn Kay and Gerald Peary, 153–168. New York: E. P. Dutton, 1977.

Keil, Charles. "The Story of Uncle Josh Told: Spectatorship and Apparatus in Early Cinema." *Iris* 11 (Summer 1990): 63–76.

———. *Early American Cinema in Transition: Story, Style, and Filmmaking, 1907–1913*. Madison: University of Wisconsin Press, 2001.

Keil, Charlie, and Shelley Stamp, eds. *American Cinema's Transitional Era: Audiences, Institutions, Practices*. Berkeley: University of California Press, 2004.

Kendall, Elizabeth. *Where She Danced: The Birth of American Art-Dance*. Berkeley: University of California Press, 1984.

Kirby, Lynne. "Gender and Advertising in American Silent Film: From Early Cinema to the Crowd," *Discourse* 13, no. 2 (1991): 3–20.

———. *Parallel Tracks: The Railroad and Silent Cinema*. Durham: Duke University Press, 1996.

Koritz, Amy. *Gendering Bodies / Performing Art: Dance and Literature in Early Twentieth-Century British Culture*. Ann Arbor: University of Michigan Press, 1995.

———. *Culture Makers: Urban Performance and Literature in the 1920s*. Urbana: University of Illinois Press, 2009.

Koszarski, Richard. *An Evening's Entertainment: The Age of the Silent Feature Picture, 1915–1928*, edited by Charles Harpole. Vol. 3 of *History of the American Cinema*. New York: Charles Scribner's Sons, 1990.

Kracauer, Siegfried. *History: The Last Things before the Last*. New York: Oxford University Press, 1969.

Kraut, Anthea. "White Womanhood, Property Rights, and the Campaign for Choreographic Copyright: Loïe Fuller's Serpentine Dance." *Dance Research Journal* 43, no. 1 (2011): 3–26.

Kuhn, Annette. *Cinema, Censorship and Sexuality, 1909–1925*. London: Routledge, 1988.

Kuhn, Annette, and Jackie Stacey. "Screen Histories: An Introduction." In *Screen*

Histories: A Screen *Reader*, edited by Annette Kuhn and Jackie Stacey, 1–10. Oxford: Clarendon Press, 1998.

Kuzniar, Alice A. *The Queer German Cinema*. Stanford, Calif.: Stanford University Press, 2000.

Ladenson, Elisabeth. *Proust's Lesbianism*. Ithaca, N.Y.: Cornell University Press, 1999.

Lamar, Cecil, "The Creation of Nobles in Prussia, 1871–1918," *American Historical Review* 75, no. 3 (1970): 757–795.

Landay, Lori. "The Flapper Film: Comedy, Dance, and Jazz Age Kinaesthetics." In *A Feminist Reader in Early Cinema*, edited by Jennifer M. Bean and Diane Negra, 221–248. Durham: Duke University Press, 2002.

———. "The Mirror of Performance: Kinaesthetics, Subjectivity, and the Body in Film, Television, and Virtual Worlds." *Cinema Journal* 51, no. 3 (2012): 129–136.

Lanser, Susan S. "Sapphic Picaresque, Sexual Difference and the Challenge of Homo-adventuring." *Textual Practice* 15, no. 2 (2001): 251–268.

Lant, Antonia. "Haptical Cinema." *October* 74 (Autumn 1995): 45–73.

Laplanche, Jean, and J. B. Pontalis. *The Language of Psycho-Analysis*. London: Karnac Books and the Institute of Psycho-Analysis, 1988.

Latimer, Tirza True. "Loïe Fuller: Butch-Femme-Fatale." In *Proceedings of the Society of Dance History Scholars, 22nd Annual Conference*, 83–88. Albuquerque: University of New Mexico Press, 1999.

Leider, Emily. *Dark Lover: The Life and Death of Rudolph Valentino*. New York: Farrar, Straus and Giroux, 2003.

Lista, Giovanni. *Loïe Fuller: Danseuse de la Belle Époque*. Paris: Somogy editions d'art—Éditions Stock, 1994.

Love, Heather. *Feeling Backward: Loss and the Politics of Queer History*. Cambridge: Harvard University Press, 2009.

Lybeck, Marti M. "Gender, Sexuality and Belonging: Female Homosexuality in Germany, 1890–1933." PhD diss., University of Michigan, 2007.

Mahar, Karen Ward. *Women Filmmakers in Early Hollywood*. Baltimore: Johns Hopkins University Press, 2006.

Manning, Susan. "The Female Dancer and the Male Gaze: Feminist Critiques of Early Modern Dance." In *Meaning in Motion: New Cultural Studies of Dance*, edited by Jane Desmond, 153–166. Durham: Duke University Press, 1997.

Mannoni, Laurent. "Henri Langlois and the Musée du Cinéma." *Film History* 18 (2006): 274–287.

Marcus, Sharon. *Between Women: Friendship, Desire, and Marriage in Victorian England*. Princeton, N.J.: Princeton University Press, 2007.

Marhoefer, Laurie. *Sex and the Weimar Republic: German Homosexual Emancipation and the Rise of the Nazis*. Toronto: University of Toronto Press, 2015.

Marks, Laura U. *The Skin of the Film: Intercultural Cinema, Embodiment, and the Senses*. Durham: Duke University Press, 2000.

———. *Touch: Sensuous Theory and Multisensory Media*. Minneapolis: University of Minnesota Press, 2002.

Marsh, Carol G. "Gavotte." In *International Encyclopedia of Dance*, edited by Selma Jeanne Cohen and the Dance Perspectives Foundation, 3: 123–125. New York: Oxford University Press, 1998.

Mathews, Nancy Mowll. "The Body in Motion." In *Moving Pictures: American Art and Early Film 1880–1910*, edited by Nancy Mowll Mathews, 73–94. Manchester, Vt.: Hudson Hills Press, 2005.

Matlock, Jann. "Masquerading Women, Pathologized Men: Cross-Dressing, Fetishism, and the Theory of Perversion, 1882–1935." In *Fetishism as Cultural Discourse*, edited by Emily Apter and William Pietz, 31–61. Ithaca, N.Y.: Cornell University Press, 1993.

Mavor, Carol. *Becoming: The Photographs of Clementina, Viscountess Hawarden*. Durham: Duke University Press, 1999.

Mayer, David. "Acting in Silent Film: Which Legacy of the Theatre?" In *Screen Acting*, edited by Alan Lovell and Peter Krämer, 10–30. London: Routledge, 1999.

Mayne, Judith. *Cinema and Spectatorship*. London: Routledge, 1993.

———. *Directed by Dorothy Arzner*. Bloomington: Indiana University Press, 1994.

———. "Feminist Film Theory and Criticism." *Signs* 11, no. 1 (1985): 81–100.

———. *The Woman at the Keyhole: Feminism and Women's Cinema*. Bloomington: Indiana University Press, 1990.

McCarren, Felicia. *Dance Pathologies: Performance, Poetics, Medicine*. Stanford, Calif.: Stanford University Press, 1998.

McKernan, Luke. *Who's Who of Victorian Cinema: A Worldwide Survey*. London: British Film Institute, 1996.

McMahan, Alison. *Alice Guy Blaché: Lost Visionary of the Cinema*. New York: Continuum, 2002.

Merck, Mandy. "'Transforming the Suit': A Century of Lesbian Self-Portraits." In *Perversions: Deviant Readings*, 86–100. London: Virago Press, 1993.

Miller, D. A. "Anal *Rope*." *Representations* 32 (Autumn 1990): 114–133.

———. "The Late Jane Austen." *Raritan* 10, no. 1 (1990): 55–79.

Modern Girl Around the World Research Group, Alys Eve Weinbaum, Lynn M. Thomas, Priti Ramamurthy, Uta G. Polger, Madeleine Yue Dong, eds. *The Modern Girl Around the World: Consumption, Modernity, and Globalization*. Durham: Duke University Press, 2008.

Moon, Michael. "Flaming Closets." *October* 51 (Winter 1989): 19–54.

Morgan, Thaïs E. "Male Lesbian Bodies: The Construction of Alternative Masculinities in Courbet, Baudelaire, and Swinburne." *Genders* 15 (Winter 1992): 37–57.

Morris, Mitchell. "Admiring the Countess Geschwitz." In *En Travesti: Women, Gender Subversion, Opera*, edited by Corinne E. Blackmer and Patricia Juliana Smith, 348–370. New York: Columbia University Press, 1995.

Mulvey, Laura. "Visual Pleasure and Narrative Cinema." In *The Sexual Subject: A* Screen *Reader in Sexuality*, 22–34. London: Routledge, 1992.

Muñoz, José Esteban. "Ephemera as Evidence: Introductory Notes to Queer Acts." *Women & Performance: a journal of feminist theory* 8, no. 2 (1996): 5–16.

Musser, Charles. "American Vitagraph: 1897–1901." *Cinema Journal* 22.3 (1983): 4–46.

———. "At the Beginning: Motion Picture Production, Representation and Ideology at the Edison and Lumière Companies." In *The Silent Cinema Reader*, edited by Lee Grieveson and Peter Krämer, 15–30. London: Routledge, 2004.

———. *Before the Nickelodeon: Edwin S. Porter and the Edison Manufacturing Company*. Berkeley: University of California Press, 1991.

———. *The Emergence of Cinema: The American Screen to 1907*, edited by Charles Harpole. Vol. 1 of *History of the American Cinema*. New York: Charles Scribner's Sons, 1990.

———. "The May Irwin Kiss: Performance and the Beginnings of Cinema." In *Visual Delights 2: Exhibition and Reception*, edited by Simon Popple and Vanessa Toulmin, 96–115. Eastleigh, U.K.: John Libbey, 2005.

Muybridge, Eadweard. *Muybridge's Complete Human and Animal Locomotion: All 781 plates from the 1887 Animal Locomotion*. New York: Dover Publications Inc., 1979.

Oosterhuis, Harry. "Richard von Krafft-Ebing's 'Step-Children of Nature': Psychiatry and the Making of Homosexual Identity." In *Science and Homosexualities*, edited by Vernon A. Rosario, 67–88. New York: Routledge, 1997.

Osborne, Peter. *The Politics of Time: Modernity and the Avant-Garde*. London: Verso, 1995.

Paris, Barry. *Louise Brooks: A Biography*. Minneapolis: University of Minnesota Press, 2000.

Pearson, Roberta E. *Eloquent Gestures: The Transformation of Performance Style in the Griffith Biograph Films*. Berkeley: University of California Press, 1992.

Penley, Constance, ed. *Feminism and Film Theory*. New York: Routledge, 1988.

Pepper, Terence. *Limelight: Photographs by James Abbe*. London: National Portrait Gallery, 1995.

Petro, Patrice. *Aftershocks of the New: Feminism and Film History*. New Brunswick, N.J.: Rutgers University Press, 2002.

———. *Joyless Streets: Women and Melodramatic Representation in Weimar Germany*. Princeton, N.J.: Princeton University Press, 1989.

Petropoulos, Jonathan. *Royals and the Reich: The Princes Von Hessen in Nazi Germany*. New York: Oxford University Press, 2006.

Peukert, Detleve J. K. *The Weimar Republic: The Crisis of Classical Modernity*, translated by Richard Deveson. London: Allen Lane, The Penguin Press, 1991.

Phelan, Peggy. "'I Never See You as You Are': Invitations and Displacements in Dance Writing." In *Dancing Desires: Choreographing Sexualities On and Off the Stage*, edited by Jane Desmond, 415–422. Madison: University of Wisconsin Press, 2001.

Philip, Fiona. "Veiled Disclosures and Speaking Back: *Borderline* (1930) and the Presence of Censorship." In *Bound and Unbound: Interdisciplinary Approaches to Genders and Sexualities*, edited by Zowie Davy, Julia Downes, Lena Eckert,

Natalia Gerodetti, Dario Llinares, and Ana Cristina Santos, 146–163. Newcastle, U.K.: Cambridge Scholars Publishing, 2008.

Popple, Simon, and Vanessa Toulmin, eds. *Visual Delights: Essays on the Popular and Projected Image in the 19th Century*. Trowbridge, Wiltshire, England: Flicks Books, 2000.

———. *Visual Delights 2: Exhibition and Reception*. Eastleigh, U.K.: John Libbey, 2005.

Prosser, Jay. "Transsexuals and the Transsexologists: Inversion and the Emergence of Transsexual Subjectivity." In *Sexology in Culture: Labelling Bodies and Desires*, edited by Lucy Bland and Laura Doan, 116–131. Cambridge, U.K.: Polity Press, 1998.

Pumphrey, Martin. "The Flapper, the Housewife and the Making of Modernity." *Cultural Studies* 1, no. 2 (1987): 179–194.

Rabinovitz, Lauren. *For the Love of Pleasure: Women, Movies, and Culture in Turn-of-the-Century Chicago*. New Brunswick, N.J.: Rutgers University Press, 1998.

Raitt, Suzanne. "Sex, Love and the Homosexual Body in Early Sexology." In *Sexology in Culture: Labelling Bodies and Desires*, edited by Lucy Bland and Laura Doan, 150–164. Cambridge, U.K.: Polity Press, 1998.

Rambova, Natacha. *Rudy: An Intimate Portrait of Rudolph Valentino by His Wife Natacha Rambova*. London: Hutchinson and Co., 1926.

Reed, Christopher. "Design for (Queer) Living: Sexual Identity, Performance, and Decor in British *Vogue*, 1922–1926." *GLQ: A Journal of Lesbian and Gay Studies* 12, no. 3 (2006): 377–403.

Rentschler, Eric. "The Problematic Pabst: An *Auteur* Directed by History." In *The Films of G. W. Pabst: An Extraterritorial Cinema*, edited by Eric Rentschler. New Brunswick, N.J.: Rutgers University Press, 1990.

Rich, B. Ruby. *Chick Flicks: Theories and Memories of the Feminist Film Movement*. Durham: Duke University Press, 1998.

Roberts, Mary Louise. *Disruptive Acts: The New Woman in Fin-de-Siècle France*. Chicago: University of Chicago Press, 2002.

Rohy, Valerie. "Ahistorical." *GLQ: A Journal of Lesbian and Gay Studies* 12, no. 1 (2006): 61–83.

———. "Exchanging Hours: Dialogue on Time." *GLQ: A Journal of Lesbian and Gay Studies* 23, no. 2 (2017): 247–268.

Rosario, Vernon A. "Inversion's Histories | History's Inversions: Novelizing Fin-de-Siècle Homosexuality." In *Science and Homosexualities*, edited by Vernon A. Rosario, 89–107. New York: Routledge, 1997.

Rosen, Marjorie. *Popcorn Venus: Women, Movies and the American Dream*. London: Owen, 1975.

Ross, Sara. "'Good Little Bad Girls': Controversy and the Flapper Comedienne." *Film History* 13, no. 4 (2001): 409–423.

Rubin, Gayle. "Thinking Sex: Notes for a Radical Theory of the Politics of Sexuality." In *The Lesbian and Gay Studies Reader*, ed. Henry Abelove, Michèle Aina Barale, and David M. Halperin, 3–44. New York: Routledge, 1993.

———. "The Traffic in Women: Notes on the 'Political Economy' of Sex." In *Toward an Anthropology of Women*, edited by Rayna R. Reiter, 157–210. New York: Monthly Review, 1975.

Russell, Catherine. "New Media and Film History: Walter Benjamin and the Awakening of Cinema." *Cinema Journal* 43, no. 3 (2004): 81–85.

———. "Parallax Historiography: The Flâneuse as Cyberfeminist." In *A Feminist Reader in Early Cinema*, edited by Jennifer M. Bean and Diane Negra, 552–570. Durham: Duke University Press, 2002.

Russo, Vito. *The Celluloid Closet: Homosexuality in the Movies*. New York: Harper and Row, 1981.

Ryan, Mary P. "The Projection of a New Womanhood: The Movie Moderns in the 1920's." In *Decades of Discontent: The Women's Movement, 1920–1940*, edited by Lois Scharf and Joan M. Jensen, 113–130. Westport, Conn.: Greenwood Press, 1983.

Schivelbusch, Wolfgang. *Disenchanted Night: The Industrialization of Light in the Nineteenth Century*. Berkeley: University of California Press, 1988.

———. "The Force." *Cabinet* no. 21 (Spring 2006): 57–61.

Schor, Naomi. "Male Lesbianism." *GLQ: A Journal of Lesbian and Gay Studies* 7, no. 3 (2001): 391–399.

Schwartz, Hillel. "Torque: The New Kinaesthetic of the Twentieth Century." In *Incorporations*, edited by Jonathan Crary and Sanford Kwinter, 71–126. New York: Zone, 1992.

Schwartz, Vanessa R. "Cinema Spectatorship before the Apparatus: The Public Taste for Reality in *Fin-de-Siècle* Paris." In *Cinema and the Invention of Modern Life*, edited by Leo Charney and Vanessa R. Schwartz, 297–319. Berkeley: University of California Press, 1995.

Sears, Clare. "Electric Brilliancy: Cross-dressing Law and Freak Show Displays in Nineteenth-century San Francisco." *Women's Studies Quarterly* 36, no. 3, 4 (2008): 170–187.

Sedgwick, Eve Kosofsky. *Epistemology of the Closet*. 1990. Berkeley: University of California Press, 2008.

———. "Gender Criticism." In *Redrawing the Boundaries: The Transformation of English and American Literary Studies*, edited by Stephen Greenblatt and Giles Gunn, 271–302. New York: Modern Language Association of America, 1992.

———. *Touching Feeling: Affect, Pedagogy, Performativity*. Durham: Duke University Press, 2003.

———. *Tendencies*. Durham: Duke University Press, 1993.

Sigel, Lisa Z. "Filth in the Wrong People's Hands: Postcards and the Expansion of Pornography in Britain and the Atlantic World, 1880–1914. " *Journal of Social History* 33, no. 4 (2000): 859–885.

Silverman, Debora. *Art Nouveau in Fin-de-Siècle France: Politics, Psychology, and Style*. Berkeley: University of California Press, 1989.

Simmons, Christina. "Companionate Marriage and the Lesbian Threat." *Frontiers: A Journal of Women's Studies* 4, no. 3 (1979): 54–59.

Simms, Bryan R. "Berg's *Lulu* and Theatre of the 1920s." *Cambridge Opera Journal* 6, no. 2 (1994): 147–158.

Singer, Ben. "Feature Films, Variety Programs, and the Crisis of the Small Exhibitor." In *American Cinema's Transitional Era: Audiences, Institutions, Practices*, edited by Charlie Keil and Shelley Stamp, 76–100. Berkeley: University of California Press, 2004.

Slide, Anthony. *The Big V: The Vitagraph Company*. Metuchen, N.J.: Scarecrow Press, 1987.

———. *Inside the Hollywood Fan Magazine: A History of Star Makers, Fabricators, and Gossip Mongers*. Jackson: University Press of Mississippi, 2010.

Sloan, Kay. "Sexual Warfare in the Silent Cinema: Comedies and Melodramas of Woman Suffragism." *American Quarterly* 33, no. 4 (1981): 412–436.

Smith, Albert E. *Two Reels and a Crank*. New York: Doubleday, 1952.

Smith, Murray. *Engaging Characters: Fiction, Emotion, and the Cinema*. Oxford: Clarendon Press, 1995.

Sobchack, Vivian. "'Presentifying' Film and Media Feminism." *Camera Obscura: Feminism, Culture and Media Studies* 21, no. 1 (2006): 65–68.

Somerville, Siobhan B. "The Queer Career of Jim Crow: Racial and Sexual Transformation in *A Florida Enchantment*." In *A Feminist Reader in Early Cinema*, edited by Jennifer M. Bean and Diane Negra, 251–269. Durham: Duke University Press, 2002.

———. *Queering the Color Line: Race and the Invention of Homosexuality in American Culture*. Durham: Duke University Press, 2000.

Sommer, Sally. "Loie Fuller." In *International Encyclopedia of Dance*, edited by Selma Jeanne Cohen, 3: 90–96. New York: Oxford University Press, 1998.

Spadoni, Robert. "The Figure Seen from the Rear, Vitagraph, and the Development of the Shot/Reverse Shot." *Film History* 11, no. 3 (1999): 319–341.

Spector, Scott, Helmut Puff, and Dagmar Herzog, eds. *After the History of Sexuality: German Genealogies with and beyond Foucault*. New York: Berghahn Books, 2012.

Spring, Justin. *Secret Historian: The Life and Times of Samuel Steward, Professor, Tattoo Artist, and Sexual Renegade*. New York: Farrar, Straus and Giroux, 2010.

Stacey, Jackie. *Star Gazing: Hollywood Cinema and Female Spectatorship*. London: Routledge, 1994.

Staiger, Janet. *Bad Women: Regulating Sexuality in Early American Cinema*. Minneapolis: University of Minnesota Press, 1995.

Stamp, Shelley. *Movie-struck Girls: Women and Motion Picture Culture after the Nickelodeon*. Princeton, N.J.: Princeton University Press, 2000.

Steakley, James D. "Iconography of a Scandal: Political Cartoons and the Eulenburg Affair in Wilhelmin Germany." In *Hidden from History: Reclaiming the Gay and Lesbian Past*, edited by Martin B. Duberman, Martha Vicinus and George Chauncey, 233–263. New York: Penguin, 1990.

Stearns, Marshall, and Jean Stearns. *Jazz Dance: The Story of American Vernacular Dance*. 1968. New York: Da Capo Press, 1994.

Steedman, Carolyn. *Dust: The Archive and Cultural History*. New Brunswick, N.J.: Rutgers University Press, 2002.

Stenn, David. *Clara Bow: Runnin' Wild*. New York: Doubleday, 1988.

Stewart, Jacqueline. "What Happened in the Transition? Reading Race, Gender, and Labor between the Shots." In *American Cinema's Transitional Era: Audiences, Institutions, Practices*, edited by Charlie Keil and Shelley Stamp, 103–130. Berkeley: University of California Press, 2004.

Stockton, Kathryn Bond. *The Queer Child, or Growing Sideways in the Twentieth Century*. Durham: Duke University Press, 2009.

Straayer, Chris. *Deviant Eyes, Deviant Bodies: Sexual Re-orientations in Film and Video*. New York: Columbia University Press, 1996.

Strauven, Wanda, ed. *The Cinema of Attractions Reloaded*. Amsterdam: Amsterdam University Press, 2006.

Streible, Dan. "Female Spectators and the Corbett-Fitzsimmons Fight." In *Out of Bounds: Sports, Media, and the Politics of Identity*, edited by Aaron Baker and Todd Boyd, 16–47. Bloomington: Indiana University Press, 1997.

Studlar, Gaylyn. "Dialogue: Gaylyn Studlar Responds to Miriam Hansen's 'Pleasure, Ambivalence, Identification: Valentino and Female Spectatorship.'" *Cinema Journal* 26, no. 2 (1987): 51–53.

———. "Discourses of Gender and Ethnicity: The Construction and De(con)struction of Rudolph Valentino as Other." *Film Criticism* 13, no. 2 (1989): 18–35.

———. "The Perils of Pleasure? Fan Magazine Discourse as Women's Commodified Culture in the 1920s." *Wide Angle* 13, no. 1 (1991): 6–33.

———. *This Mad Masquerade: Stardom and Masculinity in the Jazz Age*. New York: Columbia University Press, 1996.

———. "Valentino, 'Optic Intoxication,' and Dance Madness." In *Screening the Male: Exploring Masculinities in Hollywood Cinema*, edited by Steven Cohan and Ina Rae Hark, 23–45. London: Routledge, 1993.

Sutton, Katie. *The Masculine Woman in Weimar Germany*. New York: Berghahn Books, 2011.

Thompson, Kristin. "Narration Early in the Transition to Classical Filmmaking: Three Vitagraph Shorts." *Film History* 9, no. 4 (1997): 410–434.

Thurschwell, Pamela. *Literature, Technology and Magical Thinking, 1880–1920*. Cambridge: Cambridge University Press, 2001.

Tinkcom, Matthew. *Working like a Homosexual: Camp, Capital, and Cinema*. Durham: Duke University Press, 2002.

Townsend, Julie. "Alchemic Visions and Technological Advances: Sexual Morphology in Loie Fuller's Dance." In *Dancing Desires: Choreographing Sexualities On and Off the Stage*, edited by Jane Desmond, 73–96. Madison: University of Wisconsin Press, 2001.

Trahair, Lisa. "Figural Vision: Freud, Lyotard and Early Cinematic Comedy." *Screen* 46, no. 2 (2005): 175–193.

Traub, Valerie. "The New Unhistoricism in Queer Studies." *PMLA* 128, no. 1 (2013): 21–39.

———. *The Renaissance of Lesbianism in Early Modern England.* New York: Cambridge University Press, 2002.

———. *Thinking Sex with the Early Moderns.* Philadelphia: University of Pennsylvania Press, 2016.

Trüper, Henning, Dipesh Chakrabarty, and Sanjay Subrahmanyam, eds. *Historical Teleologies in the Modern World.* London: Bloomsbury, 2015.

Tsivian, Yuri. *Early Cinema in Russia and Its Cultural Reception*, translated by Alan Bodger. London: Routledge, 1994.

Uricchio, William, and Roberta E. Pearson. *Reframing Culture: The Case of the Vitagraph Quality Films.* Princeton, N.J.: Princeton University Press, 1993.

Vasey, Ruth. "Beyond Sex and Violence: 'Industry Policy' and the Regulation of Hollywood Movies, 1922–1939." In *Controlling Hollywood: Censorship and Regulation in the Studio Era*, edited by Matthew Bernstein, 102–129. London: Athlone, 2000.

Veroli, Patrizia. *Loie Fuller.* Palermo: L'Epos, 2009.

Vicinus, Martha. *Intimate Friends: Women Who Loved Women, 1778–1928.* Chicago: University of Chicago Press, 2004.

Villiers, Nicholas De. *Opacity and the Closet: Queer Tactics in Foucault, Barthes, and Warhol.* Minneapolis: University of Minnesota Press, 2012.

Wallace, Lee. "Dorothy Arzner's *Wife*: Heterosexual Sets, Homosexual Scenes." *Screen* 49, no. 4 (2008): 391–409.

Wedekind, Frank. *Five Tragedies of Sex*, translated by Frances Fawcett and Stephen Spender. London: Vision, 1952.

Weinberg, Herman G. "The Cinema and the Censors." *Close Up* 7, no. 4 (1930): 252–259.

Weinstein, Valerie. "(Un)Fashioning Identities: Ernst Lubitsch's Early Comedies of Mistaken Identity." In *Visual Culture in Twentieth-Century Germany: Text as Spectacle*, edited by Gail Finney, 120–133. Bloomington: Indiana University Press, 2006.

Weiss, Andrea. *Vampires and Violets: Lesbians in the Cinema.* London: Jonathan Cape, 1992.

White, Patricia. "Nazimova's Veils: *Salome* at the Intersection of Film Histories." In *A Feminist Reader in Early Cinema*, edited by Jennifer M. Bean and Diane Negra, 60–87. Durham: Duke University Press, 2002.

———. *Uninvited: Classical Hollywood Cinema and Lesbian Representability.* Bloomington: Indiana University Press, 1999.

Williams, Linda. "Film Body: An Implantation of Perversions." In *Narrative, Apparatus, Ideology*, edited by Philip Rosen, 507–534. New York: Columbia University Press, 1986.

———. *Hard Core: Power, Pleasure, and the "Frenzy of the Visible."* London: Pandora Press, 1990.

———, ed. *Viewing Positions: Ways of Seeing Film.* New Brunswick, N.J.: Rutgers University Press, 1995.

Williams, Raymond. *Marxism and Literature*. Oxford: Oxford University Press, 1977.
Wollen, Peter. "Brooks and the Bob." *Sight and Sound* 4, no. 2 (1994): 22–24.
Yumibe, Joshua. *Moving Color: Early Film, Mass Culture, Modernism*. New Brunswick: Rutgers University Press, 2012.
Zaretsky, Eli. *Secrets of the Soul: A Social and Cultural History of Psychoanalysis*. New York: Alfred A. Knopf, 2004.

Index

SUSAN POTTER is lecturer in film studies at the University of Sydney.

Women and Film History International

A Great Big Girl Like Me: The Films of Marie Dressler *Victoria Sturtevant*

The Uncanny Gaze: The Drama of Early German Cinema *Heide Schlüpmann*

Universal Women: Filmmaking and Institutional Change in Early Hollywood *Mark Garrett Cooper*

Exporting Perilous Pauline: Pearl White and the Serial Film Craze *Edited by Marina Dahlquist*

Germaine Dulac: A Cinema of Sensations *Tami Williams*

Seeing Sarah Bernhardt: Performance and Silent Film *Victoria Duckett*

Doing Women's Film History: Reframing Cinemas, Past and Future *Edited by Christine Gledhill and Julia Knight*

Pink Slipped: What Happened to Women in the Silent Film Industries? *Jane M. Gaines*

Queer Timing: The Emergence of Lesbian Sexuality in Early Cinema *Susan Potter*

The University of Illinois Press
is a founding member of the
Association of American University Presses.

University of Illinois Press
1325 South Oak Street
Champaign, IL 61820-6903
www.press.uillinois.edu